John Timbs

Signs Before Death

John Timbs

Signs Before Death

ISBN/EAN: 9783337404901

Printed in Europe, USA, Canada, Australia, Japan

Cover: Foto ©Lupo / pixelio.de

More available books at **www.hansebooks.com**

SIGNS BEFORE DEATH.

A RECORD OF STRANGE APPARITIONS,

REMARKABLE DREAMS, &c.

A New Edition, Enlarged and Carefully Corrected.

> "We are such stuff
> As dreams are made on, and our little life
> Is rounded with a sleep."
> — SHAKSPEARE.

LONDON:
WILLIAM TEGG & CO., PANCRAS LANE, CHEAPSIDE.
NEW YORK:
SCRIBNER, WELFORD, & ARMSTRONG.
1875.

INTRODUCTION.

IT is more than probable that an effect has never yet been allowed to exist long without having laid to its charge, by ingenious heralds, a varying ancestry of at least a score of causes, differing in their nature as the people who create them differ, agreed only in their assertions of authenticity. The more marvellous the effect, the more numerous and absurd are these assignments Wherever mystery exists, there speculation is sure to abound ; and where speculation abounds, *there* will certainly be found also three conditions of things : (1) many ditches plentifully strewed with blind who have led each other thither, and fallen therein ; (2) much beclouded ignorance walking about disguised in all the colours of the rainbow ; and (3) a good deal of genius running wild, and increasing the confusion by subtle growths, often very beautiful, but only skin deep.

There is no greater mystery than Death, that brief period of transition, when, behind the veil—whose shadow we can see, but which no eye can penetrate, nor any hand rend— the future is coupled on to the past, and the present is abolished. Sleep has been alternately regarded as Nature's sweet restorer, and Death's twin brother; and although the one reference appears complimentary, and the other grim, yet there is an affinity between the two beyond what is usually meant by the phrases; for it is certain that sleep cures quite as much disease in the world as medicine does, and suppresses even more than it cures, and it is certain, too, that Death is the one perfect restorer of all such as long to be restored (and probably of the others too, after a process) to the state of Nature—which is a state of complete purity and love. Sleep and Death are the two greatest, and consequently the two divinest mysteries with which men are brought into contact. They are both processes, and they are both hidden. The result of the one we all have seen, and know; the joy that cometh in the morning every living being has had a share in. What comes after the other has formed the theme of endless controversy and wonder more or less intelligent, and also of one particular Book largely written by men whose minds were specially enriched for a special purpose by Him who unmistakeably knows the heart and is willing to guide the thoughts of men; and written under circumstances (positive absence of previous bias, &c.) that would be held to be satisfactory even in any modern investigation of causes. It is always bewildering, and often dangerous, to face darkness without a light; Death represents the blackness of darkness to those who are left behind; and this Book has been as the bright shining of innumerable stars—thinning the darkness with a gentle light, far more tender than that of the sun—to many many thousands of these watchers standing on the edge, gazing into the unknown but inevitable. This light has reminded them of the Source of Light, and has revealed to them sufficient to base infinite hope upon. If the mystery could be wholly interpreted, it would not be divine; but we know—enough of us to form a quorum, at any rate—that it *is* divine, and the rest we shall not know *yet*, but we shall know; and we prefer to say to all who differ, "We have a fancy—if you like to regard it as such—a very great fancy for the Bible (that is the Book) as it is (not by any means objecting to a revision of the translation, by the way) with all its mysteries, and fragmentary revelations, and promises of more by and by. And we fancy, too, that the mother who can look up quietly and say, after she has lost her baby, 'I *know* in whom I have believed, and that He is able to help those who trust Him,' has a wonderful advantage over him who says, 'I like to know what I am about; I believe what I see, or can see proved, and when I see miracles worked, or get the benefit of one, then I will believe in them and the other doubtful matters.' "

The one idea seems loving and tender, the other cold and harsh; which is about the same as saying the one seems right and the other wrong. For we know that in social life, kindliness and good-will and liberal judgment are considered the best rules for guidance, and that logical exactness and statuesque philosophy are only admired at a distance, and have no near friends. And we are sure that the Bible is with the good-natured, we are conscious of its influence right through our lives, that it is with us in every good word and kind thought, and that it tugs at us when in moments of indigestion (physical or mental) we strive to be uncharitable and rough. Please excuse us when we admit that we do not follow every controversy to what is called its 'issue;' and accept as explanation that we followed two or three representative ones, and found them such a weariness of the flesh, such a climbing up mountains of sawdust, that we determined, if we got safely out of the last, we would never run the same risk again. Without the Bible we can imagine the mother's brain giving way under the pressure, and the student throwing down his books, and asking why he should strive, to what end? Threescore years and ten, with the intermediate risks, offer but slight inducements. With the Bible we can understand the mother's calm and the student's eagerness, and the anticipations of both. We *feel* that we gain by 'believing where we cannot prove,' and that we lose by giving in to that spirit of perverseness which arogantly demands proof in defiance of a secret consciousness that the power that holds the proof can afford to smile at the impertinence, and is strong enough to crush out all opposition at any moment.

> " When He folds the cloud about Him,
> Firm within it stands His throne;
> Wherefore should His children doubt Him,
> Those to whom His love is known,
> God is with us,
> We are *never left alone.*"

II.

The foregoing are the first thoughts that came to me when I began to consider this Introduction, and I do not see that any apology need be offered for writing them down. They are not strikingly original I know; the main thought has all the advantages of age; but it is certainly true that we require to be most frequently reminded of those things that are most familiar to us, those things that are 'taken for granted'—which is merely another term for being cast into oblivion. If we thought more about the Bible, noting more carefully the vast extent and comprehensiveness of what it does reveal to us now, with its illimitable promise of more to follow—neither fact nor promise being approached by any other fact or system; if we thought more about God, of the grandeur of the conception, of the way in which He is proving every day the exact truth of the account of Him that has been handed down to us, how He is making knowledge to 'grow from more to more' with ever increasing rapidity—thus giving man the chance of proving a great many things for himself; if we were to set our minds at great thoughts such as these, and try to get an idea of their vastness, we should surely find ourselves able to overcome the temptation to stand open-mouthed in the presence of small illusions, most of which have to be carefully worked up to along a weary avenue of artifice; surely we should be strong enough to say in presence even of the strongest case, "No, no; the great God is not in that whirlwind. I may not be able to comprehend fully, but He is certainly not in Spirit-rapping, neither does he transmit his messages through Ghosts, nor sanction a special significance in the howling of dogs; Professor Anderson would be the most inspired apostle of such a God, certainly not St. Paul. But the diversions of the forces of Nature are always interesting, and frequently amusing; and inexplicable things are constantly being explained. So we will only wonder and wait."

Such then is the preliminary note in accord with which I wish the reading of the following pages to be tuned. There are many people in the world possessing good hearts but sadly weak nerves; and although those who are stronger cannot pretend to regulate their general conduct by a false standard, in order to save their neighbours from shocks, yet I think it behoves us to check their sufferings wherever a direct opportunity presents itself; and to announce the antidote when we see any risk. It would be almost wrong to send out this book with merely a word or two about the remarkable stories it contains. We must remind each other of the grounds we have for not believing in the miscellaneous working of superhuman agencies; of the appalling evidence we have daily before our eyes of the prolificness of ignorance and its spouse superstition; of the strange combinations of circumstances that are constantly being made known in every circle of friends, which look as though they had purposely interwoven themselves to create confusion amongst the parties interested, but which fall into a most natural sequence from the moment we find out the key-fact and begin our investigation at the right end. We should also remind each other at all such periods of doubt, of the enormous majority of important incidents that occur every year in every life without the slightest preparatory hint being given, which in itself seems to me to be a triumphant rejoinder to volumes of such weak questionings; of the number of times that under the influence of extreme anxiety or ill-health, we have imagined uncounted ills, not one of which has reached us; and, we might even add, of the habit human nature has somehow fallen into of dreaming of deaths, a habit that has become so general and persistent that human ingenuity—not to outdone—has ordained that to dream of a death signifies the approach of a wedding. I do not mean to say that it is in direct opposition to all we know of providential decrees and means of working that anything should at any time be done through dreams or other signs, but I do mean to say that the occasion must be very great (the simple word is the best) and the sign must bear the distinct mark of God upon it. We know that in the old time, in the beginning, dream revelations were accepted as guides to action,* but that was when Christianity, and consequently Civilization in all its highest forms were in their extreme infancy, and

---

* We might, for the sake of argument, even go so far as to say that possibly the faculty of dreaming was created for this purpose, and after the special need for such aids had ceased—Christianity becoming sufficiently established and Civilization growing—the faculty was not withdrawn lest we of later times should fail to understand the ancient process.

more than one able writer has shewn how many agencies were required then to aid, support, and defend the young growths that would be utterly foolish and futile now. Fingers were made before forks, and served the purpose; but now we have the improved means let us use them and be thankful.

The only super-humanity there is any need that we should recognise now, is, the super-humanity of science, and of knowledge generally. All science was super-human once and there are probably a number of inoffensive forces of nature—not meaning to make people uncomfortable, but simply going on with their work—which we have not yet reached; and the forces with which we are upon tolerably friendly terms may indulge occasionally in combinations undreamt of in our philosophy. Bear in mind, too, that, by silly affright and superstitious reverence on your part whenever anything strange occurs, you are reducing yourself to the level of the most savage tribes that have yet been discovered, and that even the most untutored of these could make your experience pale into mere matter-of-fact beside the gorgeous visions and intricate miracles he could relate as vouchsafed to him. Mr. Tylor remarks that 'the religious beliefs of all the lower races are based upon visions and dreams.'

III.

But to set aside the fact of superstition, and all the marvellous and suggestive stories connected with the history of it, as unworthy of notice, would be just as foolish as to urge or encourage belief in it. This history has always been of increasing interest, increasing as the light that could be thrown upon it has increased; for it has seemed to the thoughtful that superstition is in the main faith misdirected, and that all this uneasiness about spiritual manifestations, &c., has a thread, long drawn out, yet connecting it with that inborn yearning which, however much neglected, lingers in the heart of man, stretching some of the thoughts of it towards the Infinite Hereafter—that Hereafter being another inborn bit of knowledge.

The earliest glimpses of human sense—the first excursions beyond the line of Instinct—are found in the records of mythology: and they reveal to us the existence of a constant feeling of fear lest evil deeds requiring redress should be committed, and a terrible anxiety to atone without loss of time or chance for any such mishaps. Mythology, which is the basis from whence arises the whole fabric of modern fable, in its earliest developments showed a keen discrimination between right and wrong, and unhesitatingly dismissed the wrong to frightful penalties—to be scorched up by the sun, whose heat was insatiable; to be eaten up of dragons whose appetites were equal to any emergency. This idea of the punishment of wrong-doing is the first principle by which humanity is distinguished, it is embedded in the constitution of the lowest types. In it was involved the possibility of right-doing; if wrong must be punished, it followed, as a matter of course, that right must be rewarded. Hence, we find that the most careful regard was shown to the supposed feelings of the Sun and the Dragon; and, as it is useless to cry out after you are hurt (or at anyrate unavailing), we know that no efforts were spared to conciliate those powerful and voracious elements—or rather Deities, which is the more exact description.

This may be regarded as the time when the sentiment of Reverence was beginning life, and it was certainly blind in its youth, as very many now living, who have not carefully cultivated a later acquaintance with it, are always unconsciously testifying. The visible indifference of the sun, and the assumed indifference of the dragon, to these oblations, only excited these victims of a dawning conscience (if the term may be allowed) to still wilder excesses. The reaction came after a time, but it brought little light with it. The only new element it introduced was curiosity: superstition was rampant as ever, but some of the elementary forms of fear had given place, and the first suggestions of wonder were experienced. From that time the business was carried on by curiosity, superstition, wonder, fear, and reverence conjointly, the latter being a sleeping partner, but largely interested.

IV.

Now, this principle of Wrong being punishable and Right being laudable, and this desire to conciliate the powers that were, involved, as we have already hinted, the further notion of a Hereafter; otherwise men would have felt a certain security in the knowledge that, if the worst came to the worst, and especially if unwittingly they did wrong, they could cancel the whole business by putting an end to themselves. But the knowledge was implied that no such obliteration was possible; and this is strengthened by the whole subsequent development of curiosity, which certainly signifies something to be discovered. This new phase did not however bring with it any new power of penetration, I have said: it did little more than re-assert the facts about Right and Wrong, Punishment and Reward, a Present and a Future, &c., and left them unqualified and unsupported. I will quote here two brief passages which I noted the other day when seeking out some of the earlier utterances upon this great subject of human hopes and fears, anticipations and horrors, and which bear directly upon the preceding remarks. A French writer, Boismont, in his treatise "Des Hallucinations," published more than 20 years ago, said, " The savage who dreams of the Great Spirit and boundless hunting grounds of another life ; the man of the middle ages who knelt at the entrance of the purgatory of St. Patrick ; the Arab who wanders amid the enchanted Palaces of the *Thousand-and-One Nights ;* the Hindoo absorbed in the incarnations of Brama ; the inhabitant of the civilized world who in public believes in nothing, and consults the pythoness or fortune-teller in secret, or seeks for revelations of the future in magnetism ; all obey the same law of necessity—that of believing in something ;" and this important intuition if not properly trained and dieted, runs wild and entangles itself with other unchecked growths. " If," wrote Hobbes, " this superstitious fear of spirits were taken away, and with it prognostics from dreams, false prophecies, and many other things depending thereon, by which crafty and ambitious persons abuse the simple people, men would be much more fitted than they are for civil obedience. And this ought to be the work of the Schools."

Fear is always highly imaginative and includes the principle of Reverence in a greater or less degree ; there is something beautiful in the eager efforts of the Savage to hinder or assuage the anger of the sun, and something highly poetical in the notion of an insatiable dragon engaged in purging his part of the world of the evil that lurked therein. But curiosity in all its lower and most popular forms has nothing of the kind to temper its excesses, the majority of which become in consequence completely gross—entirely unideal ; it is an effect of civilization and culture, although in many hundreds of instances it may not be connected with its cause by even a single nerve. That is what I mean when I say that passing from the region of Fear into that of Curiosity we realise a change of atmosphere but no fresher air, until we get away from where the people congregate, and reach the outlying hills in pursuit of the minority. How enormous is the majority even now, who use this great intuition only for the meanest purposes of every-day life, instead of cherishing it as the birth-right of humanity, and the weapon whereby mountains can be removed if it be intelligently wrought with.

Just as it is possible for a woman to attain to the highest reach or to touch the lowest depth that is within the compass of humanity, so does Curiosity (the secret spring of all culture) develop under right training into the steady and unfailing guide of the Intelligence, leading it to elevated places whence full and fair views can be obtained, taking it round to the back of the infinite number of Hypocrises while they are ignorantly playing their little games before the world, shewing it even a long way into the mystery of Godliness; or, it degenerates into an instrument of torture, to the possessor quite as much as to the most sensitive witness or victim; its reflections are inverted, and he so becomes filled with distorted views of the men and things about him, with calumnies in the place of revelations of the progress of truth and righteousness, until he is unable to weigh an action, to follow the current of a motive, or to estimate the approximate value of anything that is not obvious. He wants everything explained to him and then refuses to accept explanations unless they exhaustively *account for* the matter in hand; he must have everything accounted for to his satisfaction or, he says, *he won't believe in it*—as if that mattered! How the forces of nature must laugh in their own delightful way at some of our airs and graces, our terrible threats of scepticism, of shewing them up if they don't behave better, and so on.

I sometimes think that the old established firm to which I have alluded on p. xiii. is very much extending its operations without offering any improvement in the quality of its productions; and that the education of curiosity must be very seriously neglected in many parts. For instance, when I read such utterances as the following :—"Afterwards the question should be put, 'are we sitting in the right order to get the best manifestations?' Probably some members of the circle will then be told to change seats with each other, and the signals will be afterwards strengthened. Next ask, 'Who is the medium?' When spirits come, asserting themselves to be related or known to anybody present, well-chosen questions should be put to test the accuracy of the statements, *as spirits out of the body have all the virtues and all the failings of spirits in the body.*" This is one of the *rules* laid down for the regulation of a spiritualistic seance.

In these absurd efforts (to use a very mild term) to pry into the region beyond nature, the greatest results obtained are so paltry when compared with the everyday achievements of common sense, that they would be entitled only to take rank amongst the heavier forms of practical joking, and we should be justified in referring them thither, but for the number of people we see who are seriously influenced by them. It is not my intention to speak in this place with any detail upon the great subjects of Latent Thought, and the independent working of the brain—Unconscious Cerebration; but the mere mention of such vast and important departments of scientific research is reassuring; and to think for a moment of what Sir Wm. Hamilton and Dr. Carpenter have already unravelled, or rather how much they have revealed, of these greatest mysteries of men's minds is surely enough to allay any passing excitement that anything we can regard as a phenomenon may arouse, and to cause us to agree with the latter gentleman when he says that in view of the great scientific discoveries that have been already granted to us, we ought to "look to an increased acquaintance with Nature, rather than to supernatural agencies, for the explanation of phenomena that seems beyond the scope of ordinary knowledge." There are so many more things in heaven and earth than are dreamt of by the most comprehensive philosopher; and it is to be hoped, my friend, whoever you are, that there are more and greater ideas in your head than have ever yet come out of it, and how they got there you don't know, nor ever will know. There is nothing more wonderful in the world than that. "We know that when any given object is seen, there is an image of that object, be it tree, man, or animal, painted on the retina in rays of light; but how that image is communicated to the brain, and from it to the sentient principle—what is the mechanical change produced on the nerve fibres during its transmission—what different change is required to convey the different images of a tree or a dog to the mind; of all these things we are utterly ignorant." So spake an anonymous but thoughtful writer 12 years ago, and as many of the incidents recorded in the following pages are cases of hallucination, as seeing things that are invisible, the passage may be read to advantage twice.

Before closing, I must give just one more, to me very striking, instance, shewing at once how many delusions occur and how they might be prevented. Mr. Home, the celebrated medium, declared, amongst other assertions, that he could see the light issue from a magnet. Dr. Carpenter says calmly—that if certain conditions could be complied to, this assertion would "be entitled to rank as an ascertained scientific fact. But," he continues, "this, after all, would merely prove that magnetic force, acting through Mr. Home's nervous system, could produce the sensation of light; which would not seem more unlikely to those who know the correlation of those forces, than that certain persons should be apprised of a change of wind or the approach of a thunderstorm, by feelings of which ordinary people have no experience." Of course none but a man of high cultivation could defend himself or his opinion with such an explanation as this. And does not this also show that even the exhibitor may himself be taken in—that is to say, deceived as to the nature of the properties exhibited in and through him? And am I not right, when I say again, be content to wonder and wait? And do disabuse your minds, you who are under the influence of that absurd postulate, that it is necessary to form a definite and final opinion without delay upon everything that presents itself with a claim upon your attention; don't send it away without notice, but do not be afraid to say "I'll think it over, and let you know in a year or two."

> We have but faith; we cannot know;
> For knowledge is of things we see;
> And yet we trust it comes from Thee,
> A beam in darkness, let it grow.

It remains to be stated that Horace Welby's '*Signs before Death*,' forms the basis of this volume. But none of his stories are simply reprinted; antiquated forms of expression have been modified as far as seemed desirable, absurd comments by no means essential have been expunged, and some new matter added.

W. B. T.

LONDON, 1874.

INDEX.

	PAGE
Apparition to a Highwayman	3
A Mysterious Memorandum	27
Apparition at Belfast	29
A Mother's Appearance to her Son	54
An Experience of a Professor	90
Appearance of Henry Jacob to his cousin	101
Anecdote of Lady Hastings	102
A Fortunate Dream	104
A Member of Parliament warned of Arrest	118
Apparition seen by R. Bovet	120
Apparition seen in York Cathedral	128
An Awful Admonition	131
Apparitions recorded by Boswell	132
Ann Taylor of Tiverton	134
Apparition seen by Lady Pennyman	135
Apparition seen by Mr. Walker	152
Apparition of Lord Tyrone	160
Apparition to Mr. W. Lilly	168
Apparition of Mr. Thomkins	172
Apparition to M. Mercato	190
Apparition seen at Portnedown Bridge	191
Apparition of Major Blomberg	194
Apparition to Lady Fanshaw	211
Apparition to Melancthon	213
Apparition to Mrs. Veal	215
Apparition to Mr. Bezuel	227
A Hint to Judge Brograve	233
Apparition of Mr. Barlow's Huntsman	237
Apparition to Ninon de L'Enclos	244
A Dream Fulfilled	272
A New Miracle	274
Apparition to Miss Hepburn of Garleton	247

Contents.

	PAGE
Apparition to Mr. Weston	249
Belfast, Apparition at	29
Blandy, Omens of the Murder of Mr.	34
Beaumont's Confession	126
Booty (Mr.) and the Ship's Crew	223
Barlow's (Mr.) Huntsman	237
Councillor John Bourne of Dudley	33
Captain Porteous	36
Cashio Burroughs and the Courtesan	97
Captain Roger's Dream	98
Captain Bell and Luther's Table-Talk	114
Confession of John Beaumont	126
Charles II., Omen to	233
Conversion of Henry de Joyense	243
Discovery of a Murder at Chester	1
Drummer of Tedworth	15
Durley, John Bourne of	33
David Hunter's Vision	59
Duchess of Mazarine and Madame Beauclair	65
Doune, Dr. and Mrs.	72
Dr. Scott and the Title-Deed	75
Dorothy Dingley of Lancaster	82
Dream, A Fortunate	104
Discovery of Murderers of Mr. Stockden	106
Dream Revelations of Murder	107
Dominica, Apparition to the Governor of	194
Dream of Rev. J. Wilkins	225
Desfontaines, Apparition of	227
Death of Commissioner	234
Dream of Miss Hutton	242
Duel Prevented	256
Dream Fulfilled, A	272
Evidence of an Apparition	238
Farrer (Dr.) and his Daughter	14
Ficinus, Apparition of	190
Goddard (T.) of Marlborough	50
Gast's House	55
Hastings (Lady Elizabeth), Anecdote of	102
Haddock (James) to F. Traverner	109

	PAGE
Henry III.'s Death Prognosticated	241
Hutton (Miss) Remarkable Dream of	242
Hepburn (Miss) of Garleton, Apparition to	247
James IV., Warning to	28
Jacob (Dr.), Apparition to	101
Johnson (Dr.), Apparition recorded in Life of	132
Joyense (Henry de), Conversion of	243
Lee's (Sir Charles) Daughter	32
Letter by Earl of Marlborough	44
Luther's Table-Talk, Captain Bell and	114
Lady Davies's Prognostics	115
Londonderry, Apparitions to the Marquis of	123
Lindsay (R.) of Edinburgh	128
Lady Beresford, Apparition to	160
Lilly (Mr. W.), Apparitions seen by	168
Lady Fanshaw, Apparition to	211
Lord Lyttleton	234
Murder at Chester, Discovery of	1
Merchant's Apprentice, The	30
Marlborough's Letter to Sir H. Portland	44
Middleton (Lord) and the Laird	100
Murder, Dream Revelations of	107
Mohun (Lord) to his Mistress	116
Melancthon, Apparition to	213
Massacre of St. Bartholomew	240
Miracle, A New	274
Ninon de L'Enclos, Apparition to	244
Omen of Murder of Mr. Blandy	34
Omen to Mrs. Stephens	117
Orrery (Lord) and his Butler	157
Owen, Sir John and Lady	229
Omen to Charles II.	233
Porteous, Captain	36
Prognostics, Lady Davies's	115
Pitcairne's (Dr.) Dream	190
Portnedown Bridge, Apparition seen at	191
Peden, Alexander	242
Rochester Apparition, The	94
Radiant Boy, Appearance of the	123

	PAGE
Remarkable Dream of Rev. J. Wilkins	225
Sir Charles Lee's Daughter	32
Spider (The) and the King	36
Sydenham (Major) and Captain W. Dyke	42
Sherbroke (Sir John) and General Wynyard	45
Sherring's Story of Gast's House	55
Strange Presages at Woodstock	60
Scott (Dr.) and the Title-Deed	75
Singular Vision to Mrs. Lowe	88
Stockden, Discovery of Murderers of	106
Strange Experiences of the Wesley Family	173
Sword Signs	210
Second Sight	250
Stampford Ghost	261
The Two Brothers	11
Tedworth, The Drummer of	15
The Merchant's Apprentice	30
The Spider and the King	36
Theodosius, Vision of	39
Thornton of Fulham	73
The Midnight Storm	142
Tyrone (Lord) Appearance of	160
The Abbey Vault	196
The Disobedient Son	200
The Yatton Demoniac	202
Vision of Theodosius	39
Vision of David Hunter	59
Villiers, Duke of Buckingham	69
Vision to Mrs. Lowe	88
Wicked Step-Mother, The	4
Warning to James IV	28
Wynyard (General) and Sir J. Sherbroke	45
Woodstock, Strange Presages at	60
Warning to an M.P.	118
Warren (Rev. Mr.) Apparition to	172
Wesley Family, Strange Experiences of	173
Weston (Mr.), Apparition to	249
York Cathedral, Apparition in	128
Yatton Demoniac, The	202

SIGNS BEFORE DEATH.

I.

Discovery of a Murder at Chester.

ABOUT the year 1632, near Chester-in-the-street, there lived one Walker, a yeoman of good estate, and a widower, with a handsome young house-keeper, who was by the neighbours suspected to be with child. Towards the dusk one evening in autumn, she was sent away in company with a man named Mark Sharpe. After this she was not heard of for a long time. In the following winter, one James Graham, or Grime, a miller, residing about two miles from the place where Walker lived, was one night alone very late in the mill, grinding corn. About twelve o'clock he came down stairs, having finishing putting corn in the hopper, when there stood before him a woman, with her hair hanging loose about her head, and stained with blood. Upon her head were five large wounds. He asked her who she was, and what she wanted? She replied, "I am the spirit of ———, who lived with Walker; and having been seduced by him, he promised to send me to a private place, where I should be well attended to until I was brought to bed and well again, when I should return and keep his house. Accordingly," continued the Apparition, "I was one night sent away late, with one Mark Sharpe, who upon a moor (naming a place which the miller knew) slew me with a pick (such as men use in digging coals), and gave me these five wounds, and afterwards threw my body into a coal-pit hard by, and hid the pick under a bank; and his shoes and stockings being bloody, he endeavoured to wash them, but seeing the blood would not wash out, he hid them there." The Apparition further told the Miller that he must be the man to reveal the crime, or else she must still appear and haunt him. The Miller returned home very sad and heavy, but told no one of what he had seen.

Shortly afterwards, and again towards dusk, the Apparition met him a second time, and threatened that if he did not reveal the murder, it would continually pursue and haunt him. He still said nothing of what had happened until just before Christmas, when walking one evening in his garden, it appeared again, and so threatened and terrified him, that he faithfully promised to reveal the whole matter next morning.

In the morning he went to a magistrate, and told what he knew. A diligent search was made, the body was found in a coal-pit, with five wounds in the head, and the pick, the shoes, and stockings, still marked, were also found under a bank close by. Walker and Mark Sharpe were both apprehended, but would confess nothing. At the following Durham assizes they were arraigned before Judge Davenport, found guilty, condemned, and executed. During the trial, one Mr. Fairbair gave it in evidence upon oath, that he saw the likeness of a child stand upon Walker's shoulders!
—*From H. Welby.*

II.

The Apparition and the Highwayman.

In the year 1780, Mr. Bower, an aged man, living at Guildford in Surrey, was, upon the highway, not far from the town, found barbarously murdered, having one great cut across the throat, and another down his breast. Two men were taken up on suspicion, and imprisoned in Guildford gaol, with another, who had before been committed for robbery. During the night, this third man was awakened about twelve o'clock, and greatly terrified by a vision of an old man, who had a wide gash across his throat, almost from ear to ear, and a wound down his breast. He came in stooping, and holding his hand to his back. The thief called to his new companions, who grumbled at him, but made no answer.

In the morning he retained so lively an impression of what he had seen, that he spoke to them again, but they told him it was nothing but his fancy. But he was so fully persuaded of the reality of this apparition, that he told others of it, and it reached the ears of a magistrate of Surrey, who was cousin to the murdered gentleman.

He immediately sent for the prisoner, and asked him, in the first place, whether he was born or had lived near Guildford? To this he answered no. Secondly, he enquired if he knew any of the inhabitants of that town, or of the neighbourhood? He replied that he was an entire stranger to all that part of the country. He then enquired if he had ever heard of one Mr. Bower? He said he had not. After this he asked for what the other two men were imprisoned? He said he supposed for some robbery, but did not know positively.

The magistrate then desired him to tell him what

he had seen in the night, which he immediately did. He said the old gentleman had a picked beard, rough cheeks, and that the hair on his face was black and white. The magistrate said that he himself could not have given a more exact description of Mr. Bower.

He, however, concealed this story from the jury at the assizes, knowing it would not be evidence according to law. The friends of the murdered gentleman had been very rigid in their search, and had discovered several suspicious circumstances; one of which was, that these two men had washed their clothes, but some stains of blood still remained; another, that one of them had denied ever having heard that Mr. Bower was dead, having in another place talked about it two hours before. Upon this, and similar evidence, the men were condemned and executed, but they both denied all knowledge of the murder to the last moment.

Some time after a tinker was hanged, who, at his death said, that the murder of Mr. Bower, at Guildford, was his greatest trouble; for he had a hand in it. He then confessed that he struck the blow on the back, which brought Mr. Bower from his horse, and when he was down, the other two men who had been arraigned and executed, cut his throat, and robbed him.—*From Dr. H. More.*

III.

The Wicked Step-mother.

A gentlemen of good position married a lady of fortune, by whom he had one son and one daughter. After a few years the lady died. He then married a second wife with less fortune than the other, who maltreated the children he had by his first wife.

The first misunderstanding between the parties was

owing to the eldest son's wish to go abroad, which the mother-in-law would gladly have acquiesced in, had it not been for the expense, which she feared might prove very heavy. The young gentleman not obtaining leave, applied to his own mother's brother, and, finding his plan approved, set out on his intended journey, contrary to the wish of his father.

The father received intelligence from him regularly for some time, and had made him a reasonable allowance; but owing to the influence of his step-mother, this remittance was suddenly discontinued, after which the correspondence ceased for four years.

During this long silence, the mother-in-law exerted herself in several ways: she first intimated to his father that he must be dead; and, consequently, that his estate should be settled upon *her* eldest son, she having several children. His father opposed this proposition very firmly, but the wife became importunate, arguing that, if he were dead, then there could be no room to object to her son's being heir-at-law. If he were alive, his neglect of his father was inexcusable, and he ought to resent it, and settle the estate as though he were dead.

The father withstood the importunities of his wife for a long time. Her restless solicitations, however, at last produced this provisional arrangement: that if he did not hear from his son within four years, he would consent to resettle the estate. She became dissatisfied with this conditional agreement, and he grew angry at her discontent. Still she teazed him so continually that at last she reduced the time to one year; but before she brought him to this agreement, she told him one day in a passion, that she hoped the spirit of his son would appear to him, and tell him that he was dead and that he ought to do justice to his other children. He replied that he hoped his son's spirit, if he were not dead, would appear to her and tell her he was alive, before the time expired.

It happened one evening soon afterwards that they had a violent quarrel upon this subject, when suddenly a hand appeared at the casement, endeavouring to open it. The gentleman did not see it, but his wife did, and she presently started up, as if frightened, and, forgetting the quarrel, exclaimed, "Dear me! there are thieves in the garden." Her husband ran immediately to the door of the room, and, opening it, looked out.

"There is nobody in the garden," said he; and then shut the door again, and returned to his seat.

"I am sure I saw a man there," she said.

"It must be a ghost then," he replied, "for I am sure there is nobody in the garden."

"I am certain," added his wife, "I saw a man put his hand up to open the casement; but finding it fast, and I suppose seeing us in the room, he walked off."

"It is impossible he could have got away in the time. Did not I run to the door immediately, and you know the garden walls on both sides would prevent escape."

"No, I am not so easily mistaken," replied she; "if 'twas a ghost, 'twas the ghost of your son, who perhaps may be come to tell you he is gone."

"If it was my son," replied he, "he is come to tell us he is alive, I warrant you; and to ask how you can be so wicked as to desire me to disinherit him," and with these words "*Alexander*," he cried aloud, repeating it twice, "if you are alive, show yourself, and don't let me be vexed thus daily with the story of your being dead."

At these words the casement flew open, and his son Alexander looked in, and staring directly upon the mother with an angry countenance, cried out, "*Here*," and then vanished! The wife gave a terrified scream; the maid ran into the parlour to see what was the matter, and found her mistress had fainted away.

The husband ran immediately from the parlour into the garden, and from thence to two other doors which opened out of his garden, one into the stable-yard and another into the field beyond the garden, but found them all fast shut and barred. On returning into the garden, he found his gardener and a boy: he asked them if any other person had been in the garden, but they both solemnly affirmed that none had been there.

Upon this he returned to the room, seated himself, and remained silent for some time. After a while his wife recovered herself, when the first words she said were, "What was it?" "Indeed," said her husband, "'twas Alexander." She fell again into a fainting fit, and continued very ill for several days afterwards.

This put an end for some considerable time to her solicitations about disinheriting her son-in-law. But time wore on, and she began to revive the old cause again, though not at first so eagerly as before. This gave rise to serious disputes, in which the husband alluded to the recent apparition, and threatened to recall it. The enraged wife at length indicted him as a wizard, and accused him of horrible traffickings in witchcraft and sorcery. At length, for what will not the discontent of woman effect, she so far prevailed on him, that he offered to refer the dispute to indifferent persons, or friends on both sides; and they met several times, but could bring the matter to no conclusion. His friends said that he called for his son, and some one opened the casement and cried *Here;* asserting that there was not the least evidence of witchcraft in that, and insisting that she could make nothing of it. She offered to swear that he had threatened her before with his son's ghost; that now he had visibly raised a spectre, for that upon calling his son, the spirit immediately appeared. After much altercation they were reconciled again, and accordingly he gave her the writing; but when he delivered it to her, in the presence of her two arbitrators, he thus addressed her:—" Look you, you have worried me into this agreement by your fiery temper, and I have signed it against justice, conscience, and reason ; but depend upon it I shall never perform it."

One of the arbitrators said, " Why, Sir, this is all to no purpose ; for if you resolve not to perform it, where is the utility of the writing ? Why do you promise what you do not intend to perform ? This will but kindle a new flame to begin with, when the time expires." " Because," said he, " I am satisfied in my mind that my son is alive." " Come," said his wife, speaking to the gentleman who had argued with her husband, "let him sign the agreement, and leave me to make him perform it." "Well," replied the husband, "you shall have the writing, and you shall be let alone, but I am satisfied you will never ask me to perform it." At the end of four months she challenged the performance ; accordingly a day was appointed, and her two friends, the arbitrators, were invited to dinner. Accordingly the writings were brought forth, engrossed, and read over; and the husband being won over, executed the deeds. When they had settled the particulars, and the new deeds were read over, she took up the old writings to cancel them ; and, on her tearing off the seal, they suddenly heard a rushing noise in the parlour where they sat, as if somebody had come in at the door of the room which opened from the hall, and passed through the room towards the garden door, which was shut.

They were all much surprised at it, for the noise was very distinct; but they saw nothing. The woman turned pale, and became very nervous; however, as nothing was seen, she soon recovered, and said to her husband, "What, have you laid your plot to bring up more devils ?" The man sat composed, though he was not less surprised. One of the gentlemen said to him, "What is the meaning of all this?" "I protest, Sir," he replied, "I know no more of it than you do." "What can it it be then?" said the other gentleman. "I cannot conceive," said he, "for I am utterly unacquainted with such things." "Have you heard nothing from your son?" asked the gentleman. "Not one word these five years," replied the father. "Have you not written to him about this transaction?" said the gentleman. "Not a word, for I know not where to address a letter to him," he answered. "Sir," said the gentleman, "I have heard much of apparitions, but I never saw one in my life, nor did I ever believe there was any such thing possible, and indeed I have seen nothing now; but the passing of some body or spirit across the room just now was evident; I heard it distinctly." "Nay," said the other arbitrator, "I felt the wind of it as it passed by me. Pray," he added, turning to the husband, "did you see anything yourself?" "No," he replied. The first arbitrator enquired, "Have you seen anything at any other time, or heard any voices or noises, or had any dreams about this matter?" "Indeed I have several times dreamt my son was alive, and that I had spoken with him, and once I had asked him why he was so undutiful as not to let me hear from him in so many years, seeing he knew that I had it my power to disinherit him," he answered. "Well, Sir, and what answer did he give?" "I never dreamt so far on as to have his answer." "And what do you think of it yourself," said the arbitrator, "do you think he is dead?" "No, indeed," said the father, "I believe he is alive, and that I am about to commit myself." "Truly," said the second arbitrator, "it begins to shock me; I don't care to meddle any more with it." The wife having somewhat recovered her spirits, and being specially encouraged because she saw nothing, now started up

—" To what purpose is all this discourse," said she, "is it not already agreed upon? What do we come here for?" The first arbitrator agreed; "I think we meet now not to enquire into why it is done, but to execute things according to agreement; and what are we frightened at?" "I am not frightened," said the wife; "come, sign the deed, I'll cancel the old writings if forty devils are in the room." Upon this she took up one of the deeds, and was about to tear off the seal.

At that moment the same casement again flew open, and the shadow of a body was seen standing in the garden, the head reaching up to the window, and the face looking into the room, staring directly at the woman with a stern countenance: "*Hold*," said the spectre, as if speaking to the woman, and immediately shut the casement, and disappeared.

It is impossible to describe the consternation which this second apparition created in the whole company; the wife screamed out, fell into hysterics, and let the writing drop from her hands: the two arbitrators were exceedingly terrified, and one of them took up the award signed by them, in which they empowered the husband to execute the deed disinheriting the son.

"I dare say," said he, "be the spirit a good or a bad one, it will not be against cancelling this," and he tore his name out of the award; the other did the same, and both of them rose from their seats and said they would have no more to do in the affair. This put an end to the whole business.

In about four or five months after the second apparition, the son arrived from the East Indies, whither he had sailed four years before, in a Portuguese ship from Lisbon. Upon being particularly enquired of about these things, and especially whether he had any knowledge of them, or had seen any apparition, or other extraordinary intimation concerning what was going on against him at home; he constantly affirmed that he had not, except that he once dreamt his father had written him a very angry letter, threatening him, that if he did not come home, he would disinherit him, and cut him off without a shilling. This, he added, was one of the principal reasons of his desire to return to England upon the first opportunity.— *From Moreton's History of Apparitions.*

IV.

The Two Brothers.

Mr. R—— N——, and Mr. J—— N——, brothers, whose education had been equally liberal, they having been members of the University of Oxford, displayed, at the conclusion of their college days, tastes diametrically opposite. The former was for venturing everything, and running all hazards, in order to push his fortune; whilst the maxim of the other was to regulate his conduct by the strictest prudence and economy, and leave nothing to chance.

When their studies were finished, they both returned to their father, an eminent merchant of Bristol. For some time after their return, they were entirely occupied with deliberations what professions they should adopt, what plan of life they should pursue for the remainder of their days.

In the midst of these golden dreams, the father, by a sudden and unexpected turn of fortune, failed, and took so to heart the loss of his wealth, that he died in a few days, leaving his two sons in a state of indigence. The eldest brother declared, that he was resolved rather to risk death than to stay at Bristol, where he had formerly lived in affluence.

The brothers accordingly took leave of each other, the former bent upon buffeting fortune, and the latter resolving to avail himself of the slight resources which he might find in the place of his nativity.

He accordingly went to live with a merchant, an acquaintance of his father, by whom he was employed as clerk. Mr. R—— N—— went to London, where his money was soon exhausted, and he became reduced to such an extremity that having been four days without food, he one evening wandered about St. James's Park in despair, and presently sat down upon one of the benches, and taking a knife out of his pocket, was upon the point of committing suicide, when suddenly looking up, he saw a figure of great beauty. It appeared to him to be a handsome youth, whose eyes shone with a starry brightness, and a glory seemed to play about his hair.

Lifting up his eyes to this angelic appearance, he heard these words distinctly pronounced: "*Hold, rash mortal!*" The despairing man immediately desisted, and the phantom advancing forward beckoning him, he rose up and followed it: it suddenly vanished, and he walked on with an exultation he could not account for, till at last he met a soldier, who pressed him to enter a public-house, which was the rendezvous of a recruiting party.

Here the mirth but little suited the more serious mood of Mr. R—— N——; but as he was quite destitute, he readily accepted the proposal to enlist. The regiment which he joined was soon after ordered abroad, and he signalized himself at the siege of Quebec, and upon several other occasions, and soon rose to a lieutenancy. Upon his return to England, he found himself reduced to half-pay, which proved insufficient to meet the demands of his pleasure.

The greatest source of expense was, as usual, an unhappy attachment. This led him to frequent all the places of amusement, and to expend large sums of money upon dress and jewellery.

But her attractions served only to render her more dangerous : in truth, she possessed the most fascinating loveliness, which was greatly heightened by her conversational charms. In the meantime her gay admirer, by gentlemanly appearance and plausible address, easily obtained credit to a large amount ; but, at length, his creditors became so importunate, that he was in the greatest perplexity, and the thought of having imposed upon persons who had so generously obliged him, drove him almost into a phrenzy. His evil genius now suggested to him a course almost equally desperate as that of suicide, which he had already attempted, namely, that of going upon the highway.

He accordingly provided himself with pistols, and one evening went to Blackheath. He rode to and fro in the utmost perturbation of mind; his terror still increasing as the night approached, till at last he beheld the same angelic appearance that he had seen before, which seemed to point to the road to London. Even in the darkness of the night the whole figure appeared very manifest, and no sooner had Mr. R—— N—— beheld it, but all his agitation and disorder subsided, and, with the utmost composure of mind, he returned to London, having taken the precaution of throwing away his pistols, lest they might give rise to any suspicion of the purpose which he had in leaving town.

Upon his return to his lodgings, he broke up his connexion with the pernicious woman who had given him such terrible advice.

The grand source of his inquietude still remained. He was apprehensive every moment of being arrested, and thrown into jail by his creditors. He now formed a resolution to go over to Ireland, thinking he could there be secure from his creditors. Whilst his mind was occupied with these thoughts he was arrested, and there being several actions against him at the same time, he was obliged to get himself removed to the Fleet by Habeas Corpus. A man of his high tone of mind could but ill brook confinement. The days hung heavily on his hands, and he was obliged to have recourse to wine to dispel the gloom by which his mind was overcast. Whilst Mr. R—— N—— led this life of care and inquietude, he one night had a dream, which revived his drooping spirit. He dreamed that the same vision which had appeared to him twice before came in the night, and opened the gates of his prison; and the ideas which passed in his imagination took so strong a hold upon his mind, that when he awoke in the morning, he could not for some time be persuaded that he was still in prison. The delusion soon vanished, but he retained his cheerfulness, and this seemingly groundless joy was soon followed by a real one.

About noon he heard himself enquired for, and immediately knew the voice to be that of his brother. He rushed into his arms, and embraced him with the utmost transport. When their first emotions of joy were somewhat subsided, Mr. J—— N—— gave his brother to understand that he had accumulated a fortune by East India trade; and enquiring into the state of his affairs, and the sum for which he was in confinement, he paid the debt and set him at liberty that evening.—*From H. Welby.*

V.

Dr. Farrer and his Daughter.

In 1678, Dr. Farrar, physician to Charles the Second, made a compact with his daughter, Mrs. Pearson, that the first of them that died, if happy, should appear, after death, to the survivor.

Some time after, the daughter, who lived at Gillingham Lodge, two miles from Salisbury, fell in labour, and owing to a noxious draught being given instead of another prepared for her, she suddenly died.

Her father lived in London, and the night on which she died, she opened his curtains and gazed upon him. He had before heard nothing of her illness; but upon this apparition confidently told his maid that his daughter was dead, and two days after he received the news.—*From Dr. H. More.*

VI.

The Drummer of Tedworth.

Every one has heard of the comedy of " *The Drummer, or the Haunted House,*" celebrated enough in its day; but the popularity of which ceased when the affair was no longer a topic of public conversation. The circumstances which gave rise to this performance are detailed as follows, by Glanvil, by whose statement it appears that the matter turned out to be no farce for Mr. Mompesson, the proprietor of the house.

Mr. John Mompesson of Tedworth, being in March, 1661, at a neighbouring town, called Ludgarshal, and hearing a drum beat there, he inquired what it meant. The bailiff, at whose house he was told him, that they had been for some days troubled with an idle drummer, who demanded money of the constable by virtue of a pretended pass, which he thought was counterfeit. Upon this Mr. Mompesson sent for the fellow, and asked him by what authority he went up and down the country in that manner with his drum. The drummer answered, he had good authority, and produced his pass, with a warrant under the hands of Sir William Cawley and Colonel Ayliff, of Gretenham. Mr. Mompesson knowing the handwriting of these gentlemen. discovered the pass and warrant to be counterfeit, and thereupon commanded the vagrant to give up his drum, and charged the constable to carry him before the Justice of the Peace. The fellow then confessed the cheat, and begged earnestly to have his drum. Mr. Mompesson told him, that if he understood from Colonel Ayliff, whose drummer he said he was, that he had been an honest man, he should have it again, but in the meantime he would secure it; so he left the drum with the bailiff, and the drummer in the constable's hands, who it seems was prevailed on by the fellow's entreaties to let him go.

About the middle of April following, when Mr. Mompesson was preparing for a journey to London, the bailiff sent the drum to his house; on his return from his journey, his wife told him that they had been much frightened in the night by thieves, and that the house had very nearly been entered. He had not been at home above three nights, when the same noise was heard that had disturbed his family in his absence —a very great knocking at the doors. Hereupon he got up, and went about the house with a brace of pistols in his hands; he opened the door where the great knocking was, and then he heard the noise at another door, he opened that also, and went out round the house, but could discover nothing, only he still heard a strange noise. When he got back to bed the noise was continued on the top of the house for some time, and then by degrees subsided.

After this the noise of thumping and drumming was very frequent, usually five nights together, and then it would intermit three. It was on the outside of the house, which was built chiefly of wood. It constantly came as they were going to sleep, whether early or late. After a month's disturbance outside, it came into the room where the drum lay, four or five nights after they were in bed, and continued almost two hours. The sign of it just before it came was, a hurling in the air over the house, and, at its going, like that at the breaking up of a guard. It continued in this room for the space of two months, which time Mr. Mompesson himself lay there to observe it. In the fore part of the night, it used to be very troublesome, but after two hours all was quiet.

Mrs. Mompesson being brought to bed, there was but little noise during her confinement, nor any for three weeks after, till she had recovered her strength. But after this cessation it returned in a ruder manner than before, and followed and vexed the youngest children, beating their bedsteads with much violence. By placing the hands on them, one could feel no blows but could see the beds shake; for an hour together it would beat Round-heads and Cuckolds, the Tat-too, and several other points of war, as well as any drummer. After this, a scratching under the children's beds was heard, as if by something that had iron talons. It would also lift the children up in their beds, follow them from one room to another, and for a while haunted none particularly but them.

There was a loft in the house whither they removed the children, putting them to bed while it was daylight, but they were no sooner laid down than their troubler was with them as before.

On the fifth of November, 1661, a great noise was heard, and a servant observing two boards in the children's room seeming to move, he bid the unseen agency to bring him one of them; upon which the board came (nothing moving it that he saw) within a yard of him; the man added, "Nay let me have it in my hand;" upon which it was pushed quite close to him again, and so up and down, to and fro, at least twenty times together, till Mr. Mompesson forbad his servant such familiarities. This was in the day-time, and seen by a whole room-full of people. That morning it left a sulphurous smell behind it, which was very offensive. At night the minister, one Mr. Cragg, and divers of the neighbours, came to the house on a visit. The minister went to prayers with them, kneeling at the children's bedside, where it was then very troublesome and loud. During prayer-time it withdrew, but returned as soon as prayers were done, and then in sight of the company the chairs walked about the room of themselves, the children's shoes were hurled over their heads, and every loose thing moved about the chamber. At the same time a bed-staff was thrown at the minister, which hit him on the leg, but so gently that a bit of wool could not fall more softly, and it was observed, that it stopt just where it fell, without rolling or moving from the place.

Mr. Mompesson perceiving that it so much persecuted the little children, lodged them out at a neighbour's house, taking his eldest daughter, who was about ten years of age, into his own chamber, where it had not been for a month. As soon as she was in bed the disturbance began there again, and continued three weeks. After this the house where the children lodged out, happening to be full of strangers, they were taken home, and no disturbance having been known in the parlour, they were lodged there, where also their persecutor found them and plucked them by the hair and night-clothes, but made no noises.

It was noted, that when the noise was loudest, and came with the most sudden and surprising violence, no dog about the house would move, though the knocking was often so boisterous and rude, that it had been heard at a considerable distance from the house. The servants sometimes were lifted up in their beds and let gently down again without hurt, at other times it would lie like a great weight upon their feet.

About the latter end of December, 1661, the drumming was less frequent, and then they heard a noise like the jingling of money.

After this it desisted from the ruder noises, and employed itself in trifling, and less troublesome tricks. On Christmas-eve, a little before day, one of the young boys arising out of his bed, was hit on a sore place upon his heel with the latch of the door, although the pin that it was fastened with was so small that it was a difficult matter to pick it out. The night after Christmas-day, it threw some clothes about the room, and hid a bible in the ashes. In such silly tricks it frequently indulged.

After this, it was very troublesome to a servant of Mr. Mompesson's, who was a stout fellow, and of sober conversation; this man lay within during the greatest disturbance, and for several nights something would endeavour to pluck his clothes off the bed, so that he was fain to tug hard to keep them on, and sometimes they would be plucked from him by main force, and his shoes thrown at his head; and now and then he would find himself forcibly held as if bound hand and foot, but whenever he could make use of his sword, and struck with it, the spirit quitted its hold.

A little after these contests a son of Mr. Thomas Bennet, whose workman the drummer had sometimes been, came to the house and told Mr. Mompesson of some words that he had spoken, which it seems were not well received; for as soon as they were in bed, the drum was beat up very violently and loudly; the gentleman arose and called his man to him, who was in the same room with John, just mentioned. As soon as Mr. Bennet's man was gone, John heard a rustling noise in his chamber like the movements of a person in silk, and something came to his bedside; the man presently reached after his sword, which he found held from him, and it was with difficulty and much tugging that he regained it, but as soon as he had done so the unseen power left him : it was always observed that it avoided a sword.

About the beginning of January, 1662, they were wont to hear a singing in the chimney before it came down ; and one night, about this time, lights were seen in the house. One of these came into Mr. Mompesson's chamber ; this light seemed blue and glimmering, and caused great dazzling in the eyes of those who saw it. After the light, something was heard coming up the stairs, as if without shoes. The light was seen also four or five times in the children's chamber ; and the maids confidently affirm that the doors were at least ten times opened and shut in their sight, and when they were open they heard a noise as if half a dozen had entered together, after which some were heard to walk about the room, and one always with the same rustling noise. Mr. Mompesson himself once heard these noises.

During the time of the knocking, when many were present, a gentleman of the company said, "Satan, if the drummer set thee to work, give three knocks and no more ; " this it did very distinctly, and stopped. Then the gentleman knocked to see if it would answer him as it was wont, but it did not ; for further confirmation, he bid it, if it were the drummer, give five knocks and no more that night, which it did, and left the house quiet. This was done in the presence of Sir Thomas Chamberlain, of Oxfordshire, and divers others.

On Saturday morning, an hour before day, January 10, a drum was heard to beat outside Mr. Mompesson's chamber, from whence it went to the other end of the house, where some gentlemen strangers slept, played at their door four or five tunes, and then ceased.

One morning, Mr. Mompesson rising early to go on a journey, heard a great noise in the room where the children lay, and running down with a pistol in his hand, heard a voice crying, " A witch, a witch." Upon his entrance all was quiet. This cry had been heard once before.

Having one night played some little tricks at the foot of Mr. Mompesson's bed, it went to another, where one of his daughters lay; there it went from side to side, lifting her up as it passed under. At one time there were three kinds of noises in the bed, they thrust at the places whence the sounds came with a sword, but it shifted, and seemed carefully to avoid the thrust, sometimes getting under the child. The night after, it came panting like a dog out of breath; upon which one took a bed-staff to strike at it, which was caught out of her hand and thrown away, and, company coming up, the room was presently filled with a noisome smell and became very hot, though it was winter time and there was no fire. It continued in the bed panting and scratching for an hour and a half, and then went into the next chamber, where it knocked a little, and seemed to rattle a chain; this continued for two or three nights together.

After this, the lady's bible was found in the ashes, the paper sides being downwards. Mr. Mompesson took it up, and observed that it lay open at the 3rd chapter of St. Mark, where there is mention of the unclean spirits falling down before our Saviour, and of his giving power to the twelve to cast out devils, and of the scribe's opinion, that he cast them out through Beelzebub.

The next night they strewed ashes over the chamber, to see what impressions it would leave; in the morning they found in one place the resemblance of a great claw, in another of a lesser, some letters in another, which they could make nothing of, besides many circles and scratches in the ashes.

"About this time," says Glanvil, "I went to the house to enquire the truth of those things of which there was so loud a report. It had ceased from its drumming and ruder noises before I came, but most of the more remarkable circumstances before related, were confirmed to me there by several of the neighbours together, who had been present at the time. At this time it used to haunt the children, beginning as soon as they were in bed. They went to bed the night I was there about eight o'clock, a maid-servant came down immediately afterwards and told us *it* was come. The neighbours who were there, and two ministers who had seen and heard it frequently, went away, but Mr. Mompesson and I, and a gentleman who came with me, went up. I heard a strange scratching as I went up the stairs, and when we came into the room I perceived it was just behind the bolster of the children's bed, and seemed to be against the tick. It was as loud a scratching as one with long nails could make upon a bolster. There were two little girls in the bed, between seven and eight years old. I saw their hands out of the clothes, and they could not contribute to the noise that was behind their heads; they had become used to it, and had always somebody or other in the chamber with them, and therefore seemed not to be much troubled. I, standing at the bed's head, thrust my hand behind the bolster, directing it to the place whence the noise seemed to come, whereupon the noise ceased there, and was heard in another part of the bed; but when I had taken out my hand it returned, and was heard in the same place as before. I had been told it would imitate noises, and made trial by scratching several times upon the sheet, as five, and seven, and ten, which it followed, always stopping at my number. I searched under and behind the bed, turned up the clothes to the bed-cords, grasped the bolster, sounded the wall behind, and made all the search possible, to find if there were any trick or contrivance, or common cause of it; so also did my friend, but we could discover nothing. I was then verily persuaded, and am so still, that the noise was made by some demon or spirit. After it had scratched about half an hour or more, it went into the midst of the bed under the children, and there seemed to pant like a dog out of breath, very loudly. I put my hand to the place, and felt the bed bearing up against it, as if something within had thrust it up. I grasped the feathers, to feel if any living thing were in it. I looked under and everywhere about, to see if there were any dog or cat or any such creature in the room, and so did we all, but found nothing. The motion it caused by this panting was so strong, that it shook the room and windows very sensibly. It continued thus more than half-an-hour, while my friend and I stayed in the room. During the panting, I thought I saw something moving in a linen-bag, that hung up against another bed in the room. I stepped forward and caught it by the upper end with one hand, with which I held it, and drew it through the other, but found nothing in it. There was nobody near to shake the bag, or if there had, no one could have caused such a movement, which seemed to be from within, as if a living creature had moved in it. This passage I mention incidentally, because it depended on my single testimony; but having told it to learned and inquisitive men, who thought it not altogether inconsiderable, I have now added it here.

"It will I know, be said by some that my friend and I were under some fright, and so fancied noises and sights that were not. This is the eternal evasion,

But I certainly know for my own part, that during the whole time of my being in the room, and in the house, I was under no more constraint of fear than I am while I write this relation. And if I know that I am now awake, and that I see the objects that are before me, I know that I heard and saw the particulars I have told. There is, I am sensible, no great matter for story in them, but there is so much as convinceth me that there was somewhat extraordinary, and what we usually call preternatural, in the business.

"I shall now briefly mention two or three other incidents of my visit to Tedworth. My friend and I lay in the chamber where the first and chief disturbance had been. We slept well all night, but early in the morning I was awakened (and I awakened my bed-fellow) by a loud knocking just without our chamber door. I asked who was there several times, but the knocking still continued without answer. At last I said, 'In the name of God who is it, and what would you have?' To which a voice answered, 'Nothing with you.' We, thinking it had been some servant of the house, went to sleep again. But speaking of it to Mr. Mompesson when we came down, he assured us that no one of the house slept that way, or had business thereabout, and that his servants were not up till he called them. They all affirmed, much later, that the noise was not made by them. Mr. Mompesson had told us before that it would be gone in the middle of the night, and come again divers times early in the morning, about four o'clock, and this I suppose was about that time."

But to proceed with Mr. Mompesson's own particulars. There came one morning a light into the children's chamber, and a voice crying, "A witch, a witch," at least an hundred times.

Mr. Mompesson, at another time (during the day), seeing some wood move that was in the chimney of a room where he was, as of itself, discharged a pistol into it, after which they found several drops of blood on the hearth, and in places on the stairs.

For two or three nights after the discharge of the pistol, there was a calm in the house, but soon the invisible agent came again, applying itself now to a little child newly taken from nurse, which it so persecuted, that it would not let the poor infant rest for two nights together, nor allow candles to remain in the room, but carried them away lighted, up the chimney, or threw them under the bed. It so scared this child by leaping upon it, that for some hours it could not be recovered from the fright, so that they were forced again to remove the children out of the house. The night after this removal, something about midnight came up stairs, and knocked at Mr. Mompesson's door, but he lying still, it went up another pair of stairs, to his man's chamber, to whom it appeared, standing at his bed's foot; the exact shape and proportion he could not discover, but he said he saw a great body, with two red glaring eyes, which, for some time, were fixed steadily upon him, and at length disappeared.

About the beginning of April, 1663, a gentleman who slept in the house had all his money turned black in his pockets; and Mr. Mompesson, coming one morning into his stable, found the horse he was wont to ride lying on the ground with one of his hinder legs in his mouth, and so fastened there that it was only with difficulty that several men succeeded in getting it out with a lever. After this there were some other remarkable things, but the account goes no farther; only Mr. Mompesson positively asserted that afterwards the house was several nights beset with seven or eight somethings in the shape of men, who, as soon as a gun was discharged, would shuffle away together.

The drummer was tried at the assizes at Salisbury

upon this occasion. He was committed first to Gloucester gaol for stealing, and a Wiltshire man coming to see him, he asked what news in Wiltshire; the visitor said he knew of none. "No?" saith the drummer, "do not you hear of the drumming at a gentleman's house at Tedworth?" "That I do enough," said the other. "I," quoth the drummer, "have plagued him (or to that purpose) and he shall never be quiet until he hath made me satisfaction for taking away my drum." Upon information of this, the fellow was tried for a witch at Sarum, and all the main circumstances here related were sworn at the assizes, by the minister of the parish and divers others of the most intelligent and substantial inhabitants, who had been eye and ear witnesses of them, time after time, for several years together.

The fellow was condemned to transportation, and accordingly sent away but by some means (it is said by raising storms and affrighting the seamen) he made a shift to come back again. During all the time of his restraint and absence, the house was quiet, but as soon as he was set at liberty, the disturbance returned.

He had been a soldier under Cromwell, and used to talk much of gallant books he had of an old fellow, who was accounted a wizard.

This is the sum of Mr. Mompesson's account, partly from his own mouth, related before many persons, who had been witnesses of all, and who confirmed his relation; and partly from his own letters, from which the order and series of things is taken. The same particulars he sent also to Dr. Creed, who was at that time Doctor of the Chair in Oxford.

Mr. Mompesson suffered by it in his name, in his estate, in all his affairs, and in the general peace of his family. The unbelievers in spirits and witches took him for an impostor. Many others regarded the permission of such an extraordinary evil to be the judgment of God upon him for some notorious wickedness or impiety. Thus his name was continually exposed to censure, and his estate suffered, by the concourse of people from all parts to his house, by the diversion it gave him from his affairs, and by the discouragement of servants by reason of which he could hardly get any to live with him.

The drummer of Tedworth met with great opposition when first narrated, and several violent controversies took place.

VII.

A Mysterious Memorandum.

Towards the end of the last century, a clergyman, in Lancashire, about to begin to read prayers at his church, saw a paper lying in his book, which he supposed to be the banns of marriage. He opened it, and saw written in a fair and distinct hand, the following: "John P. and James D. have murdered a travelling man, have robbed him of his effects, and buried him in (such an) orchard." The minister was extremely startled, and asked his clerk hastily if he had placed any paper in the prayer-book. The clerk declared he had not. The minister prudently concealed the contents of the paper, for the two names therein contained were those of the clerk and sexton of the church.

The minister then went directly to a magistrate, told him what had happened, and took the paper out of his pocket to read it, when, to his great surprise, nothing appeared thereon! The magistrate now said that his head must certainly have been distempered, when he imagined such strange contents upon a blank piece of paper. The clergyman, by earnest entreaties, however, prevailed on the justice to grant his warrant against the clerk and sexton; who were taken up on suspicion, and separately confined and examined, when many contradictions appeared in their statements; the sexton, who kept an alehouse, owned having lodged such a man at his house, and the clerk said he was that evening at the sexton's. It was now thought proper to search their houses, in which were found several pieces of gold, and goods belonging to men that travel the country; yet they gave so tolerable an account of these that no positive proof could be made out, till the clergyman, recollecting that the paper mentioned the dead body to be buried in such an orchard, a circumstance which had before escaped his memory, the place was searched and the body was found; on hearing which the sexton confessed the fact, accusing the clerk as his accomplice, and they were both executed accordingly.—*From H. Welby.*

VIII.

Warning to James IV. at Linlithgow.

While James IV. stayed at Linlithgow, to gather up the scattered remains of his army, which had been defeated by the Earl of Surrey at Flodden-field, he went into the church of St. Michael there, to hear evening prayer. While he was at his devotion, a remarkable figure of an ancient man of reverend aspect, with flowing amber-coloured hair hanging over his shoulders, his forehead high, and inclining to baldness, his garments of a fine blue colour, somewhat long and girded together with a fine white cloth, was seen enquiring for the king; when his majesty being pointed out to him, he made his way through the crowd till he came to him, and then, with a clownish simplicity, leaning over the canon's seat, he addressed him in the following words :—" Sir, I am sent hither to entreat you to delay your intended expedition for this time, and proceed no farther, for if you do, you will be unfortunate, and not prosper in your enterprise, nor any of your followers. I am further charged to warn you not to follow the acquaintance, company, or counsel of women, as you value your life, honour, and estate." After giving him this admonition, he withdrew himself back again through the crowd, and disappeared. When service was ended, the king enquired earnestly after him, but he could not be found or heard of any where, neither could any of the bystanders feel or perceive how, when, or where he passed from them, having in a manner vanished from their sight.—*From Buchanan's History of Scotland.*

IX.

Apparition at Belfast in Ireland.

There was once a long contest between Lemuel Matthews, archdeacon in the county of Down, and Claudius Gilbert, minister of Belfast, about their right to Drumbeg, a small parish near Belfast; and it proved troublesome to the parishioners, who had paid their dues to Mr. Gilbert, the incumbent. The archdeacon claimed it to be paid to him also, for which he procured a warrant; and in the execution of it by his servants, at the house of one Charles Loftin, they offered some violence to his wife, who refused entrance, and who died of the injury a few weeks after. Mrs. L. being an infirm woman, little notice was taken of her death till some time after, when, by her strange appearance to one Thomas Donelson, a witness of the violence done to her, he was induced to commence a prosecution against Robert Eccleson, the criminal. She appeared several times, but chiefly upon one

Sunday evening. Before her last coming (for she appeared three times that day), several neighbours were called in, to whom he gave notice that she would re-appear, she again charged him to prosecute Eccleson; and the voice, as also Donelson's reply, the people heard, though they saw no shape. Upon this Donelson deposed what he knew, before Mr. Randal Brice, a justice of the peace, and confirmed all at the assizes at Down, in the year 1685, where the several witnesses were sworn; and their examinations were entered in the records of the assize, to the amazement of all the country, and of the judges. Eccleson hardly escaped with his life, but was burnt in the hand.

In 1796 there were many witnesses of this circumstance yet alive, particularly Sarah, the wife of Charles Loftin, son to the deceased woman; and one William Holiday and his wife.—*From Baxter's World of Spirits*, 1796.

X.

The Merchant's Apprentices.

A certain merchant having formed a trading establishment in one of the English colonies in America, he prepared to send over several of his servants. One of these already fitted out, and prepared to embark, his cargo actually being on board the ship at Gravesend, was engaged in the office with his master who, being called away, asked him to remain until his return. When he returned his man was seated there, with the book-keeper also, writing as he left him.

At this moment, the merchant had occasion to return to the dining-room, from whence he came; leaving the youth in the counting-house.

When he reached the top of the stairs, the young man was seated at dinner with the other servants; the room they dined in being a small parlour, which opened against the stairs, he could see him from the upper part of the staircase, and could not be deceived.

The master did not speak to him ; but he sent his servant immediately to look, and he also saw the youth at dinner.

The young gentleman sailed in the vessel just mentioned, and arrived safely in America. He left his elder brother in London, who was at that time studying physic. Shortly after, this brother had an accidental reconnoitre with a gentleman in Short Street, leading from Fleet Street into Salisbury Square; and being a complete master of his weapon, he wounded his antagonist, and drove him into a tavern in the street ; whence came out two other men also with swords ; but both of them found the gentleman so much an overmatch for them, that they left him as fast as the first. A fourth now came out with a fire-poker, taken hastily out of the tavern-kitchen, and running at this gentleman with it, knocked him down and fractured his skull, of which wound he afterwards died.

While this was done in London, his brother wrote from Boston, to his master the merchant, to the following effect :

" I beg you will be pleased, in your return to this, to let me have some account, as much as conveniently may be, how my brother does, and what condition he is in ; which importunity I hope you will excuse, when you read the following account:—

"On the 30th of June last, about six o'clock in the morning, lying in bed, and broad awake, my brother or an apparition of my brother, came to the bed's feet and opened the curtain, looking full in my face, but did not speak. I was very much frightened ; but however, I so far recovered as to say to him, Brother, what is the matter with you ?

"He had a napkin-cap on his head, which was very bloody; he looked very pale and ghastly, and said, 'I am basely murdered by one (naming the person); but I shall have justice done me;' and then disappeared."

This letter was so dated, that it was impossible any account of the disaster could have reached America within that time.—*From Moreton on Apparitions.*

XI.

Sir Charles Lee's Daughter.

Sir Charles Lee, by his first lady, had only one daughter, of which she died in child-birth. After her death, her sister, Lady Everard, desired to have the child left in her charge till she was marriageable. When this time arrived a match was concluded for her with Sir William Perkins, but was prevented in the following extraordinary manner.

One Thursday night, Miss Lee imagined that she saw a light in her chamber after she was in bed, when she rang for her maid, and asked why she had left a candle burning in her chamber. The maid said she left none, and there was none, but what she brought with her at that time. She then said it was the fire; but the maid told her that the fire was quite out. About two o'clock she was awaked again, and saw the apparition of a little woman between her curtain and her pillow, who told her she was her mother, that she was happy, and that by twelve o'clock that day she should be with her. She again rang for the maid, called for her clothes, and when dressed, went into her closet, and did not quit it till nine; when she brought out with her a letter sealed to her father, gave it to her aunt, the Lady Everard, told her what had happened, and desired that, as soon as she was dead, it might be sent to him. Her aunt, judging her to be delirious, sent to Chelmsford for a physician, who came immediately. He could discern no indication of what the lady imagined, or any indisposition. The young lady insisted upon being bled and then desired that the chaplain might be called to read prayers, and when prayers were ended, she took her guitar and psalm-book, and played and sang melodiously. About twelve o'clock, she rose and seated herself in an armchair, and immediately expired. This event took place in 1662, at Waltham in Essex, three miles from Chelmsford, and the letter was sent to Sir Charles at his house in Warwickshire. It was communicated by him to the Lord Bishop of Gloucester, and was first published by Beaumont, in his " Treatise on Spirits.'

XII.

Councillor John Bourne of Durley.

Mr. John Bourne, for his skill and integrity, was made by his neighbour, John Mallet, Esq. of Enmore, the chief of his trustees for his estate. In 1654, Mr. Bourne fell sick at his house at Durley, when his life was pronounced by a physician to be in immediate danger. Within twenty-four hours, when the doctor and Mrs. Carlisle, a relation of Mr. Bourne (whose husband he had made one of his heirs), were sitting by his bedside, the doctor opened the curtains at the bed-foot to give him air; when suddenly a great iron chest with three locks, standing by the window (in which were all the writings and evidences of Mr. Mallet's estate), began to open, lock by lock. The lid of the iron chest then lifted itself up, and stood wide open. Mr. Bourne, who had not spoken for twenty-four hours, raised himself, and looking upon the chest, cried, "you say true, you say true, you are in the right, I'll be with you by and bye." The patient then lay down and spoke no more. The chest closed again, and locked itself lock by lock, and Mr. Bourne died within an hour afterwards.—*From H. Welby.*

XIII.

Omens of the Murder of Mr. Blandy.

Several striking presages are said to have alarmed the family of the unfortunate Mr. Blandy, of Henley, in Oxfordshire, previous to his untimely death. A few days before the death of his wife, a grand chorus of music was heard by the daughter and several of the servants at midnight, as if proceeding from the garden behind the apartment where Mrs. Blandy lay. This was succeeded by three distinct knocks on the window of Miss Blandy's chamber, adjoining that of her mother. Meanwhile the old lady, though insensible of these sounds, was horribly frightened by a dream, in which she saw her husband drinking a cup administered by her daughter; presently he swelled to a monster, and instantly expired. When she awoke in the morning, she told the dream to her waiting maid, and died the same day. This happened about two years before the memorable murder of Mr. Blandy, of the approach of which he had several ominous presages.

The story of this dreadful parricide is briefly as follows:—Mr. Blandy was an eminent attorney, and by his practice had accumulated several thousand pounds: he had an only child, his daughter, Miss Mary, whom he gave out to be worth thirty thousand pounds. Captain William Cranston, brother of Lord Cranston, of Scotland, a short time before the death of Mrs. Blandy, was upon a recruiting party in Oxfordshire, and hearing of the lady's fortune, found means to introduce himself to the family. He soon gained an ascendency over the mother; and the daughter discovered a very sensible feeling for the soldier. But there was an almost insuperable obstacle in the way of their mutual happiness. The captain had been privately married in Scotland. This, however, he hoped to get over by a decree in the supreme court of session. That expectation proving but ill-founded, Mr. Blandy would not assent to the union of his daughter with such a man, however honourable by birth.

The mother died suddenly. The father remained inexorable, and could not be induced to grant his consent. This sent the Captain's sanguine soul to work. The affection of Miss Blandy for this profligate, almost double her age, was violent. He imposed upon her credulity; sent her from Scotland a pretended love-powder, which he enjoined her to administer to her father, in order to gain his affection, and procure his consent. This injunction she declined, on account of a frightful dream, in which she fancied her father falling from a precipice into the ocean. The captain wrote a second time; told her his design in words rather enigmatical, but easily understood by her.

She decided to administer the powder, and mixed it in his tea; the father drank, and soon after swelled enormously.—" What have you given me, Mary?" cried the unhappy dying man, "you have murdered me; of this I was warned, but alas, I thought it was a false alarm!" Thus he died, a most melancholy spectacle. Miss Blandy was taken while attempting to run away, conducted to Oxford Castle, lay there till the assizes, was found guilty, and executed. Captain Cranston went abroad, and died in a miserable state of mind soon afterwards.—*From H. Welby.*

XIV.

The Spider and the King.

Bruce, the restorer of the Scottish monarchy, in the reign of Edward II. of England, having been out one day to reconnoitre the enemy, lay that night in a barn belonging to a loyal farmer. In the morning, still reclining his head on the straw pillow, he beheld a spider climbing a beam of the roof. The insect fell to the ground and immediately made a second essay to ascend. This attracted the notice of the hero, who with regret saw the spider fall a second time from the same eminence. It made a third attempt without success; and, in short, the monarch, not without a mixture of concern and curiosity, beheld the insect no less than twelve times baffled in its aim: but the thirteenth trial carried its success. The spider gained the summit; when the king, starting from his couch, thus exclaimed in soliloquy: " Behold this despicable insect has taught me perseverance! I will follow its example. Have not I been twelve times defeated by the superior force of the enemy? On one fight more hangs the independency of my kingdom." In a few days was fought the memorable battle of Bannockburn, in which Bruce proved victorious, slew thirty thousand of the invading enemy, and restored the monarchy of Scotland.—*From Horace Welby.*

XV.

Captain Porteous.

The following narrative was found, in 1796, in the study of an eminent divine of the Church of Scotland:—

A married lady lately saw, one day at noon, in a

vision, a child, then in embryo in her womb, rise to an elevated situation in the world, having the command of soldiers, dragged to a dungeon, tried for murder, condemned, pardoned, but soon after torn to pieces by the populace. After this she imagined much confusion arose in the country, till the name of her son was rendered odious and detestable to the whole nation.

The child, agreeable to the prediction, proving a son, much care was taken in his education, at one of the public schools of Edinburgh. When he grew up he discovered a strong inclination for travelling. He went abroad without the consent of his parents, remained many years in the king's service, and after obtaining his discharge, resided for some years in London. All this time he was totally unmindful of his filial duty, and indeed he never took the least notice of his parents, who now lived in a secluded situation about ten miles west from Edinburgh; to which city the hero of the story returned about the year 1735, and was, by the interest of a gentleman, appointed to the command of the city guard.

One day, as he was mustering his men in a field adjacent to the city, he cast his eyes upon a man of Musselburgh, who was reputed to possess the second sight. The captain called the augur aside, and required him to fortell his destiny. The poor soothsayer, with much reluctance, informed the curious enquirer that his time would be but short; that he would be *a midnight market-man*. This threw the officer into a violent rage; and had not the sage softened the sentence, by an explanation which gave a different turn to it, he certainly would have suffered a severe flagellation.

Soon after this, two notorious smugglers were condemned to die at Edinburgh, for breaking into the king's storehouse at Leith, and carrying away goods which had been seized by the officers of the revenue. These men, on the Sunday preceding the day of execution, were conducted to one of the churches, as was customary, under a guard. During the sermon, notwithstanding the vigilance of Captain Porteous, one of the prisoners found means to make his escape, and get clear off. The other was executed on the Wednesday following in the Grassmarket, contrary to the desire of the populace. As soon as the execution had taken place, the boys began to pelt the executioner; and the impetuous captain, who had attended with a strong party, commanded the men to level their pieces, and follow his example. He himself fired upon a young gentlemen of a good family from the Highlands, and killed him upon the spot; and the men instantly discharging their muskets, killed several of the citizens, who were beholding from their windows the dreadful spectacle.

The captain was seized by order of the Lord Provost, conducted to the Tolbooth, tried by the Lords of Justiciary, and being found guilty on the clearest evidence, received sentence of death.

It was at this time that his mother, who alone was living, heard of the awful situation of a man whom she knew to be her son, by a letter which she received from him during his troubles. The lady readily recollected her dream, flew to Edinburgh in the utmost distress, and would have been quite distracted, had she not been informed that great interest was making at London in favour of the captain.

In a few days a respite arrived from the Queen (for George II. was then at Hanover), with an order to secure the captain in the castle. This quite altered the face of affairs with the captain and his mother, who began to ridicule the prediction of the dream, and the soothsayer. That evening they made merry with several friends in the prison, till the captain became intoxicated, and consequently unprepared to meet the awful fate which awaited him. He was instantly alarmed by a report that the city was up in arms, and intent on his destruction. The noise of sledge hammers on the iron doors soon convinced him that the alarm was not false. In short, the enraged multitude gained entrance, dragged forth the captain, led him in triumph along the High street, procured a rope, reached the usual place of execution, and after suffering him to say a short prayer, hung him upon a projecting pole ; which proved an almost literal accomplishment of the visionary prediction of the mother, who did not long survive the death of her son.

The confusion in the established national church, occasioned by the Queen's proclamation being read by some, and burnt by others, is well known.—*From Horace Welby.*

XVI.

Vision of Theodosius the Roman Emperor.

The following is well attested by Theodoret and Livy :—

In the Western Empire lived one Eugenius, an aspiring man, who from keeping a grammar school had risen to the office of Lord High Treasurer. Eugenius being elated with the extraordinary reputation of his eloquence and merit, entered into a plot with one Abrogastes, a Frenchman by birth, to possess himself of the emperorship, and, by his assurances and great promises, prevailed upon the eunuchs of the emperor's bed-chamber to strangle their master Valentinian while he was sleeping. Having perpetrated this horrible murder, he next consulted the diviners and and astrologers, who gave him every assurance that he should obtain a complete victory, gain the empire, and extirpate the Christian religion.

Upon this, he soon assembled forces, and made himself master of the Julian Alps, where he lay securely encamped amongst the mountains. This news surprised and perplexed Theodosius; who, after conferring the imperial title on his son Honorius, mustered a considerable number of troops, and arriving in Gaul, found Eugenius ready to oppose him with a very superior army. The emperor's officers, at the same time, advised him to avoid the battle till he might bring an army into the field more numerous than that of the usurper.

About sunrise he fell asleep upon the ground and dreamed he saw two men clothed in white garments, and riding on white horses, who bade him lay aside all solicitude, and draw up his army in order of battle very early that morning and attack the enemy. They told him they were John the Evangelist and Philip the Apostle; and they were sent to fight for him at the head of his troops. The emperor waked and renewed his devotions, and addressed himself to heaven with greater fervency than before this vision. His men marched down with great alacrity and courage from the mountains; and the two armies came to a battle at a river called Frigidas, about thirty-six miles from Aquileia. Romans now engaged Romans, the action was very hot and obstinate and many fell on both sides; but the Eugenians pressed hard upon the barbarians, who had flocked from Thrace and offered themselves in great numbers in this expedition.

At length the emperor, seeing all hope cut off, threw himself prostrate on the ground, and recommended his cause to God. The officers of the parties that lined the mountains now sent him assurances, that they would come over to him if he would promise that they should hold the same posts under him that they held under Eugenius; and this he had no sooner done under his own hand, than they came over to him. Bacurius also, one of the emperor's generals, inspired with sudden resolution, put himself in front of the retreating troops, broke the enemy's ranks and routed them; and there arose on a sudden a violent storm of wind, so violent that it not only carried the weapons of the emperor's army with redoubled force upon the enemy, and returned those of the rebels upon themselves, but even forced their shields out of their hands and whirled them back again, and raised such violent clouds of dust as almost put out their eyes; in a word, it entirely disarmed them and put them into confusion, so that the greater part of them were either killed upon the spot or overtaken in the rout and made prisoners; as many as threw down their arms and implored pardon obtained it.

Thus the usurper lost the day, and those from whose hands he expected the person of his sovereign were sent by his master to fetch him down from his hill. As soon as he saw them climbing it, and approaching towards him, he asked them whether they had brought Theodosius along with them. Their answer was, they had come by the appointment of God to carry him to Theodosius; and immediately they pulled him from his seat and carried him to the emperor, who severely reproached and expostulated with him for the murder of Valentinian, and for all his treason and rebellion. In conclusion, the soldiers struck off his head as he was begging quarter at the emperor's feet, where he hoped to save his life. The day of this overthrow and execution was the 6th of September, in Arcadius's third and Honorius's second consulate. The traitorous General Arbogastes, the principal agent in this mischief, after he had preserved himself by flight for three days, finding it impossible to escape the stroke of justice, put an end to his life by his own sword.

XVII.

Major Sydenham and Captain William Dyke.

Major George Sydenham resided at Dulverton, in the county of Somerset, and Captain William Dyke at Skilgate, in the same county. Shortly after the death of the former, a doctor was desired to attend a sick child at the major's house. On his way thither he called on the captain, who willingly accompanied him to the place. Soon after their arrival they were conducted to the room they were both to occupy. After they had lain a while the captain knocked and bade the servant bring him two large candles lighted. The doctor inquired what he meant by this? The captain replied, " You know what disputes the major and I used to have touching the being of a God and the immortality of the soul. On these points we could never agree. It was finally agreed between us that he who died first should, the third night after his funeral, between the hours of twelve and one, come to the summer-house in the garden, and there give a full account to the survivor touching these matters. This," said the captain, " is the night, and I am come to fulfil my promise." The doctor dissuaded him, reminding him of the danger of following such strange counsels. The captain replied that he had solemnly engaged, and nothing should discourage him ; he was resolved to watch, that he might be sure to be present at the hour appointed. As soon as he perceived that it was half-past eleven, he arose, and taking a candle in each hand, went out by a back door and walked to the garden-house, where he continued two hours and a half, and, at his return, declared that he had neither seen nor heard anything more than usual.

About six weeks afterwards, the captain rode to Eton, accompanied by the doctor. They lodged there at an inn, staying two or three nights, but not sleeping together as at Dulverton. The morning before their return the captain stayed in his chamber longer than usual before he called the doctor. At length he entered the doctor's chamber, but with his hair erect, his eyes staring, and his whole body shaking and trembling. The doctor, filled with surprise, inquired, "What is the matter, captain?" The captain replied, "I have seen the major." The doctor smiled, when the captain immediately added, "If ever I saw him in my life I saw him just now." He then related what had passed in these words: "This morning, soon after it was light, some one came to my bedside, and suddenly drawing back the curtains, called, 'Cap. cap.' (this being the term of familiarity by which the major used to call the captain), to whom I replied, 'What, major?' He answered, 'I could not come at the time appointed, but I am now come to tell you that there is a God, and a very just and terrible one; and if you do not turn over a new leaf you will find it so.' On the table there lay a sword which the major had formerly given me. After the apparition had paced about the chamber he took up the sword, drew it out, and finding it not so clean and bright as usual, 'Cap. cap.,' said he, 'this sword was not used to be kept after this manner when it was mine.' After these words he suddenly disappeared."

The captain was not only thoroughly persuaded of the truth of this narrative, but was from that time observed to be much affected by it during the remaining two years of his life.—*From Aubrey's Miscellanies.*

XVIII

Letter written by James Earl of Marlborough, a short time before his Death, in the Battle at Sea on the Coast of Holland, 1665, directed to the Right Hon. Sir Hugh Portland, Comptroller to His Majesty's Household.

SIR,—I believe the goodness of your nature, and the friendship you have always borne me, will receive with kindness the last office of your friend. I am in health enough of body, and (through the mercy of God) well disposed in mind. This I premise, that you may be satisfied that what I write proceeds not from fantastic terror of mind, but from a sober resolution of what concerns myself, and earnest desire to do you more good after my death, than my example (God of his mercy pardon the badness of it) in my lifetime may do you harm. I will not speak out of the vanity of this world; your own age and experience will save that labour: but there is a certain thing that goeth up and down the world, called religion, dressed and pretended fantastically, and to purposes bad enough, which yet, by such evil dealing, looseth not its being: the great good God hath not left it without a witness, more or less, sooner or later, in every man's bosom, to direct us in the pursuit of it; and for the avoiding of those inextricable disquisitions and entanglements our own frail reason would perplex us withal, God, in his infinite mercy hath given us his holy word; in which as there are many things hard to be understood, so there is enough plain and easy, to quiet our minds, and direct us concerning our future being. I confess to God and you, I have been a great neglecter, and, I fear, great despiser of it: God of his infinite mercy pardon me the dreadful fault. But when I retired myself from the noise and deceitful vanity of the world, I found no true comfort in any other resolution than what I had from thence: I commend from the bottom of my heart the same to your (I hope) happy use. Dear Sir Hugh, let us be more generous than to believe we die as the beasts that perish; but with a Christian, manly, brave resolution, look to what is eternal. I will not trouble you farther. The only great God, Father, Son, and Holy Ghost, direct you to an happy end of your life, and send us a joyful resurrection.

So prays your true friend,

MARLBOROUGH.

Old James, near the Coast of Holland,
April 24, 1665.

I beseech you commend my love to all my acquaintance; particularly, I pray you that my cousin Glascock may have a sight of this letter, and as many friends besides as you will, or any else that desire it. I pray grant this my request.

This letter, weighty in matter, and serious in its phraseology, is most remarkable for the time in which it was written, namely, but a few days before the Earl died.

XIX.

Sir John Sherbroke and General Wynyard.

These gentlemen were, as young men, officers in the same regiment, which was employed on foreign service. They were connected by similarity of tastes and studies, and spent together in literary occupation much of their vacant time. They were one afternoon sitting in Wynyard's apartments. It was about four o'clock; they had dined, but neither of them had taken wine, and they had retired early from the mess to continue together the occupations of the morning. The apartment in which they were had two doors in it, the one opening into a passage, and the other leading into Wynyard's bed-room. There was no way of entering the sitting-room but from the passage, and no egress from the bed-room but through the sitting-room; so that any person passing into the bed-room must have remained there, unless he returned by the way he entered. This point is of consequence to the story.

As these two young officers were pursuing their studies, Sherbroke, whose eye happened accidentally to glance from the volume before him towards the door that opened to the passage, observed a tall youth, of about twenty years of age, whose appearance was that of extreme emaciation, standing beside it. Struck with the presence of a perfect stranger, he immediately turned to his friend, who was sitting near him, and directed his attention to the guest who had thus strangely broken in upon their studies. As soon as Wynyard's eyes were turned towards the mysterious visitor, his countenance became suddenly agitated. "I have heard," says Sir John Sherbroke, " of a man being as pale as death, but I never saw a living face assume the appearance of a corpse, except Wynyard's at that moment."

As they looked silently at the form before them,— for Wynyard, who seemed to apprehend the import of the appearance, was deprived of the faculty of speech, and Sherbroke, perceiving the agitation of his friend, felt no inclination to address it,—as they looked silently upon the figure, it proceeded slowly into the adjoining apartment, and, in the act of passing them, cast its eyes with an expression of somewhat melancholy affection on young Wynyard. The oppression of this extraordinary presence was no sooner removed, than Wynyard, seizing his friend by the arm and drawing a deep breath, as if recovering from the suffocation of intense astonishment and emotion, muttered in a low and almost inaudible tone of voice, "Great God! my brother!" "Your brother!" repeated Sherbroke, "What can you mean, Wynyard? there must be some deception—follow me;" and, immediately taking his friend by the arm, he preceded him into the bed-room, which, as before stated, was connected with the sitting-room, and into which the strange visitor had evidently entered. Imagine the astonishment of the young officers, when, entering the bed-room, they found no one in it. Wynyard's mind had received an impression that the figure which he had seen was the spirit of his brother. Sherbroke still persevered in strenuously believing that some delusion had been practised.

They took note of the day and hour in which the event had happened; but they resolved not to mention the occurrence in the regiment, and gradually they persuaded each other that they had been imposed upon by some artifice of their fellow-officers, though they could neither account for the reason, nor suspect the author, nor conceive the means of its execution. They were content to imagine any thing possible, rather than admit the possibility of a supernatural appearance. But Wynyard could not help expressing his solicitude with respect to the safety of the brother whose apparition he had either seen, or imagined himself to have seen; and the anxiety which he exhibited for letters from England, and his frequent mention of his fears for his brother's health, at length awakened the curiosity of his comrades, and eventually betrayed him into a declaration of the circumstances which he had, in vain, determined to conceal. The story of the silent and unbidden visitor was no sooner bruited abroad than the destiny of Wynyard's brother became an object of universal and painful interest to the officers of the regiment; there were few who did not inquire for Wynyard's letters before they made any demand for their own. At length the long-wished for vessel arrived; all the officers had letters except Wynyard. Still the secret was unexplained. They examined the several newspapers, but they contained no mention of any death, or of any other circumstance connected with his family that could account for the preternatural event. There was a solitary letter for Sherbroke still unopened. The officers had received their letters in the mess-room at the hour of supper. After Sherbroke had broken the seal of his last packet, and cast a glance on its contents, he beckoned his friend away from the company and departed from the room. All were silent. The feeling of interest was now at its height; the impatience for the return of Sherbroke was inexpressible. They doubted not but that the letter contained the long-expected intelligence. After the interval of an hour Sherbroke joined them. No one dared be guilty of so great a rudeness as to enquire the nature of his correspondence; but they waited in mute attention, expecting that he would himself touch upon the subject. His mind was manifestly full of thoughts that pained, bewildered, and oppressed him. He drew near to the fire-place, and leaning his head on the mantel-piece, after a pause of some moments said in a low voice to the person who was nearest to him, "Wynyard's brother is no more!" The first line of Sherbroke's letter was, "Dear John, break to your friend Wynyard the death of his favourite brother." He had died on the day, and at the very hour on which the friends had seen the vision pass so mysteriously through the apartment.

So strong was Sherbroke's conviction against the possibility of any preternatural intercourse with the souls of the dead, that he still entertained a doubt of the report of his senses, although their testimony was supported by the coincidence of vision and event.

Some years later, on his return to England, he was walking with two gentlemen in Piccadilly, when, on the opposite side of the way, he saw a person bearing the most striking resemblance to the figure which had been disclosed to Wynyard and himself. His companions were acquainted with the story; and he instantly directed their attention to the gentleman opposite, as the individual who had contrived to enter and depart from Wynyard's apartment without their being conscious of the means. Full of this impression, he immediately went over, at once addressed the gentleman, and now fully expected to elucidate the mystery. He apologized for the interruption, but excused it by relating the occurrence which had induced him to the commission of this solecism in manners. The gentlemen received him as a friend. He had never been out of the country; but he was the twin brother of the youth whose spirit had been seen.

This story is related with several variations. It is sometimes told as having happened at Gibraltar, at others in England, at others in America. There are also differences with respect to the conclusion. Some say that the gentleman whom Sir John Sherbroke afterwards met in London, and addressed as the person whom he had previously seen in so mysterious a manner, was not another brother of General Wynyard, but a gentleman who bore a strong resemblance to the family. But, however, the leading facts in every account are the same. Sir John Sherbroke and General Wynyard, two gentlemen of veracity were together present at the spiritual appearance of the brother of General Wynyard; the appearance took place at the moment of dissolution; and the countenance and form of the ghost's figure were so distinctly impressed upon the memory of Sir John Sherbroke—to whom the living man had been unknown—that on accidentally meeting with his likeness

he perceived and acknowledged the resemblance.—
From H. Welby.

XX.

Thomas Goddard of Marlborough, Wilts.

The following interesting deposition of Thomas Goddard of Marlborough, Wilts, weaver, made the 23rd Nov., 1674—is taken from Glanvil's "Saducissimus Triumphatus." On Monday the 9th inst., as he was going to Ogborn, at a stile on the highway near Mr. Goddard's ground, about nine in the morning, he met the apparition of his father-in-law, one Edward Avon, of this town, glover, who died in May last, having on, to his appearance, the same clothes, hat, stockings, and shoes he usually wore when he was living. He was standing by and leaning over the stile. When he came near, the apparition spoke to him, with an audible voice, these words, "Are you afraid?" To which he answered, "I am thinking on one who is dead and buried, whom you are like." To which the apparition replied with the like voice, "I am he that you are thinking on; I am Edward Avon, your father-in-law; come near to me, I will do you no harm." To which Goddard answered, "I trust in him who hath bought my soul with his precious blood, you shall do me no harm." Then the apparition said, "How stand cases at home?" Goddard asked what cases? Then it asked, "How are William and Mary?"—meaning, as he conceived, his son William Avon, a shoemaker here, and Mary his daughter, Goddard's wife. Then it said, "What! Taylor is dead," meaning one Taylor of London, who married his daughter Sarah, which Taylor died the Michaelmas before. Then the apparition held out its hand, and in it, as Goddard con-

follow me." He said, "should both of us come, or but one of us?" It answered, "Thomas, do *you* take up the sword." And so he took up the sword and followed the apparition about ten lugs (poles) farther into the copse, and then turning back, he stood still about a lug and a-half from it, his brother-in-law staying behind at the place where they first laid down the sword. Then Goddard, laying down the sword upon the ground, saw something stand by the apparition like a mastiff dog, of a brown colour. Then the apparition, coming towards Goddard, he stepped back about two steps, and the apparition said to him, "I have something to say to you, but will not touch you; and then it took up the sword, and went back to the place where it stood before, mastiff dog still with it, and pointed the tip of the sword in the ground, and said, "In this place lies buried the body of him which I murdered in the year 1635, which is now rotten and turned to dust." Whereupon Goddard said, "I adjure you in the name of the Father, Son, and Holy Ghost, wherefore did you commit this murder?" and it answered, "I took money from the man, and he contended with me, and so I murdered him." Goddard asked who was confederate in the said murder? and it said, "None but myself." Then Goddard enquired, "What would you have me do in this thing?" And the apparition said, "This is that the world may know that I murdered a man, and buried him in this place, in the year 1635."

The apparition then laid down the sword on the bare ground, whereon nothing grew, but seemed to Goddard to be as a grave sunk in. It rushed further into the copse, and he saw it no more. Whereupon Goddard, and his brother-in-law Avon, leaving the sword there and coming away together, Avon told Goddard he heard the voice, and understood what was said, and also heard other words distinct from his, but could not understand any of it, nor see any apparition at all. The deposition was signed

> In the presence of Christ. Lypyatt, *Mayor;* Rolf Bayly, *Town-Clerk;* Joshua Sacheveral, *Rector of St. Peter's,* in Marlborough.
>
> Examined by me,
> WILL. BAYLY.

XXI.

A Mother's appearance to her Son while at Sea.

A woman, who lived on Rhode Island, in America, whilst on her death bed, and just before she expired, expressed a great desire to see her only son, who was then a mariner, navigating in the West India seas, and to deliver him a message. She informed the persons near her what she wanted to say to her son and died immediately. About that instant she appeared to him, as he was standing at the helm, it being a bright moonlight night. She first appeared on the shrouds, and delivered her message; and afterwards walked over some casks that lay on the deck, then descended the side regularly to the water, where she seemed to float for a while, and at last sunk and wholly disappeared. The young man immediately recorded the time and day, and the substance of her message, and found on his arrival at Rhode Island, that she died at the very time when she was seen by him; and the words she spoke to him corresponded exactly with those she delivered to the persons around her.

XXII.

Relation of James Sherring, taken concering the matter at old Gast's House, of Little Burton, June 23, 1677.

On June 23, 1677, the following circumstances occured at the house of a man named Gast, at Little Burton, in Somersetshire.

The first night that the narrator was there with two others, Hugh Mellmore and Edward Smith, they heard as it were someone washing in water over their heads. Then taking a candle and going up the stairs, there was a wet cloth thrown at them, but it fell on the stairs. They going up farther there was another thrown as before. And when they were come up into the chamber there stood a bowl of water, some of it sprinkled over, and the water looked white, as if there had been soap used in it. The bowl just before was in the kitchen, and could not have been carried up but through the room where they were. The next thing that they heard the same night was a terrible noise also upstairs as if it had been a clap of thunder, then they heard great scratching about the bedstead, and after that great knocking with a hammer against the bed's-head, so that the two maids that were in bed cried out for help. Then they ran up stairs, and there lay the hammer on the bed, and on the bed's-head there were near a thousand prints of the hammer, which the violent strokes had made. The maids said that they were scratched and pinched by a hand with very long nails that was put into the bed. They said the hammer was locked up fast in the cupboard when they went to bed.

The second night one of the company sat down in the chimney to fill a pipe of tobacco; he made use of the firetongs to take up a coal to light his pipe, and by and by the tongs were drawn up the stairs, and after they were in the chamber the tongs were made to snap as if in some one's hands, and were then thrown upon the bed. Although the tongs were so near him downstairs he never perceived them to go away. The same night one of the maids left her shoes by the fire, and they were carried up into the chamber and the old man's brought down and set in their place. The same night there was a knife carried up into the chamber, the bed's head was scratched and scraped all the night, and when they went up into the chamber, the knife was found in the loft. As they were going up the stairs there were many things thrown at them which were just before in the low room, and when they went down the stairs the old man's breeches were thrown down after them.

The third night, as soon as the people were gone to bed, the servants' clothes were taken and thrown at the candle and put it out, and immediately after they cried out with a very hideous cry that 'They should be all choked if they were not presently helped.' When assistance came, it was found that a quantity of the feathers had been plucked out of the bolster that lay under their heads, and some thrust into their mouths, until they were almost choked. The feathers were then thrown about the bed and room. They were plucked out of a hole no bigger than the top of one's little finger. Some time after they were vexed with a very hideous knocking at their heads as they lay on the bed. Then James Sherring and Thomas Hillary, who had gone up, took the candle and stood at the bed's feet, and the knocking continued. Then they saw a hand with an arm-wrist hold the hammer which kept on knocking against the bedstead. Then James Sherring going towards the bed's-head, the hand and hammer fell down behind the bolster, and could not be found; although they turned up the bed-clothes and searched thoroughly. But as soon as they went down stairs the hammer was thrown out into the middle of the chamber.

The fourth and fifth nights there was but little done more than knocking and scratching.

The sixth and seventh nights all was quiet as at other houses; and upon the eighth day Sherring and Hillary left the house.

The circumstances that follow are what James Sherring heard the people of the house report.

There was a saddle hanging up in the house belonging to their Uncle Warren of Leigh (which it seems they had detained wrongfully), that would come off the nail and hop about from one place to another, and from one table to another. Jane Gast and her kinswoman took this saddle and carried it to Leigh, and as they were going along the broad common there were sticks and stones thrown at them, which made them very much afraid, and walking close together for fear, the whittles which were on their shoulders became knit. They carried the saddle to the house which was old Warren's, and left it, and returned home very quiet. But at night, the saddle was brought back from Leigh (which is a mile and a half at least from old Gast's house), and thrown upon the bed where the maids lay. After that, the saddle was very troublesome to them, until they broke it in small pieces and threw it out into the highway.

There was a coat belonging the owner of the saddle, which hung on the door in the hall, and it came off from the place and flew into the fire and lay some considerable time before they could get it out. For it was as much as three of them could do to pluck it out of the fire, because of the ponderous weight that seemed to lay on it. Nevertheless there was no mark of the fire upon it.

One night there were two of this old Gast's granddaughters in bed together, one of them, about twelve or thirteen years of age, and the other about sixteen or seventeen. They said they felt a hand in bed with them, which they bound up in the sheet, and took bedstaves and beat it until it was as soft as wool, then they took a stone which lay in the chamber, about a quarter of an hundred weight, and put on it, and were quiet all the night. In the morning, they found it as they left it. Then the eldest of the maids swore that she would burn the Devil, and fetched a furze faggot to burn it, but when she came again, the stone was thrown away, and the cloth was found wet.

The following is the relation of Jane Winsor, of Long Burton, she being there three nights, taken the 3rd day of July, 1677 :—

She heard or saw nothing as long as the candle burned, but as soon as it was out something seemed to fall down by the bedside, and by and by it began to hit about the bed's-head with a staff, and struck Jane Winsor on the head. She put forth her hand and caught it, but was not able to hold it fast. She got out of the bed to light a candle, and there was a great stone thrown after her, but it missed her. When the candle was lighted, they arose and went down to the fire. One of them went up to fetch the bed-clothes to make a bed by the fire, and there lay a heap of stones on the bed whereon they lay just before. As soon as the bed was made, and they had laid down to take their rest, there was a loud scratching on the form that stood by them. Then something came and heaved up the bolster under their heads, and endeavoured to throw them out of bed. At last it got hold of one end of the pillow, and set it on end, and there it stood for some considerable time, at last falling down in its place ; after this they were not disturbed.
—*From Horace Welby.*

XXIII.

David Hunter's Vision.

The following circumstantial narrative was given to the Bishop of Down and Dromore, in whose service Hunter lived at Neatherd, at Portmore, in Ireland, 1663. The facts were narrated by him, day by day as they occurred, to the Bishop, and to Lady Conway, then on a visit at Portmore.

One evening as David Hunter was carrying a log of wood into the dairy, there appeared to him an old woman; the fright made him throw away his log of wood and run into the house. The next night she appeared again to him; and he could not choose but follow her all night, and thus almost every night for three quarters of a year. He was drawn after her through the woods at a good rate, until the poor fellow came to look quite bewitched and weary. When in bed with his wife, if she appeared, he was compelled to rise and go. And when his wife found she could not hold him back, she went too, and walked after him till day, though she saw nothing. His little dog became so well acquainted with the apparition, that he would follow her as well as his master.

One day as David was going over a hedge into the highway, she came just against him, and he cried out, "Lord bless me, would I was dead; shall I never be delivered from this misery?" "And the Lord bless me too," replied the apparition, "It was very happy you spoke first, for till then I had no power to speak, though I have followed you so long." "My name," said she, is "Margaret ———, I lived here before the war, and had one son by my husband; when he died I married a soldier, by whom I had several children, which that former son maintained, else we must all have starved. He lives beyond the Ban-water; pray go to him, and bid him dig under such a hearth, and there he shall find twenty-eight shillings. Let him pay what I owe in such a place, and place the rest to the charge unpaid at my funeral; and go to my son that lives here, which I had by my latter husband, and tell him, that he lives a wicked and a dissolute life, and is very unnatural and ungrateful to his brother that maintained him, and if he does not mend his life, God will destroy him."

David Hunter told her he never knew her. "No," said she, "I died seven years before you came into the country;" still she charged him to deliver her message and she would never hurt him. But he deferred doing as the apparition bid him, and she appeared the night after as he lay in bed, and struck him on the shoulder very hard; at which he cried out, and asked her if she did not promise she would not hurt him? She said, that was if he obeyed her; if not, she would kill him. He told her he could not now, as the waters were out. She said, she was content that he should stay till they were abated; but charged him afterwards not to fail her. When the waters were abated he delivered her message, and afterwards she appeared and gave him thanks. "For now," said she, "I shall be at rest, therefore pray lift me up from the ground, and I will trouble you no more." David Hunter now lifted her up from the ground, and he said she felt just like a bag of feathers in his arms; she then disappeared, and he saw no more of her from that time—*From Horace Welby.*

XXIV.

Strange Presages at Woodstock.

In 1649, during the visit of the Commissioners of Woods and Forests to survey the manor-house, park, deer, woods, and other demesnes belonging to the Manor of Woodstock, in Oxfordshire, the following circumstances occurred. They are related with much accuracy and precision as to time and place in the Natural History of Oxfordshire, a work of great reputation.

The Commissioners, October 13, 1646, with their servants, took up their lodging in the king's own rooms, the bed-chamber, and withdrawing room. On the 16th October there came, as they thought, something into the bed-chamber where two of the Commissioners and their servants lay, in the shape of a dog, which, going under their beds, seemed to gnaw their bedcords, but on the morrow, finding them whole, and a quarter of beef which lay on the ground untouched, they were much surprised.

October 17.—Something to their thinking, removed a quantity of wood out of the dining-room into the presence chamber, and hurled the chair and stools up and down that room. From thence it came into the two chambers where the Commissioners and their servants lay, and hoisted up their bed's-feet so much higher than their heads, that they thought they would have been thrown out; it then let them fall down with such a force that their bodies rebounded from the bed, after this the bedstead shook violently.

October 18.—Something came into the bed-chamber and walked up and down, fetched the warming-pan out of the withdrawing-room, and made so much noise that they thought five bells could not have made more.

October 19.—Trenchers were thrown up and down the dining-room, and at the people therein, whereof one of them being shaken by the shoulder, and awakened, put forth his head to see what was the matter, and had trenchers thrown at it.

October 20.—The curtains of the bed in the withdrawing-room, were drawn to and fro, and much shaken, and eight great pewter dishes and a number of trenches thrown about the bed-chamber again. This night they also thought whole armfuls of wood had been thrown down in their chambers, but in the morning they found nothing.

October 21.—The keeper of their ordinary and his dog lay in one of the rooms with them, this night they were not disturbed at all. But October 22, though the dog kenneled there again, to which they had ascribed their former night's rest, both they and it were greatly disturbed, the dog barking with a whining fearful yelp. October 23.—They had all their clothes plucked off them in the drawing-room, and bricks fell out of the chimney into the room. October 24.—They thought, in the dining-room, that all the wood of the King's oak had been brought thither and thrown down close by their bedside; the noise of which being heard by those in the drawing-room, one of them rose to see what was the cause, fearing indeed that his fellow Commissioners had been killed, but found no such matter; whereupon returning to his bed again, he found two dozen of trenchers thrown into it, and carefully covered with the bed-clothes.

October 25.—The curtains of the bed in the drawing-room were pulled to and fro, and the bedstead shaken as before, and, in the bed-chamber, glass flew about so thick (and yet not a pane of the chamber windows was broken) that it might have rained glass. Whereupon they lighted candles, but to their grief they found nothing but the pieces. October 29.—Something walked in the drawing-room about an hour, and going to the window opened and shut it; then going into the bed-chamber, it threw great stones for about half-an-hour, some of which lighted on the high bed, others on the truckle bed, to the number of 70 or 80 in all. This night there was also a very great noise, as if several pieces of ordnance had been shot off together. During these noises, which were heard in the two rooms at once, both Commissioners and servants were struck with so great horror that they cried out to one another for help; and one of them snatched up a sword and nearly killed one of his brethren standing in his shirt, whom he took for the spirit that did the mischief. At length they got all together, but the noise continued so great and so terrible, and shook the walls so much, that they thought the whole manor would have fallen on their heads. At its departure it took all the glass and fled away.

November 1.—Something, as they thought, walked up and down the drawing-room, and then made a noise in the dining-room. The stones that were left before, and laid up in the withdrawing-room, were all fetched away this night, and a great deal of glass (not like the former) thrown about again. November 2.—Something came into the drawing-room, treading, as they thought, much like a bear, which at first only walked about a quarter of an hour; at length it made a noise about the table, and threw the warming pan so violently, that it quite spoiled it. It also threw glass and great stones about again, and the bones of horses; and all so violently, that the bedstead and walls were bruised by them. This night they set candles all about the rooms, and made fires up to the mantle-pieces of the chimneys, but all were put out, nobody knew how; pieces of burnt wood being thrown up and down the rooms. The curtains were torn from their beds, and the bed-posts pulled away, so that the tester fell down upon them, and the feet of the bedstead were cloven in two. Upon the servants in the truckle bed that lay all this time quaking with fear, there came first a little water which made them begin to stir, but before they could get out, there came a whole bowl as it were of stinking ditch water down upon them, so green that it stained their night dresses.

The same night the windows were all broken, and there were most terrible noises in the three several places together, to the extraordinary surprise of all who lodged near; nay, the very coney-stealers that were abroad that night, were so affrighted with the dismal thundering, that in haste they left their ferret in the coney-burroughs behind them, beyond Rosomand's Well. Notwithstanding all this, one of the witnesses had the boldness to ask in the name of God what it was? What it would have? and what they had done, that they should be disturbed in this manner? To this no answer was given, but the noise ceased for a while. At length it came again, and worse than ever. Whereupon one of them lighted a candle and set it between the two chambers in the door-way, on which another of them fixing his eyes, saw the similitude of a hoof striking the candle and candlestick into the middle of the bed-chamber, and making three scrapes on the snuff to put it out. Upon this the same person drew his sword, but he had scarce got it out, when there was another invisible hand had hold of it too, and tugged with him for it, and prevailing, struck him so violently with the pummel, that he was stunned with the blow.

Then began great noises again, so great, that calling one another together, they went into the presence chamber, where they said prayers and sung psalms; notwithstanding all this, the thundering noise still continued in other rooms. November 3.—After this they removed their lodgings over the gate, and next day they went to Ewelin but returning on Monday, the devil (for that was the name they gave their nightly guest) left them not unvisited, nor on the Tuesday following, which was the last day they sojourned at Woodstock.—*From H. Welby.*

XXV.

The Duchess of Mazarine, and Madame de Beauclair.

The Duchess of Mazarine was one of the most celebrated of the mistresses of the gay and licentious court of King Charles II. Waller distinguishes her as one of the favourites of that monarch in the following lines—

> " When through the world fair Mazarine had run,
> Bright as her fellow-traveller the sun,
> Hither at last the Roman eagle flies,
> As the last triumph of her conquering eyes."

Madame de Beauclair was equally admired and loved by his brother and successor, James II.; between these two ladies there existed an intimate friendship.

They were both women of excellent ability, who had enjoyed all the luxuries of this world, and were arrived at an age when they might be supposed to despise all its follies.

After the burning of Whitehall, these two ladies were allotted very handsome apartments in the Stableyard, St. James's, but the face of public affairs being then wholly changed, and a new set of courtiers as well as rules of etiquette having come into vogue, they were left almost entirely to themselves.

About this time the doctrine of the immortality of the soul was warmly disputed in all circles, especially among those whose mere rank in life served as a specious pretext for their interference in such matters. The doctrine was too much discussed, not to be frequently a subject of conversation with these ladies; and the plausible arguments for and against used by persons of high reputation for their learning, had such an effect on both as to raise great doubts in their minds. In one of these serious consultations on this topic, it was agreed between them, that whichever should be first called from this world, should return (if there was a possibility of doing so) and give the other an account in what manner she was disposed of. This promise, it seems, was often repeated, and the Duchess happening to fall sick, and her life being despaired of by all about her, Madame de Beauclair reminded her of her compact, to which her grace replied, "you may depend upon my performance." These words passed between them about an hour before the death of the Duchess, and were spoken before several friends and attendants who were in the room.

Some years after the Duchess's decease, the narrator of these facts, during a visit to Madame de Beauclair, referring to the topic of a future life, she expressed her disbelief of it with great warmth; which surprising me, I offered some arguments to prove the reasonableness of depending on a life to come: to which she answered, that not all that the whole world could say should ever persuade her to that opinion; and then she related the compact made between herself and the Duchess of Mazarine.

A few months afterwards, I happened to be at the house of a person of rank with whom since the death of the Duchess of Mazarine Madame de Beauclair was very intimate. We had just set down to cards about nine o'clock in the evening, when a servant came hastily into the room, and acquainted the lady I was with, that Madame de Beauclair had sent to entreat she would come that moment to her, adding, that if she desired ever to see her more in this world she must not delay her visit.

So odd a message might naturally surprise the person to whom it was delivered. She asked who brought it, and being told it was Madame de Beauclair's groom of the chamber, she ordered that he should come in, and demanded of him if his lady was in good health, or if he knew of anything extraordinary that had happened to her, which should occasion this hasty summons. The groom answered, that he was entirely unable to explain, as he had not heard his lady complain of any indisposition.

"Well then," said the lady, rather pettishly, "I desire you will make my excuse, as I have really a cold, and am fearful the night-air may increase it; but tomorrow I will not fail to wait on her very early in the morning.

On the departure of the groom, we began to form several conjectures on this message from Madame de Beauclair, but before we had time to agree on a reasonable conclusion, he returned again, accompanied this time by Mrs. Ward, her waiting-woman, and both were very much confused and almost breathless.

"Oh, Madam," cried she, "my lady expresses great concern at your refusing this request, which she says will be her last. She says that she is convinced she will not be in a condition to receive your visit to-morrow; but as a token of her friendship she bequeaths you this little casket containing her watch, necklace, and other jewels, which she desires you will wear in remembrance of her."

We immediately left the house, but, as no mention was made of me in the message, on arriving at Madame de Beauclair's house I waited in a lower apartment till she might give orders for my admittance.

She was no sooner informed of my presence than she desired I would come up. I did so, and found her sitting in an easy chair near her bed-side, and, in the opinion of all present, in perfect health.

We enquired if she felt any inward disorder, she replied in the negative; "yet," said she, with a little sigh, "you will soon, very soon, behold me pass from this world into that eternity which I once doubted, but am now assured of."

As she spoke these last words she looked steadfastly in my face.

I told her I was heartily glad to find so great a change in her ladyship's sentiments, but that I hoped she had no reason to imagine the conviction would be fatal. She only answered with a gloomy smile; and a clergyman of her own persuasion who had been sent for, coming in at that moment, we quitted the room.

In half an hour we were called in again, and she appeared to be more cheerful than before; her eyes sparkled with uncommon vivacity, and she told us she should die with the more satisfaction, because she was enjoying in her last moments the presence of two persons the most agreeable to her in this world, and in the next would be sure of enjoying the society of one whom in life she had dearly cherished.

We now began to dissuade her from giving way to such conversation, when she interrupted us by saying, "talk no more of that,—my time is short, and I would not have the small space allowed me wasted in vain delusion: know," continued she, "I have seen my dear Duchess of Mazarine; I perceived not how she entered, but turning my eyes towards yonder corner of the room, I saw her stand in the same dress she was accustomed to wear when living. I would fain have spoken, but had not the power of utterance: she took a circuit round the chamber, seeming rather to swim than walk: then halting beside the Indian chest, and looking on me with her usual sweetness, 'Beauclair,' said she, 'between the hours of twelve and one this night you shall be with me.' My surprise being a little abated, I began to ask some questions concerning that future world I was so soon to visit, but on the opening of my lips for that purpose, she vanished from my sight."

The clock now struck twelve, and as she discovered not the least symptoms of any illness, we again endeavoured to remove all apprehensions of death; but we had scarce began to speak when on a sudden her countenance changed, and she cried out, " Oh! I am sick at heart!" Mrs. Ward, who during this time stood leaning on her chair, applied some salts, but to no effect; she grew still worse, and in about half an hour expired; it being exactly the time the apparition foretold.

I have been thus particular in relating all the circumstances of this affair, as well to prove that I could not be deceived in it, as to show that Madame de Beauclair was neither melancholy nor superstitious. This lady was far from any such apprehensions, looking upon them as ridiculous and absurd, and could have been convinced by nothing but the testimony of her own eyes and ears.—*From H. Welby.*

XXVI.
Villiers, Duke of Buckingham.

Most of our readers are familiar with the history of the above nobleman, and the tragical termination of his life. The following narrative, as connected with this event, will therefore be read with much interest.

There were many stories scattered abroad at this time relating prophecies and predictions of the duke's untimely and violent death; amongst the rest there was one that gained some credit. There was an officer in the king's wardrobe in Windsor Castle, named Parker, about the age of fifty. This man had, in his youth, been bred in a school in the parish where Sir George Villiers, the father of the Duke lived, and had been much cherished by Sir George, but whom he had never seen since his youth. About six months before the assassination of the Duke of Buckingham, at midnight, this man was in his bed at Windsor, and in good health, when there appeared to him on the side of his bed a man of a venerable aspect, who drew the curtains aside, and fixing his eyes upon him, asked him if he knew him.

The poor man, half dead with fear and apprehension, being asked the second time whether he remembered him, and having in that time called to his memory the presence of Sir George Villiers, he answered that he thought him to be that person. He replied, he was the same, and that he expected a service from him; which was, that he should go to his son, the Duke of Buckingham, and tell him, if he did not somewhat ingratiate himself with the people, or at least abate the extreme malice which they had against him, he would be suffered to live but a short time.

After this discourse he disappeared, and the poor man slept well till morning, when he believed all this to be a dream.

The next night, the same person appeared to him again in the same place, and about the same time of the night, and asked him whether he had done as he required of him; and perceiving he had not, severely reprimanded him, and said, that if he did not perform his commands he should enjoy no peace of mind, but should always be pursued by him; upon this he promised to obey. But the next morning, waking out of a good sleep, though he was exceedingly perplexed with the lively representation of all the particulars in his memory, he was still willing to persuade himself he had only dreamed; and considered that being the Duke's inferior he did not know how to gain admission to his presence. At length he resolved to do nothing in the matter.

The same vision appeared to him a third time, and bitterly reproached him for not performing his promise. The poor man had by this time gained courage to tell him that he had deferred the execution of his commands upon considering how difficult it would be for him to get any access to the Duke; and if he should obtain admission to the Duke, he never would be able to persuade him that he was sent to warn him of approaching danger.

The spectre replied, as he had done before, that he should never find rest till he had performed what he required, and therefore he had better despatch it; that the access to his son was known to be very easy, and that few men waited long for him.

In the morning, the poor man more confirmed by the last appearance, started for London, where the court was then held. He now called on Sir Ralph Freeman, one of the Masters of Requests, who had married a lady nearly allied to the Duke; and was well received by him. Through the interest of Sir Ralph, Parker obtained a promise of an interview with the Duke, who according to his usual condescension told him that he was the next day to hunt with the King; that his horses would attend him at Lambeth-bridge, where he should land by five o'clock in the morning, and if the man attended him there at that hour, he would speak with him.

Sir Ralph presented Parker to the Duke at his landing, who received him courteously, and conversed with him nearly an hour.

Parker told Sir Ralph in his return over the water, that when he mentioned certain particulars the Duke's colour changed, and he swore that he could come at that knowledge only by the devil; for that those particulars were only known to himself and to another.

The Duke joined in the chase, but was observed to ride all the morning with great pensiveness and in deep thought, without any delight in the exercise; and before the morning was spent, he left the field, and alighted at his mother's lodgings in Whitehall, with whom he was shut up for two or three hours. When the Duke left her, his countenance appeared full of trouble mixed with anger, and the Countess was found overwhelmed in tears, and in deep agony.

When the news of the Duke's murder, which happened within a few months afterwards, was brought to his mother, she seemed not surprised, but received it as if she had foreseen it; nor did she afterwards express such a degree of sorrow as was expected from a mother for the loss of so valuable a son.

This story is related in Clarendon's History of the Rebellion, and is also told by Lilley in his Observations on the Life and Death of King Charles the First.

A considerable time before this happened, Sir Clement Throckmorton dreamed that an assassin would kill his Grace. He therefore took the first opportunity to advise him to wear a privy coat; the Duke thanked him for his counsel very kindly, but gave him this answer, that he thought a coat of mail would signify little in a popular commotion, and from any single person he apprehended no danger.—*Relique Wotton.*

XXVII.

Dr. and Mrs. Donne.

Doctor Donne and his wife resided for some time with Sir Robert Drury, at his house in Drury Lane. Sir Robert and the Doctor having agreed to accompany Lord Hay upon an embassy to the Court of France, the Doctor left his wife, who was then pregnant, in Sir Robert's house. Two days after they had arrived at Paris, Dr. Donne happened to be left alone in the room where they had dined, but in about half an hour Sir Robert returned, when noticing the sad air of the Doctor, Sir Robert earnestly requested him to state what had befallen him in his short absence?

The Doctor replied, "Since you left me I have seen a frightful vision, I have seen my dear wife pass by me in the room, with her hair hanging about her shoulders, and a dead child in her arms." Sir Robert replied, "Surely, Sir, you have slept since I left you, and this is the result of some melancholy dream, which I would have you forget, for you are now awake" Dr. Donne replied, "I cannot be more sure that I now live than that I have not slept, that I have seen my wife, and that she stopped short, looked me in the face, and then fled away." This he affirmed the next day with more confidence, which induced Sir Robert to think that there might be some truth in it. Sir Robert immediately dispatched a servant to Drury-house, to ascertain whether Mrs. Donne was alive or dead; and if alive in what state of health. On the twelfth day the messenger returned, stating that he had seen Mrs. Donne, that she was very ill; and that after a long and painful labour, she had been delivered of a dead child; and upon examination it proved that the delivery had been on the day Dr. Donne saw the apparition in his chamber.—*Isaac Walton.*

XXVIII.

Mr. Thornton of Fulham.

Mr Thornton was one night extremely agitated by a dream. It appeared to him that he saw the gardener of his family in the act of murdering the cook. He awoke, but endeavoured to dismiss this vision from his remembrance, and attempted to compose himself to sleep. His eyes were scarcely closed, when again the same dreadful picture presented itself to his imagination. Alarmed by the extraordinary, the distinct, and the repeated intimation, he arose, and taking his night-lamp in his hand, left his room with the intention of proceeding to the spot indicated in his dream. The hour was about four o'clock. The morning was clear, moonlight, and frosty.

The reader will conceive what his surprise must have been, when, on entering the kitchen, on his way to the garden, he perceived the cook dressed in white, putting on her bonnet and cloak, as if preparing for a journey. To his inquiries respecting her presence at such an unaccustomed hour, and in such extraordinary attire, she replied that she was on the point of being married to the gardener,—that they were going to a neighbouring village for that purpose,—and that Mark was waiting for her at the end of the garden with a horse and tax-cart to convey her to church. Mr. Thornton told her that he of course could have no objection to their marriage, though he remonstrated against the secrecy of the proceeding; he desired her to wait a few moments till his return, as he was desirous of speaking to Mark previously to their setting off. He did not delay a moment: his mind much misdoubted the good intentions of the paramour, and he was not a little struck with the coincidence of his dream and the preparations which he witnessed. He first went to the bottom of the garden—to the spot mentioned by the maid-servant as the place where Mark was waiting for her coming. All was still. There was no Mark; no horse; no chaise. He then proceeded to the place marked out to him by the vision. Here he was destined to behold a proceeding of a very doubtful character; working with an indefatigable and hurried hand, and with his back turned towards him, Mr. Thornton perceived a man digging a pit. As he stood at his work, the pit appeared to be about three feet deep, and about the same in width, and about six feet in length; it had all the appearance of a grave.

Mr. Thornton approached silently, and laid his hand with a sudden and violent grasp on the man's shoulder. Mark turned his eyes upon his master, shuddered, and fainted. Were the indications of that dream the suggestions of a lying spirit?—*From H. Welby.*

XXIX.

Dr. Scott and the Title Deed.

One evening Dr. Scott was seated by the fire reading at his house in Broad Street when accidentally raising his head, he saw in an elbow chair, at the opposite side of the fireplace, a grave gentleman in a black velvet gown, a long wig, looking with a pleasing countenance towards the doctor, as if about to speak to him.

The doctor was much disturbed. According to his narrative of the fact the spectre it seems spoke first, and desired the doctor not to be alarmed, that he came to him upon a matter of great importance to an injured family which was in great danger of being ruined; and though he (the doctor) was a stranger to the family, yet knowing him to be a man of integrity he had chosen him to do this act of charity and justice.

The doctor was not at first composed enough to enter into the business with due attention, but seemed rather inclined to get out of the room if he could, and once or twice made an attempt to knock for some of the family to come up. The doctor having at length recovered himself, said, "In the name of God, what art thou?" After much importunity on the part of the doctor the apparition made the following statement:—

"I lived in the county of Somerset, where I left a very good estate, which my grandson enjoys at this time. But he is sued for the possession by my two nephews, the sons of my younger brother.

[*Here he gave his own name, the name of his younger brother, and the names of his two nephews.*]

The doctor then asked him how long the grandson had been in possession of the estate; he told him seven years, intimating that he had been so long dead.

He then went on to explain that his nephews would be too strong for his grandson in the suit, and would deprive him of the mansion-house and estate; so that he would be in danger of being entirely ruined, and his family reduced.

The doctor then said, "And what am I able to do in it if the law be against him?"

"Why," said the spectre, "it is not that the nephews have any right; but the grand deed of settlement, being the conveyance of the inheritance, is lost: and for want of that deed they will not be able to make out their title to the estate."

"Well," said the doctor, "and still what can I do in the case?"

"Why," said the spectre, "if you will go down to my grandson's house, and take some persons with you whom you can trust, I will give you such instructions, that you shall find out the deed of settlement, which lay concealed in a place where I put it, and where you shall direct my grandson to take it out in your presence."

"But why then can you not direct your grandson himself to do this?"

"Ask me not about that," said the spectre, "there are divers reasons which you may know hereafter. I can depend upon your honesty in the meantime, and matters shall be so disposed that you shall have your expenses paid you and be handsomely rewarded for your trouble."

Having obtained a promise from Dr. Scott, the

spectre told him he might apprise his grandson that he had formerly known his grandfather and ask to see the house; and that in a certain upper room or loft he would see a quantity of old lumber, coffers, chests, &c., which had been thrown aside, to make room for more fashionable furniture.

That in a certain corner he should find an old chest with a broken lock upon it and a key in it, which could neither be turned in the lock nor pulled out. In this chest lay the grand deed or charter of the estate, which conveyed the inheritance and without which the family might be ejected. The doctor having promised to despatch this important commission, the spectre disappeared.

After a lapse of some days, and within the time limited by the proposal of the spectre, the doctor went into Somersetshire, and having found the house alluded to he was very courteously invited in. They now entered upon friendly discourse, and the doctor pretended to have heard much of the family and of his grandfather, from whom, he said, he perceived the estate descended to its present occupier.

"Aye," said the gentleman, shaking his head, "my father died young, and my grandfather left things so confused that for want of one principal writing, which is not yet come to hand, I have met with great trouble from two cousins, my grandfather's brother's children, who have put me to very great expense about it."

"But I hope you have got over it, sir?" said the doctor.

"No," said the gentleman, "to be candid with you, we shall never get quite over it, unless we can find this old deed; which, however, I hope we shall find, for I intend to make a general search after it."

"I wish with all my heart you may find it, sir," said the doctor.

"I do not doubt but we shall; I had a strange dream about it last night," said the gentleman.

"A dream about the writing!" said the doctor, "I hope it was that you should find it then."

"I dreamed," said the other, "that a strange gentleman came to me, and assisted me in searching for it. I do not know but that you are the man."

"I should be very glad to be the man," said the doctor.

"Nay," replied the gentleman, "you may be the man to help me to look after it."

"Aye, sir," said the doctor, "I may help you to look after it, indeed, and I will do that with all my heart; but I would much rather be the man that should help you to find it; pray when do you intend to search?"

"To-morrow," said the gentleman, "I have appointed to search for it."

"But," said the doctor, "in what manner do you intend to search?"

"Why," replied the gentleman, "it is our opinion that my grandfather was so very much concerned in preserving this writing and had so much jealousy as to its safety, that he hid it in a secret place; and I am resolved to pull half the house down, but I will find it, if it is above ground."

"Truly," said the doctor, "he may have hid it, so that you may pull the whole house down before you find it. I have known such things utterly lost by the very care taken to preserve them."

"If it was made of something the fire would not destroy," said the gentleman, "I would burn the house down, but I would find it."

"I suppose you have searched all the old gentleman's chests, trunks, and coffers over and over," said the doctor.

"Aye," said the gentleman, "and turned them all

inside outward, and there they lay in a heap up in a loft or garret with nothing in them; nay, we knocked three or four of them in pieces to search for private drawers, and then I burnt them for anger, though they were fine old cypress chests that cost money enough when they were in fashion."

"I am sorry you burnt them," said the doctor.

"Nay," said the gentleman, "I did not burn a scrap of them till they were all split to pieces, and it was not possible there could be any thing in them."

This made the doctor a little easy, for he began to be surprised when he told him he had split some of them and burned them.

"Well," said the doctor, "if I cannot do you any service in your search, I will come to see you again to-morrow, and wait upon you during it with my best good wishes."

"Nay," says the gentleman, "I do not design to part with you, since you are so kind as to offer me your assistance; you shall stay all night, then, and be at the commencement of the search."

The doctor had now gained his point so far as to make an intimacy with the family; and after much entreaty he consented to sleep in the house.

A little before dark, the gentleman asked him to take a walk in the park, but he declined; "I would rather, sir," said he smiling, "that you show me this fine old mansion house, that is to be demolished to-morrow; methinks I would fain see the house once before you pull it down."

"With all my heart," said the gentleman. He took him immediately up stairs, showed him the best apartments, and his fine furniture and pictures; and coming to the head of the staircase, offered to descend.

"But, sir," said the doctor, "shall we not go higher?"

"There is nothing there," said he, but garrets and

old lofts full of rubbish, and a place leading to the turret and the clock-house."

"O, let me see it all, now we are here," said the doctor, "I love to see the old lofty towers and turrets, the magnificence of our ancestors, though they are out of fashion now; pray let me see them."

After they had rambled over the mansion, they passed by a great lumber room, the door of which stood open.

"And what place is this?" said the doctor.

"O! that is the room," said the gentleman, "where all the rubbish, the chests, coffers, and trunks lie; see how they are piled one upon another almost to the ceiling."

Upon this the doctor began to look around him. He had not been in the room two minutes before he found everything precisely as the spectre in London had described; he went directly to the pile he had been told of, and fixed his eye upon the very chest with the old rusty lock upon it, which would neither turn round nor come out.

"On my word, sir," said the doctor, "you have taken pains enough, if you have searched all these drawers, chests, and coffers, and everything that may have been in them."

"Indeed, sir," said the gentleman, "I have examined them myself, and looked over all the musty writings one by one; and they have all passed through my hand and under my eye."

"Well, sir," said the doctor, "will you gratify my curiosity by opening and emptying this small chest or coffer?"

The gentleman, looking at the chest, said, smiling, "I remember opening it; and turning to his servant, he said, "William, do you not remember that chest?"

"Yes, sir," replied the servant, "I remember you were so tired, that you sat down upon the chest when everything was out of it; that you shut the lid, and sat down and sent me to my lady to bring you a dram of citron; and that you said you were ready to faint."

"Well, sir," said the doctor, "its only a whim of mine, and probably it may contain nothing."

"You shall see it turned upside down before your face, as well as the rest."

Immediately the coffer was dragged out and opened. When the papers were all out, the doctor turning round, as if looking among them, but taking little or no notice of the chest, stooped down as if supporting himself with his cane, struck the same into the chest, but snatched it out again hastily as if it had been a mistake, and turning to the chest, he shut the lid, and seated himself upon it. Having dismissed the servant, " Now, sir," said he, " I have found your writing ; I have found your grand deed of settlement ; and I will lay you a hundred guineas I have it in this coffer."

The gentleman took up the lid again, handled the chest, looked over every part of it; but could see nothing; he was confounded and amazed! "What do you mean?" said he to the doctor, "here is nothing but an empty coffer."

"Upon my word," said the doctor, "I am no magician, but I tell you again the writing is in this coffer."

The gentleman knocked and called for his servant with the hammer, but the doctor still sat composed upon the lid of the coffer.

At length the man came with a hammer and chisel, and the doctor set to work upon the chest, knocking upon the flat of the bottom. "Hark!" says he, "don't you hear it sir? don't you hear it plainly?"

"Hear what?" said the gentleman; "I do not understand you."

"Why the chest has a double bottom, sir, a false bottom," said the doctor, "don't you hear it sound hollow."

In a word, they immediately split the inner bottom open, and there found the parchment spread abroad flat on the whole breadth of the bottom of the trunk.

It is impossible to describe the joy and surprise of the gentlemen, and of the whole family; the former sent for his lady and two of his daughters to come into the garret among the rubbish, to see the place and manner in which the writing was found.—*From H. Welby.*

XXX.

Dorothy Dingley of Launceston, Cornwall.

In the beginning of the year 1665, a disease happened in this town, and some of my scholars (the minister of the town is speaking) died of it. Among others who fell victims to its malignity was John Elliott, the eldest son of Edward Elliot of Treberse, Esq., a stripling about sixteen years of age, but of uncommon abilities. At his particular request, I preached at his funeral, which happened on the 20th day of June, 1665. In my discourse I spoke some words in commendation of the young gentleman. An old gentleman, who was then in the church, was much affected with the discourse, and was often heard to repeat the same evening a line which I quoted from Virgil:—

Et puer ipse contrari dignus.

The cause of this old gentleman's concern was the application of my observations to his own son, who being but a few months younger than Mr. Elliot, was now by a strange accident quite beyond hope of recovery.

The funeral ceremony being over, on leaving the church, I was courteously accosted by this old gentleman; and with unusual importunity, almost forced against my will to his house that night, nor could I have even declined his kindness had not Mr. Elliot interposed. I excused myself for the present, but was constrained to promise to wait upon him at his own house the Monday following. This then seemed satisfactory, but before Monday I received a message requesting that if possible I would be there on the Sunday. This second attempt I resisted, by answering that it was inconvenient. The gentleman sent me another letter on the Saturday enjoining me by no means to fail coming upon the Monday. I was indeed startled at so much eagerness, and began to suspect that there must be some design in this excess of courtesy.

On Monday I paid my promised visit, and met with a reception as free as the invitation was importunate. There also I met a neighbouring minister, who pretended to call in accidentally, but by the sequel I supposed it otherwise. After dinner this brother of the cloth undertook to show me the gardens, where, as we were walking, he intimated to me the main object of this treat.

First he apprised me of the unhappiness of the family in general, and then instanced the youngest son in particular. He related what a hopeful youth he had been, and how melancholy he was now grown, deeply lamenting that his ill-humour should so incredibly subdue his reason. " The poor boy," said he, " believes himself to be haunted by ghosts, and is confident that he meets with an evil spirit in a certain field about half a mile from this place, as often as he goes that way to school." In the midst of our discourse, the old gentleman and his lady came up to us. The clergyman continued the narrative, and the parents of the youth confirmed what he said, and they all desired my opinion and advice on the affair.

I replied, that what the youth had reported to them

was strange, yet not incredible, and that I knew not then what to think or say on the subject; but if the lad would explain himself to me, I hoped to give them a better account of my opinion the next day.

The youth was called immediately, and I soon entered into a close conference with him. At first I was very cautious not to displease him, but endeavoured to ingratiate myself with him. But we had scarce passed the first salutation and begun to speak of the business, before I found him very communicative. He asserted that he was constantly disturbed by the appearance of a woman in an adjacent field, called Higher Brown Quartils. He next told me in a flood of tears, that his friends were so unkind and unjust to him as neither to believe nor pity him; and that if any man would go with him to the place he might be convinced that his assertion was true.

"This woman who appears to me," said he, "lived neighbour to my father, and died about eight years since; her name was Dorothy Dingley." He then stated her stature, age, and complexion: that she never spoke to him, but passed by hastily, and always left him the foot-path, and that she commonly met him twice or three times in the breadth of the field.

"Two months had elapsed," he continued, "before I took any further notice of it, and though the face was in my memory, yet I could not recal the name; but I concluded that it was some woman who lived in the neighbourhood, and frequently passed that way. Nor did I imagine otherwise, until she met me constantly morning and evening, and always in the same field, and sometimes twice or thrice in the breadth of it.

"The first time I noticed her was about a year since; and when I began to suspect and believe it to be a ghost, I had courage enough not to be afraid. I often spoke to it, but never had a word in answer.

I then changed my way and went to school by the under horse road, and then she met me in the narrow lane, between the quarry park and the nursery-ground.

At length I began to be terrified at it, and prayed continually that God would either free me from it, or let me know the meaning of it. Night and day, sleeping or waking, the shape was ever running in my mind; and I often repeated these passages of Scripture (Job. vii. 14) "Thou scarest me with dreams, and terrifiest me through visions;" and (Deut. xxviii. 67) "In the morning thou shalt say, would God it were evening, and at evening thou shalt say, would God it were morning, for the fear of thine heart, wherewith thou shalt fear, and for the sight of thine eyes which thou shalt see."

I was much pleased with the lad's ingenuity, in the application of these pertinent texts of scripture to his condition, and desired him to proceed, which he did as follows:—

"By degrees I grew very pensive, insomuch that I was noticed by all our family; being questioned closely on the subject I told my brother William of it, and he privately acquainted my father and mother.

"They however laughed at me, and enjoined me to attend to my school, and keep such fancies out of my head.

"I accordingly went to school regularly, but always met the woman in the way."

Our conference ended in my offering to accompany him to the field, which proposal he received with ecstasy, and we accordingly went.

The gentleman, his wife, and Mr. Williams, were impatient to know the result, insomuch that they came out of the parlour into the hall to meet us; and seeing the lad look cheerful, the first compliment from the old man was, "Come, Mr. Ruddle, now you have talked with Sam I hope he will have more wit; an idle boy, an idle boy!" At these words the lad ran up stairs to his chamber without replying, and I soon stopped the curiosity of the three expectants, by telling them I had promised silence and was resolved to be as good as my word, but that they should soon know all.

The next morning, before five o'clock, the lad was in my chamber, when I arose and went with him. The field he led me to was some twenty acres in extent, in an open country, and about three furlongs from any house. We had not proceeded above a third part over the field, before the spectre, in the shape of a woman, exactly as he had described her to me in the orchard the day before, met us and passed by. I was somewhat surprised at it; and though I had firmly resolved to speak to it, yet I had not the power, nor indeed durst I look back. We walked to the end of the field, and returned, but the spectre did not then meet us again. On our return home, the lady waited to speak with me; I told her that my opinion was, that her son's complaint was not to be slighted, nor altogether discredited.

On the morning of the 27th day of July, 1665, I went to the haunted field alone, and walked the breadth of it without any encounter. I returned and took the other walk, and then the spectre appeared to me at about the same place I saw it before when the young gentleman was with me; in my idea it moved swifter than the time before, and was about ten feet distant from me on my right hand.

On the evening of this day I proposed that the parents and the son should go with me to the place next morning, and it was decided to do so. In the morning, lest we should alarm the servants, they went under the pretence of seeing a field of wheat, and I took my horse, and met them at the place appointed.

Thence we all four walked leisurely into the Quartils,

and had passed about half the field before the spectre made its appearance. It then came over the stile just before us, and moved with such swiftness that by the time we had gone six or seven steps it had passed by. I immediately turned my head and ran after it, with the young man by my side; we saw it pass over the stile at which we entered, and disappear. I stepped upon the hedge at one place and he at another, but could discern nothing, whereas I dare aver that the swiftest horse in England could not have conveyed himself out of sight in that short space of time. Two things I observed in this day's appearance :—

1. That a spaniel dog who followed the company unregarded, barked and ran away as the spectre passed by.

2. That the motion of the spectre was not by steps or moving of the feet, but by a kind of sliding as children upon the ice, or a boat down a swift river, which exactly answers the descriptions the ancients gave of the motion of their lemurs.

This ocular evidence convinced, but strangely frightened, the old gentleman and his wife, who knew Dorothy Dingley in her lifetime, were at her funeral, and plainly saw her features in this present apparition. I was resolved to proceed, and use such means as learned men have successfully practised in these uncommon cases.

The next morning being Thursday, I went out very early by myself, and walked for about an hour's space in meditation and prayer in the field's adjoining the Quartils. Soon after five I stepped over the stile, into the disturbed field, and had not gone above thirty or forty paces before the spectre appeared at the farther stile. I spoke to it with a loud voice, whereupon it approached but slowly, and when I came near, it moved not. I spoke again, and it answered in a voice neither very audible nor intelligible. I was not in the least terrified, and therefore persisted, until it spoke again, and satisfied me.

On the evening of the same day, an hour after sunset, it met me again near the same place, and after a few words on each side it quietly vanished, and neither appeared since nor ever will more to any man's disturbance. The conversation in the morning lasted about a quarter of an hour.

These things are true, and I know them to be so with as much certainty as eyes and ears can give me; and until I can be persuaded that my senses deceive me; and by that persuasion deprive myself of the strongest inducement to believe the Christian religion, I must and will assert, that these things in this paper are true. I know full well with what difficulty relations of so uncommon a nature and practice obtain belief.

Such is the narrative of the Rev. Mr. Ruddle, a clergyman of some note at Launceston, in Cornwall. It wants neither name, date, nor place, but every particular seems to be detailed with the utmost precision and fidelity.—*From H. Welby.*

XXXI.

Singular Vision to Mrs. Lowe.

One morning in the summer of 1745, Mrs. Jane Lowe, housekeeper to Mr. Pringle, of Clifton Park, in the south of Scotland, beheld the apparition of a lady walking in the avenue, on the margin of a rivulet, which runs into Kale water. The form resembled a daughter of her master, who had long been absent from the family, at the distance of about a hundred miles south of Paris. As Mrs. Lowe walked down the avenue and approached the rivulet, this resemblance impressed her so strongly that, seeing her master in an enclosure adjoining, she went and told him what she had seen. Mr. Pringle laughed, and said, "you simple woman, that lady is Miss Chattow of Morebattle." However, Mrs. Lowe prevailed upon him to accompany her to the place, which they had nearly reached, when the apparition sprung into the water and instantly disappeared.

Mr. Pringle and Mrs. Lowe, on returning to the hall, apprized the family of the vision, and for their pains were heartily laughed at. The Rev. Mr. Turnbull, minister of Linton, happened to breakfast that morning with Mr. Pringle, his lady, and two young daughters, who joined in the laugh. About three months afterwards, the same reverend gentleman honoured the family with his company; when standing at a window in the lower room, he observed a poor, ragged, lame, lean man, slowly approaching the house. "Here comes another apparition," cried Mr. Turnbull, with a kind of contemptuous smile. This drew the immediate attention of all present, and Mr. Pringle quickly recognised the person to be his second son, whom he had not seen before for above ten years.

On his arrival, he soon convinced them he was not an apparition, declaring that he had narrowly escaped with his life from Tunis, in the vicinity of which he had been a slave to the Algerines seven years, but had happily been ransomed at the critical moment when he was ordered to be put to death for mutiny. He added, that on his return home through France, he called at the place where he had heard that his sister resided, and to his unspeakable grief found that she died on the 25th of May, the same summer, about five o'clock in the morning, which he recollected to have been the precise time when he was saved from the jaws of death, and when he thought he beheld his sister. Mrs. Lowe, who was present in the room, on hearing his declaration, added her testimony by affirming that the day alluded to was that on which she had shown Mr. Pringle the apparition; and this was confirmed by the reverend divine, in whose study this narrative was found after his death.—*From H. Welby.*

XXXII.

An Experience of a Konigsberg Professor.

"I am not so decidedly sceptical on the possibility of supernatural appearances," said Count Falkesheim to Sir Nathaniel Wraxall, "as to treat them with ridicule, because they may appear to be unphilosophical. I received my education in the University of Konigsberg, where I had the advantage of attending lectures in ethics and moral philosophy, delivered by a professor who was esteemed a very superior man in those branches of science. He had, nevertheless, though an ecclesiastic, the reputation of being tinctured with incredulity on various points connected with revealed religion. When, therefore, it became necessary for him in the course of his lectures to treat on the nature of spirit as detached from matter, to discuss the immortality of the soul, and to enter on the doctrine of a future state, I listened with more than ordinary attention to his opinions. In speaking of all these mysterious subjects, there appeared to me to be so visible an embarrassment, both in his language and in his expressions, that I felt the strongest curiosity to question him further respecting them. Finding myself alone with him soon aftterwards, I ventured to state to him my remarks on his deportment, and entreated him to tell me if they were well founded or only imaginary suggestions.

"The hesitation which you noticed," answered he, "resulted from the conflict that takes place within me, when I am attempting to convey my ideas on a subject where my understanding is at variance with the testimony of my senses. I am equally, from reason and reflection, disposed to consider with incredulity and contempt the existence of apparitions. But an appearance, which I have witnessed with my own eyes, as far as they, or any of the perceptions can be confided in, and which has even received a sort of subsequent confirmation from other circumstances connected with the original facts, leave me in that state of scepticism and suspense which pervaded my discourse. I will communicate to you its cause. Having been brought up to the profession of the church, I was presented by Frederick William the First, late King of Prussia, to a small benefice, situated in the interior of the country, at a considerable distance south of Konigsberg. I repaired thither in order to take possession of my living, and found a neat parsonage house, where I passed the night in the bed-chamber which had been occupied by my predecessor.

"It was in the longest days of summer; and on the following morning, which was Sunday, while lying awake, the curtains of the bed being undrawn and it being broad daylight, I beheld the figure of a man habited in a sort of loose gown, standing at a reading desk on which lay a large book, the leaves of which he appeared to turn over at intervals; on each side of him stood a little boy, in whose faces he looked earnestly from time to time, and as he looked he seemed always to heave a deep sigh. His countenance, pale and disconsolate, indicated some distress of mind. I had the most perfect view of these objects, but being impressed with too much terror and apprehension to rise or to address myself to the appearance before me, I remained for some minutes a breathless and silent spectator, without uttering a word or altering my position. At length the man closed the book, and then taking the two children, one in each hand, he led them slowly across the room; my eyes eagerly followed him till the three figures gradually disappeared or were lost behind an iron stove which stood at the furthest corner of the apartment.

"However deeply and awfully I was affected by the sight which I had witnessed, and however incapable I was of explaining it to my own satisfaction, yet I recovered sufficiently the possession of my mind to get up, and having hastily dressed myself, I left the house. The sun was long risen, and directing my steps to the church, I found that it was open but the sexton had quitted it; on entering the chancel my mind and imagination were so strongly impressed by the scene which had recently passed, that I endeavoured to dissipate the recollection by considering the objects around me. In almost all the Lutheran churches of Prussian dominions, it is the custom to hang up against the walls or some part of the building, the portraits of the successive pastors or clergymen who have held the living. A number of these paintings, rudely performed, were suspended in one of the aisles. I had no sooner fixed my eyes on the last on the range, which was the portrait of my immediate predecessor, than they became rivetted to the object, as I instantly recognised the same face which I had beheld in my bed-chamber, though not clouded by the same deep impression of melancholy and distress. The sexton entered as I was still contemplating this interesting head, and I immediately began a conversation with him on the subject of the persons who had preceded me in the living. He remembered several incumbents, concerning whom respectively I made various inquiries, till I came to the last relative to whose history I was particularly inquisitive. 'We considered him,' said the sexton, 'one of the most learned and amiable men that had ever resided among us. His character and benevolence endeared him to all his parishioners, who will long lament his loss. But he was carried off in the middle of his days by a lingering illness, the cause of which has given rise to many unpleasant reports among us, and which still forms matter of conjecture. It is however commonly believed that he died of a broken heart.'

"My curiosity being still more warmly excited by the mention of this circumstance, I eagerly pressed him to disclose to me all he knew or had heard on the subject. 'Nothing respecting it,' answered he, 'is absolutely known, but scandal has propagated a story of his having formed a criminal connection with a young woman of the neighbourhood, by whom it was even asserted he had two sons. As some confirmation of the report, I know that there certainly were two children who had been seen at the parsonage, boys of about four or five years old, and who suddenly disappeared some time before the decease of their supposed father, and what has become of them we none of us know. It is equally certain that the surmises and unfavourable opinions formed respecting this mysterious business, which must necessarily have reached him, precipitated, if they did not produce, the disorder of which our late pastor died: but he is gone to his account, and we are bound to think charitably of the departed.'

"It is unnecessary to say with what emotion I listened to this relation, which recalled to my imagination, and seemed to give proof of the existence of all that I had seen. Yet unwilling to suffer my mind to become enslaved by phantoms which might have been the effect of error or deception, I neither communicated to the sexton what I had witnessed, nor even permitted myself to quit the chamber where it had taken place. I continued to lodge there without ever witnessing any similar appearance; and the recollection itself began to wear away as the autumn advanced. When the approach of winter rendered it necessary to light fires through the house, I ordered the iron stove which stood in the room, and behind which the figures which I beheld seemed to disappear, to be heated for the purpose of warming the apartment. Some difficulty was experienced in making the attempt, the stove not only smoking intolerably, but emitting an offensive smell. Having therefore sent for a blacksmith to inspect and repair it, he discovered in the inside, at the farthest extremity, the bones of two small human bodies, corresponding perfectly in size as well as in other respects with the description given me by the sexton of the two boys who had been seen at the parsonage.

"This last circumstance completed my astonishment, and appeared to confer a sort of reality on an appearance which might otherwise have been considered as a delusion of the senses. I resigned the living, quitted the place, and retired to Konigsberg; but it produced on my mind the deepest impression, and has in its effect given rise to that uncertainty and contradiction of sentiment which you remarked in my late discourse."—*From H. Welby.*

XXXIII.

The Rochester Apparition.

The following narrative was communicated in a letter from Mr. Thomas Tilson, minister of Aylesworth, in Kent, to Mr. Baxter, as a contribution to his celebrated work, "The Certainty of the World of Spirits."

"REV. SIR,—Being informed that you are writing about spectres and apparitions, I take the freedom, though a stranger, to send you the following relation:

"Mary, the wife of John Goffe, of Rochester, being

afflicted with a long illness, removed to her father's house at West-Mulling, which is about nine miles distant from her own; there she died, June 4, 1691.

"The day before her death, she grew impatiently desirous to see her two children, whom she had left at home in the care of a nurse. She prayed her husband to hire a horse, for she must go home and die with her children. When they persuaded her to the contrary, telling her she was not fit to be taken out of her bed, nor able to sit on horseback, she entreated them however to try; 'If I cannot sit,' said she, 'I will lie along upon the horse, for I must go to see my babes.'

"A minister who lives in the town was with her at ten o'clock that night, to whom she expressed good hopes in the mercies of God, and a willingness to die; 'but,' said she, 'it is my misery that I cannot see my children.'

"Between one and two o'clock in the morning she fell into a trance. One Widow Turner, who watched with her that night, says that her eyes were open, and fixed, and her jaw fallen; she put her hand upon her mouth and nostrils, but could perceive no breath; she thought her to be in a fit, and doubted whether she were alive or dead.

"The next day, this dying woman told her mother that she had been at home with her children. 'That is impossible,' said the mother, 'for you have been here in bed all the while.' 'Yes,' replied the other, 'but I was with them last night when I was asleep.'

"The nurse at Rochester, Widow Alexander by name, affirms, and says she will take her oath of it before a magistrate, and receive the sacrament upon it, that a little before two o'clock that morning, she saw the likeness of the said Mary Goffe come out of the next chamber (where the elder child lay in a bed by itself, the door being left open), and stand by her bedside for about a quarter of an hour; the younger child was there lying by her; her eyes moved, and her mouth, but she said nothing. The nurse moreover says she was perfectly awake as it was then daylight, being one of the longest days in the year. She sat up in her bed and looked stedfastly upon the apparition; she then heard the bridge clock strike two, and a little while after, said, 'In the name of the Father, Son, and Holy Ghost, what art thou?' Thereupon the appearance removed and went away; she slipped on her clothes and followed, but what became of it she cannot tell. Then, and not before, she began to be grievously affrighted, and went out of doors and walked upon the wharf (the house is just by the river side) for some hours, only going in now and then to look at the children. At five o'clock she went to a neighbour's house, and knocked at the door, but they would not rise; at six she went again, then they arose and let her in. She related to them all that had passed; they tried to persuade her that she was mistaken, or had dreamt, but she confidently affirmed, 'if ever I saw her in all my life, I saw her this night.'

"One of those to whom she made the relation, the wife of Mr. J. Sweet, had a messenger who came from Mulling that forenoon to let her know her neighbour Goffe was dying, and desired to speak with her; she went over the same day, and found her just departing. The mother, amongst other discourse, related to her how much her daughter had longed to see her children, and declared she had seen them. This brought to Mrs. Sweet's mind what the nurse had told her that morning, for, till then, she had not thought fit to mention it, but disguised it rather as the woman's disturbed imagination.

"The substance of this I had related to me by John Carpenter, the father of the deceased, next day after the burial. July 2nd, I fully discoursed the matter with the nurse and the two neighbours.

"Two days after I had it from the mother, the minister that was with her in the evening, and the woman who sat up with her that last night; they all agree in the story, and every one helps to strengthen the other's testimony.

"They all appear to be sober, intelligent persons, far enough off from designing to impose a cheat upon the world, or to manage a lie, and what temptation they should lie under for so doing, I cannot conceive.

Your most faithful and humble servant,

THOMAS TILSON.

Minister of Aylesford, near Maidstone,
in Kent.

XXXIV.

Cashio Burroughs and the Courtesan.

Sir John Burroughs being sent Envoy to the Emperor by King Charles I. took his eldest son Cashio Burroughs with him; and passing through Italy left his son at Florence to learn the language, where he became involved in an intrigue with a beautiful courtesan, mistress to the Grand Duke. Their familiarity became so public, that it came at length to the Duke's ears, who resolved to have him murdered. Cashio having timely notice of the Duke's design, immediately left the city without acquainting his mistress of his departure, and came to England. The Duke, being disappointed of his revenge, now directed towards his mistress the most reproachful language; she, resenting the sudden departure of her gallant, of whom she was most passionately enamoured, killed herself. At the same moment that she expired, she appeared to

Cashio at his lodgings at London, first rebuked him for his ingratitude to her, in leaving her so suddenly and exposing her to the fury of the Duke, then related her own tragical exit, adding that he should be slain in a duel; which accordingly happened. Thus she appeared to him frequently, even when his younger brother (who was afterwards Sir John) was in the same bed with him. As often as she appeared, he cried out with great trembling of body and anguish of mind, "Oh God! she comes! she comes!" and in this manner she haunted him till he was killed. She appeared to him in the morning before that event. "Some of my acquaintances," says Aubrey, "have told me that he was one of the handsomest men in England, and very valiant."—*Aubrey's Miscellanies.*

XXXV.

Captain Rogers' Dream.

In the year 1694, one Captain Thomas Rogers, commander of a ship called "The Society," was bound on a voyage from London to Virginia.

They had a pretty good passage, and the day before had made an observation, when the mates and officers brought their books and cast up their reckonings with the captain, to see how near they were to the coast of America. They all agreed that they were at least a hundred leagues from the capes of Virginia. After these customary reckonings, and heaving the lead, and finding no ground at an hundred fathoms, they set the watch and the captain turned into bed.

The weather was good, a moderate gale of wind blew fair for the coast, so that the ship might have run about twelve or fifteen leagues in the night after the captain went to his cabin.

He fell asleep, and slept very soundly for about

three hours, when he awoke and lay till he heard his second mate turn out and relieve the watch; he then called his chief mate, as he was going off from the watch, and asked him how all things fared; who answered that all was well, the gale fresh, and they were running at a great rate, but it was a fair wind and a fine clear night; the captain then went to sleep again.

About an hour after this he dreamed that a man pulled him, and waked him, and bade him turn out and look abroad. He, however, lay still, and was suddenly awaked again, and thus several times; and though he knew not what was the reason, yet he found it impossible to go to sleep; and still he heard the vision say, "turn out and look abroad."

He lay in this uneasiness nearly two hours, but at last he could lie no longer, so got up, put on his watch gown and came out upon the quarter-deck; there he found his second mate walking about, and the boatswain upon the forecastle, the night being fine and clear, a fair wind, and all well as before.

The mate wondering, at first did not know him; but calling, "Who is there?" the captain answered, and the mate returned, "The captain! what is the matter, sir?"

The captain said, "I don't know; but I have been very uneasy these two hours, and somebody bade me turn out, and look abroad, though I know not what can be the meaning of it.

"How does the ship cape?" said the captain.

"South-west by south," answered the mate; "fair for the coast, and the wind east by north."

"That is good," said the captain;" and after some other questions, he turned about to go back to the cabin, when somebody stood by him and said, "heave the lead, heave the lead."

Upon this he turned again to his second mate, saying, "When did you heave the lead? What water had you?"

"About an hour ago," replied the mate, "sixty fathoms."

"Heave again," said the captain.

"If you please it shall be done," said the mate.

Accordingly a hand was called, and the lead being heaved, they found ground at eleven fathoms.

This surprised them all, but much more so when at the next cast it came up seven fathoms.

Upon this the captain in a fright bade them put the helm a-lee, and about ship; all hands being ordered to back the sails, as is usual in such cases.

The proper orders being obeyed, the ship stayed presently, and came about; and before the sails filled she had but four fathoms and a-half of water under her stern; as soon as she filled and stood off, they had seven fathoms again, and at the next cast eleven fathoms, and so on to twenty fathoms; he then stood off to seaward all the rest of the watch to get into deep water, till daybreak, when, being a clear morning, the capes of Virginia and all the coast of America were in fair view under their stern, and but a few leagues distant. Had they stood on but one cable's length farther, as they were going, they would have been bump ashore, and certainly have lost their ship, if not their lives.—*From H. Welby.*

XXXVI.

Lord Middleton and the Laird Bocconi.

Sir W. Dugdale informed several gentlemen that when Major-General Middleton, afterwards created Lord, went into the Highlands of Scotland to endeavour to make a party for Charles I., an old gentleman, who was credited with the gift of second-sight, met him and told him that his attempt, though laudable, would not be successful; that they would put the king to death, and that several other attempts would be made and fail; that his son would come in, although it would be long first, and should at last be restored.

This nobleman had a great friendship for the Laird Bocconi, and they made an agreement, that the first of them that died should appear to the other in extremity. It happened that Lord Middleton was taken prisoner at the battle of Worcester, and sent up to London: while he was confined in the Tower, one morning lying pensive in his bed, Bocconi appeared to him. Lord Middleton asked him if he were dead or alive? He replied that he was dead, and had been so many years, but that he was come to revive his hopes, for that in a very short time, within three days, he should escape: this fell out as it was foretold, and he did so in his wife's clothes. When he had delivered his message, he lightly tripped about the room, and disappeared.

This account Sir William Dugdale received from the Bishop of Edinburgh, who inserted it in his miscellanies.—*Aubrey.*

XXXVII.

Appearance of Henry Jacob to His Cousin, Dr. Jacob.

Henry Jacob was a man of sound learning, of Merton College, Oxford, where he died in 1673. About a week after his death, Dr. Jacob, lying awake and the moon shining brightly, saw his cousin Henry standing by his bed in his shirt and with a white cap on.

At first the Dr. questioned himself as to the reality of his being awake, and sitting up to convince himself, for awhile looked at the phantom before him with dread and astonishment. At last he lay down, and thought to compose himself to sleep again: but curiosity would not permit this, and he again turned himself, when he saw his cousin standing there as before. Presently taking courage he rose up as at first, but yet he had not sufficient courage to speak to him. The spectre stood full half an hour before him, and then disappeared.

Dr. Jacob immediately went down stairs, and while relating the story, the cook, who had gone out to fetch wood to keep up the fire, returned in great trepidation, having seen a spectre standing "like in a shirt" upon the wood pile.

Dr. Jacob related the whole of the incident to Aubrey, when at Lord Teynham's in Kent, where he was then living as doctor.—*Wood's Athenæ Oxon.*

XXXVIII.

Anecdote of the Hon. Lady Elizabeth Hastings.

This lady was very remarkable for her piety and charity.* Archbishop Sharpe, Dr. Lucas, Mr. Nelson, and Mr. Locke, were her most intimate friends. Mr. Nelson was the first called away, and between him and this lady there subsisted a sort of religious compact for a communication of spirits in the hour of extremity, for in her last illness she was constantly anxious and in expectation of a messenger of glad tidings as she said.

For some time her friends, household, and servants, thought that the severity of the pain she suffered, which proceeded from a cancer in her breast, had rendered her delirious: but she convinced them at last that she was rational, and declared that in a short

---

*See her story in *The Tatler*, No. 42, and where her character is drawn under the name of the Aspasia.

time she would be able to tell the exact hour of her departure.

She called for a manuscript volume of notes of her own writing, and showed her brother, the Earl of Huntingdon, a memorandum, which plainly mentioned that an agreement had been made between her and Mr. Nelson that the first who died should return if possible and warn the other of the approaching termination of life.

During the whole of her illness two nurses sat up with her, relieving each other at intervals for rest in the night. On the morning of the sixth day previous to her dissolution, about four o'clock, there came visibly into the room the form and appearance of a grave and venerable looking man : the nurse saw it plainly and related how he was dressed, her account according exactly with the general appearance of the late Mr. Nelson. Lady Hastings was all the while seemingly asleep. The phantom, after standing at the side of the bed sat down in an elbow chair, which chanced to be near. The nurse after beholding it a short time, rang a bell for a servant to come to her, but not being answered, she took the light in her hand, and went to call her up, but before she could return it was gone, and Lady Hastings being then awake, rebuked her for her silly fears, and said she had now the sweet assurance of relief from her pain in six days, and in six days she died.

This story is so well attested, that it has passed into several theological works, and more than once has been mentioned in the pulpit. Mr. Thomas Barnard, who wrote her historical character, and published it, with an account of her public charities, mentions it with some additional circumstances.—*From H. Welby.*

XXXIX.

A Fortunate Dream.

A merchant of London, being on the Continent upon business, chanced to meet an old school-fellow who had turned Roman Catholic and received priest's orders. This meeting naturally recalled their former affection and friendship, and they arranged to spend the evening together. This was in French Flanders; and the wine being good, the conversation became argumentative, and religion the principal topic. This, as is too often the case between persons of different persuasions, was soon carried beyond the limits of good taste on both sides; and the merchant, who had read many polemical books, got the better of the argument in favour of the reformed religion of his country, which the other had abandoned. The priest seemed to be much chagrined, and his countenance visibly discovered the emotions of his mind. At length, however, appearing to resume his pleasantry and good nature, he invited the merchant to breakfast with him the next morning, at a convent over which he presided.

They then parted in the utmost friendship, and the merchant soon after went to bed, where soon falling asleep, he had a dream of the most frightful nature. He thought he entered a den where were ten thousand hissing serpents, one of which twisting its train round his neck, darted its sting into his bosom. The dread of this instantly awoke him, and caused him to start from his couch in the greatest agitation. His mind the remainder of the night was much too unsettled for sleep, and he lay till the sun arose, when he got up and walked out into a neighbouring field. Meeting a friend and countryman, who was a captain of a company of soldiers encamped in the vicinity, and who quickly discovered the confusion his mind was in, he told his dream, and promised to meet him again after he had breakfasted at the convent. "Although I pay but little regard to dreams in general," said the captain, "yet there is something in yours so extremely uncommon, that I verily believe it to be ominous of some disaster that awaits you this day." "And," continued he, "I would by no means advise you to go to the priest; for you may renew the argument, and he will by no means take it well to be overcome in his own convent." "As I have given my promise," said the merchant, "I must go and visit my old schoolfellow, whose friendship was always sincere, and whose company always delighted me." "My dear friend," quoth the captain, "if you will go, I wish you well back again." These singular words so struck the mind of the merchant, that he desired the captain to call upon him, as by accident, about half an hour after the time appointed, at the convent, which the captain promised to do.

At nine o'clock the merchant knocked at the gate of the convent, and was met by the priest, who welcomed him to the place with every expression of friendship. Then conducting him up a staircase, they came to a door which the priest opened. After some ceremonies, they advanced along a gallery, at the end of which were two folding doors, which, on the priest's ringing a bell, flew open, and presented a fire, and two ruffian-looking fellows with instruments of torture in their hands. The merchant gave himself up for lost, and in vain remonstrated with his false friend, who, calling him heretic, and other approbrious names, commanded the waiting villians to perform their task without farther ceremony.

At that instant a dreadful alarm was given below, which greatly surprising the priest, he went to know the cause of it and the ruffians followed him, leaving the merchant alone; who, imagining that some unhappy sufferers had gained the mastery over their tormentors, had courage enough to follow down stairs, at the bottom he was, however, agreeably surprised to meet the captain with a file of musketeers, who instantly took him under their protection and conducted him safely from the convent to the inn; the captain declaring that he was obliged to have recourse to force in order to make his way into the convent.—*From H. Welby.*

XL.

Discovery of the Robbers and Murderers of Mr. Stockden, Vitualler in Grubb Street, Cripplegate.

On the 3rd of December, 1695, about midnight, Mr. Stockden was murdered and robbed by four men then unknown; one Maynard was suspected but he got off. Soon afterwards, Mr. Stockden appeared to a Mrs. Greenwood in a dream, and showed her a house in Thames Street, near the George, saying, that one of the murderers lived there. She was somewhat alarmed, but the next morning, taking with her a friend, she went to the house which the vision had indicated, and asking for Maynard was told he was from home. Mr. Stockden appeared to her again, and then presented Maynard's face before her with a flat mole on the side of his nose (she had never seen him), and more particularly informed her that a wiredrawer should take him, and that he should be carried to Newgate in a coach. Upon inquiry they found out one of that trade, who was his intimate friend, and who for a reward of ten pounds promised to seize him; which he did as follows. He sent for Maynard to a public house, near Hockley-in-the-Hole, where he played at cards with him till a constable arrived who apprehended him, and took him before a magistrate, who committed him to Newgate, whither he was carried in a coach.

Maynard, while in prison, confessed the fact, and impeached his accomplices, who were Marsh, Bevel, and Mercer. He said that Marsh was the abettor, knowing that Mr. Stockden had money and plate, but was not present at the murder, yet he had his share of the booty. Marsh, suspecting that Maynard had confessed all he knew, left his home, but soon after this Mr. Stockden appeared again to Mrs. Greenwood, and showed her a house in Old Street (where she had not been before), saying that Marsh lodged there. Next morning she went with the same friend as before, and enquired for Marsh, but he was not at home. He was, however, soon taken at another place.

Soon after this, Mrs. Greenwood dreamed again that Mr. Stockden carried her into the Borough prison-yard, and showed her Bevel, the third criminal. Thither she went, taking with her Mrs. Footman, Mr. Stockden's kinswoman and housekeeper: they went together to the Marshalsea, and enquiring for Bevel, were informed that he had been lately brought thither for coining. They desired to see him, and when he came down, both declared that he was the man. They then applied to a peace officer who procured his removal to Newgate, where he presently confessed the horrid murder; and thus the three principal criminals were tried, condemned, and hanged. This account is testified by the Bishop of York, &c., and by the curate of Cripplegate, who published the narrative.—*From H. Welby.*

XLI.

Dream Revelations of Murder.

A young gentleman in the city of Dublin dreamed

one night that his sister (who was lately married, and lived at a small distance) had been murdered. This gave him some uneasiness; but feeling it was only a dream he went to sleep again, when the same dream was repeated. He then got up, went to another apartment, and told his dream with great agitation of mind. He was laughed at for this, and bid go to bed again. He did so, fell asleep, and dreamed the third time that his sister was murdered. He then got up, dressed himself with all speed, and hastened to his sister's house, where he found her cut and mangled in a barbarous manner. She just lived to speak a few words to her brother, and then expired, having been murdered by her husband. The villain was apprehended, tried, and hanged for the crime.

In the second year of the reign of King James I., one Anne Waters carried on certain intrigues with a young man in her neighbourhood. Finding their appointments interrupted by her husband, they agreed to strangle him with a wet napkin, so that the mark might not be perceived, which being done, they buried him under a dunghill near an adjoining cow house. The man was missed by his neighbours, but the woman dissembling grief, carried it off so well, that none suspected her in the least of so much as knowing what had become of him, but assisted her enquiries after him. After some time, conjectures being almost over, one of the inhabitants of the village dreamed that his neighbour Waters was strangled and buried under a dunghill near the cow-house; and relating his dream to others, it was resolved that the place should be searched in the presence of a constable, which being done, Water's corpse was found; and some concurring suspicions appearing, the wife was apprehended, and confessed the truth. She was burnt, according to the law in that case provided.—*Baker's Chronicle, p.* 614.

XLII.

James Haddock to Francis Taverner.
AT MICHAELMAS, 1662.

Francis Taverner, about twenty-five years old, a stout fellow, servant to Lord Chichester, Earl of Donegal, at Belfast, was riding late in the night from Hilborough homeward; near Drum Bridge his horse, though of good mettle, suddenly made a stand, and he supposing him to be taken with the staggers alighted to bleed him in the mouth, and presently remounted. As he was setting forward, there seemed to pass by him two horsemen, though he could not hear the treading of their feet, which amazed him. Presently there appeared a third in a white coat just at his elbow, in the likeness of James Haddock, formerly an inhabitant of Malone, where he died near five years before; whereupon Taverner asked him in the name of God, who he was? He replied, "I am James Haddock; and you may call me to mind by this token, that about five years ago I and two other friends were at your father's house, and you, by your father's appointment, brought us some nuts, so be not afraid," added the apparition; whereupon Taverner, remembering the circumstance, courageously asked him why he appeared rather to him than any other? He answered, because he was a man of more resolution than others; and if he would ride his way with him he would acquaint him with a business he had to deliver to him; this Taverner refused to do, preferring to go his own way, and then rode homewards.

The night after there appeared again to him the likeness of James Haddock, bidding him go to Eleanor Welsh, now the wife of one Davis living at Malone, but formerly the wife of the said James Haddock, by whom she had an only son. To this son James Haddock had by his will given a lease which he held of Lord Chichester, of which he had been deprived by Davis (who had married his mother). Taverner was to ask her if her maiden name was not Eleanor Welsh; and if it were, to tell her that it was the will of her former husband, James Haddock, that their son should be righted in the lease. But Taverner, partly loath to gain the ill-will of his neighbours, and partly thinking he should not be credited, long neglected to deliver his message, till he had been every night for about a month's space haunted with this apparition, in several forms more and more terrible. At length he went to Davis's wife, and asked her whether her maiden name was not Eleanor Welsh? If it was, he had something to say to her. She replied there was another Eleanor Welsh besides her. Hereupon Taverner returned without delivering his message.

The same night, being fast asleep in his bed, he was awakened by something pressing upon him, and saw again the apparition of James Haddock, in a white coat as at other times, who asked him if he had delivered his message? He answered that he had; upon which the apparition, looking more pleasantly upon him, bade him not be afraid, and then disappeared.

But some nights after (he not having delivered his message) it came again, and appearing in many formidable shapes, threatened to tear him in pieces if he did not do it. This made him leave the house where he resided in the mountains and betake himself to the town of Belfast, where he sat up all night at one Prince's house, and a servant or two of Lord Chichester's who were desirous to see or hear the spirit, sat with him. About midnight, as they were all by the fireside, they noticed Taverner's countenance change, and a trembling come upon him, and presently espied the apparition in a room opposite to where Traverner sat, who took up the candle and went to it, and resolutely asked in the name of God wherefore it haunted him? It replied, because he had not delivered the message, and withal threatened to tear him in pieces if he did not do it speedily; then changing itself into many prodigious shapes, it vanished in white, like a spirit; whereupon Francis Taverner became much dejected and troubled, and next day went to Lord Chichester's house, and with tears in his eyes, related to some of the family the sadness of his condition. They told the story to his lordship's chaplain, Mr. James South, who came to Taverner, and advised him to go at once and deliver punctually his message, offering to go along with him. But first they went to Dr. Lewis Downes, then minister at Belfast, who, upon hearing the relation of the whole matter, doubted at first the truth of it, attributing it rather to melancholy than any kind of reality; but he was afterwards fully satisfied of its authenticity.

They accordingly went to Davis's house, where the woman being desired to come to them, Taverner delivered his message, telling her he could not be quiet for the ghost of her former husband, James Haddock, who threatened to tear him in pieces if he did not tell her she must see John Haddock, her son by him, righted in a lease wherein she and Davis, her present husband, had wronged him. This done he presently found great quietness in his mind, and thanking the gentlemen for their company, advice, and assistance, departed to his brother's house at Drum Bridge; where, about two nights after, the apparition came to him again, and asked him if he had delivered the message? He answered, he had done so fully. It replied that he must deliver the message to the executors also, that the business might be perfected. At this meeting Taverner asked the spirit if Davis would do him any injury? To which it answered at first somewhat doubtfully, but at length threatened Davis if he attempted any thing to the injury of Taverner, and then disappeared.

The day following, Dr. Jeremiah Taylor, Bishop of Down, Connor, and Dromore, was to hold a court at Dromore, and commanded me who was then secretary to him to write for Taverner to meet him there, which he did; and there, in the presence of many, he examined Taverner strictly in this strange scene of Providence, as my lord bishop styled it. By the account given him both by Taverner and others who knew Taverner and much of the former particulars, his lordship was satisfied that the apparition was true and real, but said no more there to him, because at Hilborough, three miles from thence, on his way home his lordship was informed that Lady Conway and other persons of quality were arrived purposely to hear his lordship examine the matter. Taverner went with us to Hilborough, and there, to satisfy the curiosity of the company, after asking many things, his lordship advised him to ask these questions the next time the spirit appeared:— Whence are you? Are you a good or bad spirit? Where is your abode? What station do you hold? How are you settled in the other world? And what is the reason that you appear for the relief of your son in so small a matter, when so many widows and orphans are oppressed in the world, being defrauded of greater matters, and none of their relations appear as you do to right them?

That night Taverner was sent for to Lisburn, to Lord Conway's, three miles from Hilborough, where he was again strictly examined in the presence of many good men and women of the aforesaid matter, and was ordered to stay at my Lord Conway's all night. About nine or ten o'clock at night, standing by the fireside with his brother and many others, his countenance changed and he fell into a trembling, the usual prognostics of the apparition; and being loath to make any disturbance in his lordship's house, he and his brother went out into the court where he saw the spirit coming over the wall, which approaching nearer asked him if he had delivered his message to the executors also? He replied he had, and wondered it should still haunt him. It replied he need not fear; for it would do him no hurt, nor trouble him any more but the executor, if he did not see the boy righted. Here his brother put him in mind to ask the spirit what the bishop bid him, which he did presently; it gave him no answer, but crawled on its hands and feet to the wall again and then disappeared.

NOTE 1. That Pierce, at whose house and in whose presence the apparition was, being asked whether he saw the spirit, said he did not, but thought at that time he had a mist all over his eyes. 2. What was then spoken to Taverner was in so low and hollow a voice that they could not understand what it said. 3. At Pierce's house it stood just in the entry of a door, and as a maid passed by to go in at the door, Taverner saw it go aside and give way to the maid, though she saw it not. 4. That the lease was hereupon disposed of to the boy's use. 5. The spirit at the last, appearing at my Lord Conway's house, revealed somewhat to Taverner which he would not discover to any of us that asked him.

This Taverner, with all the persons and places mentioned in the story, I knew very well; and many wise and good men believed it, especially the Bishop and the Dean of Connor, Dr. Rust.

Witness,

Your humble servant,

THOMAS ALCOCK.

XLIII.

Captain Henry Bell and Luther's Table Talk.

Captain Henry Bell, in his narrative prefixed to Luther's Table Talk, printed in England in 1652, after having mentioned the mystery and providence of the discovery of it under ground in Germany, where it had lain hid fifty-two years, relates the following admonition relating to the translation of it into English.

Capsar Van Spar, a German gentleman having recovered the copy from the worms, desired Captain Bell, with whom he was well acquainted while he was agent for King James I. on the continent, to translate it into English and publish it in London. But Captain Bell was for some time prevented from prosecuting that design.

About six weeks after he had received the German copy, shortly after retiring to rest one night, and being in full health at the time, there appeared to him at the side of the bed, an old man clothed in a light-coloured habit, of reverend aspect, having a broad and white beard which hung as low as his girdle, who smiling at him said in a gentle manner of rebuke, "will you not take time to translate that book which is sent to you out of Germany? if you do not, I will shortly hereafter provide you both time and place to do it," and then instantly disappeared.

Captain Bell did not pay much attention to the matter afterwards. Time wore it off his memory, and he paid no more regard to what he had seen and heard, than if it had been a mere dream.

However, he had soon reason to recollect the old man's words, for soon after being at his lodgings in King Street, Westminster, at dinner with his wife, two messengers came from the Council Board with a warrant to carry him to the Gate-house, there to be confined till further orders from the Lords of the Privy Council. Upon this warrant he was detained ten years a close prisoner, whereof he spent five in the translation of the afore-mentioned work.

This narrative is extracted from the preface of Luther's Table Talk, printed in 1652, and from what Mr. Aubrey observes upon this story, which he briefly relates, it appears that whatever was the pretended cause of his confinement, the true reason of the Captain's commitment was because he had been urgent with the Lord Treasurer for his arrears, which amounted to a great sum and he being unwilling to pay, to be freed from his clamours hit upon the scheme of holding him in prison.

XLIV.

Lady Davies's Prognostics.

Sir John Davies was a very able and learned lawyer; and the author of an abridgment of Sir Edward Coke's report in French Law, which was translated into English after his decease, and published in 1651.

Sir John's lady was a very singular character, and dealt much in prophecies. An account of her predictions was published in 1649 under the title of "Strange and Wonderful Prophecies." She was reported to have foretold the death of her husband. Anthony Wood, speaking of the time of Sir John Davies's death, says, "it was then commonly rumoured that his prophetical lady had foretold his death in some manner on the Sunday going before. For while she sat at dinner by him, she suddenly burst out into tears; whereupon he asking her what the matter was, she answered, 'husband, these are your funeral tears;' to which he made reply, 'pray, therefore, spare your tears now, and I will be content that you shall laugh when I am dead.'"

Lady Davies also foretold the death of Archbishop Laud; but appears to have been mistaken as to the time. She had before spoken something unlucky of the Duke of Buckingham, importing that he should not live till the end of August, which raised her to the reputation of a cunning woman amongst the ignorant people; and now she prophesied of the new Archbishop that he should live but few days after the 5th of November; for which, and other prophecies of a more mischievous nature, she was brought into the Court of High Commission. Much pains were taken by the court to dispossess her of this spirit; but all was unavailing, till Lamb, then Duke of the Arches, shot her through and through with an arrow borrowed from her own quiver.

This was certainly the most sensible way of animadverting on the poor lady's infirmities; but to this course unfortunately her judges did not confine themselves. She was prosecuted in the High Commission Court, particularly for what was called "an enthusiastical petition to King Charles," and was treated with great rigour and cruelty. She was fined three thousand pounds, and closely imprisoned three years in the Gatehouse, Westminster. She is also said to have been confined several years in Bethlem Hospital and in the Tower of London; and she complained that during part of her imprisonment she was not allowed the use of a Bible, nor permitted to have the attendance of a female servant.—*Biog. Brit.*, vol. IV.

XLV.

Lord Mohun to his Mistress.

Lord Mohun was a dissolute young rake, and lived in the days of Charles I. According to the custom of that time, his sense of honour led him to resent in a serious manner an affront which had produced a quarrel between him and a person of the first quality, though a foreigner, in this kingdom. By appointment they met in Chelsea Fields near a place called Ebery-farm, and Lord Mohun was killed, but not without suspicions of foul play.

At the time, Lord Mohun kept company with a lady whom he supported in handsome apartments in James Street, Covent Garden. Lord Mohun was killed about ten o'clock in the morning, and at that hour his mistress, being in bed, saw him come to her bedside, draw the curtains, look upon her, and go away. She called after him, but received no answer; she then rung for her maid, asked her for Lord Mohun, but the woman replied that she had not seen him, and the key of the door was in her pocket.

About the time, Mr. Brown, brother-in-law to Lord Coningsby, discovered his being murdered to several of his friends.

Glanvil relates that his apparition was also seen by his sister and her maid, then dwelling in Fleet Street, at the hour and minute he was killed in Herefordshire. This happened in 1692.—*Aubrey's Miscellanies.*

XLVI.

Omen to Mrs. Stephens, of Spitalfields.

About the year 1611, there lived in Spitalfields one Mrs. Anne Stephens, a person at that time well known and respected for her dealings with the mercers on Ludgate Hill. While seated one evening in her house alone musing upon business, she happened by accident to look behind her, when, to her great surprise, she saw as it were a corpse lying extended upon the floor, as a dead body should be, except that the foot of one leg was fixed on the ground. She looked at it for some time, but by degrees withdrew her eyes from so unpleasing an object. However, a strange curiosity soon overcame her fears, when she ventured a second time to look that way and saw it for a considerable time longer, fixed as before. She again turned from the melancholy spectacle, and, gaining courage after a little reflection, got up with a design to satisfy herself of the reality of the vision, by going nearer to it but, lo! it was not there.

This circumstance proved an admonition to her; for taking it as a warning of her approaching dissolution, she from that hour began to settle her wordly affairs, and had just time to see them arranged when she was taken ill of a pleurisy of which she died in seven days. —*From H. Welby.*

XLVII.

A Member of Parliament warned of Arrest.

Dr. Beaumont relates that in his time, a member of parliament, anticipating that upon the recess of the house, which was not far off, he should be at liberty, withdrew himself and neglected his public duties. The House resenting it, a vote was passed ordering the secretary of state to prosecute him at law. This obliged him to resolve to leave the kingdom, and in the meantime to conceal himself—government having issued a proclamation for apprehending him, with a reward to the person who should take him.

In order to conceal himself more effectually he left his lodging where he had been hid for some time and removed to Barnet on the borders of Hertfordshire, intending, as soon as he had settled some family affairs to go into Scotland. Before he quitted, he was obliged to come to London to sign some writings to secure an estate, which it was feared might be seized.

The night before he had appointed to come to

London, he dreamed that he was in his lodgings in London where he had been concealed as above related; and in his dream he saw two men come to the door, who stated they were messengers, and produced a warrant from the secretary of state to apprehend him, and that accordingly they seized him.

The vision surprised and awaked him, and he roused Mr. D——, and told him the dream and his surprise about it. Mr. D——, seeing it was but a dream, advised him to go to sleep, which he did.

As soon as he was asleep again he was disturbed by a repetition of the dream exactly as before, and he again roused his brother; this disturbed them both very much, but being weary they both went to sleep again, and dreamed no more. He saw the men that apprehended him, their countenances, clothes, weapons, &c., and described them in the morning to his brother D——, with all the particulars.

However the journey to London being as he thought urgent, he got ready in the morning to set off, resolving to stay but one day, and then set forward for Scotland. Accordingly, he went for London in the morning, and that he might not be known he walked by private roads over Enfield Chace to Southgate, Hornsey, &c.

During his journey his mind was heavy and oppressed, and he frequently said to his brother, who walked with him, that he was certain he was going to London to be surprised, and so strong was the foreboding impression upon his mind that he once stopt at Hornsey and endeavoured to get a lodging, intending to send his brother to London to see if anything had happened there and to give him notice.

He had just secured a convenient lodging, when he saw a gentleman standing at the next door, whom he knew very well, but to whom he durst not venture to speak on that occasion; and finding on enquiry that he dwelt there, he concluded that was not a safe place for him, and resolved to go forward.

The impression upon his mind continuing, he stopt again at Islington and endeavoured to get a lodging there, but could not; at length his brother brought him word he could not get a lodging except where it was too public. Well, said he, then I must go to London; and accordingly he went, and the next morning was taken by the messengers in the manner as he had been told in his dream, by the same two men, whose faces he had seen, and with the same clothes on and weapons exactly as he had described. —*From H. Welby.*

XLVIII.

Apparition seen by Richard Bovet.

CONDENSED FROM HIS OWN NARRATIVE.

About the year 1667 I was staying with some persons of rank in the house of a nobleman in the west country, which had formerly been a nunnery. I had often heard the servants and others that inhabited or lodged there speak much of the noises and apparitions that frequently disturbed the house, but had at that time no apprehensions myself; for the house being full of strangers, the nobleman's steward, Mr. C., occupied with me a fine wainscot room, called my lady's chamber. We went to our lodging pretty early; and having a good fire in the room, we spent some time in reading, in which he much delighted; then, having got into bed and put out the candles, we observed the moon to be shining so brightly that a wager was laid between us that it was possible to read hand writting by its light as we lay upon the bed.

We had scarce finished our conversation upon that

affair, when I saw (my face being towards the door, which was locked) entering the room, five appearances of very fine and lovely women; they were of excellent stature, their dresses seemed very beautiful, were covered with light gauze, and their skirts trailed largely upon the floor. They entered in single file, and walked round the room, till the foremost came and stood by that side of the bed where I lay with my left hand over the side of the bed; for my head rested on that arm, and I determined not to alter the posture in which I was; she struck me upon that hand with a blow that felt very soft, but I could never remember whether it was cold or hot. I demanded in the name of the blessed Trinity, what business they had there, but received no answer. Then I spoke to Mr. C— "Sir, do you see what fair guests we have come to visit us?" whereupon they all disappeared. I found him in some kind of agony, and was forced to grasp him by the arm and shake him before I could obtain speech of him; then he told me he had seen the fair guests I spoke of, and had heard me speak to them; but he was not able to speak sooner to me, being extremely affrighted at the sight of a dreadful monster, which, assuming a shape betwixt that of a lion and a bear, attempted to come upon the bed's foot. I told him I thanked God nothing so frightful had presented itself to me; but I hoped (through His assisttance) to be able to meet any apparition that might present itself, however formidable. It was a long time before I could compose him to sleep; and though he had many disturbances in his own room and understood of others in the house, yet he acknowledged he had never before been so terrified during many years' abode there.

The next day at dinner he showed to many persons of quality the mark that had been occasioned by the grip I was forced to give him to get him to speak, and related all the passages very exactly; after which he protested that he would never more lie in that room; upon which I set up a resolution to lodge in it again, hoping that something of the reason of those troubles might by that means be imparted to me.

The next night, therefore, I ordered a Bible and another book to be laid in the room, and resolved to spend my time by the fire in reading and contemplation till I found myself inclined to sleep; and accordingly, having taken leave of the family at the usual hour, I addressed myself to what I proposed, not going into bed till past one in the morning. Shortly after I was in bed, I heard something walk about the room like a woman in a dress trailing about the floor: it made a mighty rustling noise but I could see nothing, though it was nearly as light as the night before. It passed by the foot of the bed, and a little opened the curtains, and thence went to a closet door on that side through which it found admittance although it was close locked; there it seemed to groan, and presently seemed to move a great chair with its foot, sit down in it and turn over the leaves of a large folio, making the usual noise that accompanies the turning over of heavy leaves. It continued in that posture, sometimes groaning, sometimes dragging the chair and clattering the book, till it was near day. Afterwards I lodged several times in this room, but was not again disturbed.

This I can attest to be a true account of what passed in that room the two nights spoken of; and though Mr. C. be lately dead, who was a very ingenious man, and affirmed the first part unto many with whom he was acquainted, I can appeal to the knowledge of those who have been inhabitants or lodgers in the said house for what remains to justify the credibility of the rest.—*From H. Welby.*

XLIX.

Appearance of the Radiant Boy to the late Marquis of Londonderry.

About twenty-five years since the late Lord Londonderry was for the first time on a visit to a gentleman in the north of Ireland. The mansion was such an one as spectres are reputed to inhabit; it was associated with many recollections of historic times; and the sombre character of its architecture and the wildness of the surrounding scenery were calculated to impress the soul with melancholy.

The apartment also which was appropriated to Lord Londonderry was especially calculated to foster such a tone of feeling from its antique appointments, from the dark and richly carved panels of its wainscot, from its yawning width and height of chimney, looking like the open entrance to a tomb, of which the surrounding ornaments appeared to form the sculptures and entablature, from the portraits of grim men and severe women arrayed in orderly procession along the walls, scowling a contemptuous enmity against the degenerate invaders of their gloomy bowers and venerable halls, and from the vast, dusky, ponderous, and complicated draperies that concealed the windows, and hung with the gloomy grandeur of funeral trappings about the hearse-like piece of furniture that was destined for his bed.

Lord Londonderry on entering his apartment might have received some painful depressions and misgivings when he found himself in the midst of such a world of melancholy images; he might have felt himself more than usually inclined to submit to the influences of superstition.

Lord Londonderry examined his chamber, he made himself acquainted with the forms and faces of the ancient possessors of the mansion as they sat upright in their ebony frames to receive his salutation; and then, after dismissing his valet, he retired to bed. His candles had not been long extinguished when he perceived a light gleaming on the draperies of the lofty canopy over his head. Conscious that there was no fire in the grate, that the curtains were closed, and that the chamber had been in perfect darkness but a few moments before, he supposed that some one must have accidentally entered his apartment; and turning hastily round to the side from which the light proceeded, saw, to his infinite astonishment, not the form of any human visitor, but the figure of a fair boy, who seemed to be garmented in rays of mild and tempered glory, which beamed palely from his slender form like the faint light of the declining moon, and rendered the objects which were nearest to him dimly and indistinctly visible. The spirit stood at some short distance from the side of the bed. Certain that his own faculties were not deceiving him, but suspecting he might be imposed on by the ingenuity of some of the numerous guests who were then visiting in the same house, Lord Londonderry proceeded towards the figure, but as he approached it retreated, as he slowly advanced the form with equal paces slowly retired, until it entered the gloomy arch of the capacious chimney, through which it appeared to sink into the earth. Lord Londonderry retired to his bed, but not to rest; his mind was disturbed by the consideration of the extraordinary event which had occurred to him. Was it real? Was it the work of the imagination? Was it the result of imposture? It was all incomprehensible.

He resolved in the morning not to mention the appearance till he should have well observed the manners and countenances of the family; he was conscious that if any deception had been practised its authors would be too delighted with their success to conceal the vanity of their triumph. When the guests assembled at the breakfast table, the eye of Lord Londonderry searched in vain for those latent smiles—those conscious looks—that silent communication between the parties, by which the authors and abettors of such domestic conspiracies are generally betrayed. Everything apparently proceeded in its ordinary course; the conversation flowed rapidly along from the subjects afforded by the moment without any of the constraint which marks a party intent upon some secret and more interesting argument and endeavouring to afford an opportunity for its introduction.

At last the hero of the tale found himself compelled to mention the occurrence of the night, prefacing it by such remarks as that it was most extraordinary, he feared that he should not be credited, and then after all due preparation the story was related. Those among his auditors who, like himself, were strangers and visitors in the house, were certain that some delusion must have been practised; the family alone seemed perfectly composed and calm. At last, the gentleman whom Lord Londonderry was visiting interrupted their various surmises on the subject by saying—" The circumstance which you have just recounted must naturally appear most extraordinary to those who have not long been inmates of my dwelling, and not conversant with the legends connected with my family; to those who are, the event which has happened will only serve as the corroboration of an old tradition that long has been related of the apartment in which you slept. You have seen the Radiant Boy—be content—it is an omen of prosperous fortunes. I would rather that this circumstance should no more be mentioned."—*From H. Welby.*

L.

Confession of John Beaumont.

Akin in authenticity and perspicuity to Glanvil's "Sadducissimus Triumphatus," quoted already, is the celebrated "Treatise on Spirits, Apparitions, &c." by John Beaumont, styled the Platonic Philosopher. This work, like that of Glanvil, is now become very scarce. The edition printed in 1705 has a frontispiece of evil and good genii, and an original representation of Jews going out in the moonshine to learn their fortune. Beaumont was a man of acute reasoning powers, and indefatigable research, as his narrative and inferences clearly show. Indeed, every page of his " Treatise" displays profound historical knowledge. His style is clear, argumentative, and unencumbered; and as specimens of these recommendations we have occasionally introduced a few of his most interesting narratives.

His *Confession* is at once curious and important, as he simply states what actually occurred to him, without attempting to expand or account for anything.

"I would not," he says, "for the whole world undergo what I have undergone from spirits coming twice to me. Their first coming was most dreadful to me, the thing being then altogether new, and consequently more surprising; though at the first coming they did not appear to me, but only called me at my chamber windows, rang bells, sang to me, and played music, &c.; but the last coming was terrible, for when they came, being only five in number, two women and three men (though afterwards there came hundreds), they told me they would kill me if I told any person in the house of their being there, which put me in some consternation; and I made a servant sit up with me four nights in my chamber before a fire—it being in the Christmas holidays—telling no person that they were there. One of these spirits, in woman's dress, lay down upon the bed by me every night, and told me if I slept the spirits would kill me, which kept me waking for three nights. In the meantime, a near relation of mine went (though unknown to me) to a physician of my acquaintance, desiring him to prescribe me somewhat for sleeping, which he did; and a sleeping potion was brought me, but I set it by, being very desirous to sleep without it.

"The fourth night I could hardly forbear sleeping, but the spirit, lying on the bed by me, told me again I should be killed if I slept, where upon I rose and sate by the fire-side, and in a while returned to my bed; and so I did a third time, but was still threatened as before; whereupon I grew impatient, and asked the spirits what they would have,—told them I had done the part of a Christian in humbling myself to God, and feared them not; and rising from my bed, took a cane, and knocked at the ceiling of my chamber, a near relation of mine lying then over me, who presently rose and came down to me about two o'clock in the morning, to whom I said, 'You have seen me disturbed these four days past, and that I have not slept; the occasion of it was that five spirits, which are now in the room with me, have threatened to kill me if I told any person of their being there, or if I slept, but I am not able to forbear sleeping longer, and acquaint you with it, and now stand in defiance of them.' And thus I exerted myself about them; and notwithstanding their continued threats I slept very well the next night, and continued so to do, though they continued with me above three months, day and night."

LI.

Robert Lindsay, Esq., of Edinburgh.

Another strange record is the following, communicated by David Laing, Esq., of Edinburgh, to Dr. Hibbert, and inserted by that gentleman in his erudite work, entitled, " The Philosophy of Apparitions."

" Robert Lindsay, grandchild or great grandchild to Sir David Lindsay of the Mouth, Lyon-King-at-Arms, &c., being very intimate with A. P., they bargained, anno 1671, that whoever died first should give account of his condition, if possible. It happened that he died about the end of 1675, while A. P. was at Paris; and the very night of his death A. P. dreamed that he was at Edinburgh, where Lindsay attacked him thus:—' Archie,' said he, ' perhaps ye heard I'm dead?' ' No, Robin.' ' Ay, but they bury my body in the Greyfriars. I am alive, though in a place whereof the pleasures cannot be expressed in Scotch, Greek, or Latin. I have come with a well-sailing small ship to Leith Road to carry you thither.' ' Robin, I'll go with you, but wait till I go to Fife and East Lothian, and take leave of my parents.' ' Archie, I have but the allowance of one tide. Farewell, I'll come for you at another time.' Since which time A. P. never slept a night without dreaming that Lindsay told him he was alive; and having a dangerous sickness, anno 1694, he was told by Robin that he was delayed for a time, and that it was properly his task to carry him off, but was unable to tell when."

LII.

Apparition seen by Mr. B. L. * *in York Cathedral.*

A few years since, Mr. B. L. accompanied some

---

* In the original MS. of this story, the name was given at length;

friends on a visit to York Cathedral. The party was numerous, and amongst them were a gentleman and his two daughters. Mr. B. L. was with the elder of these ladies exploring the curiosities of the building at some distance from the rest of their companions. On turning from the monument to which their attention had been directed, an officer in a naval uniform was observed advancing towards them. It was rather an unusual circumstance to encounter a person thus accoutred in a place so far distant from the sea, and of so unmilitary a character. Mr. B. L. was about to mention the subject to his companion, when, on turning his eyes towards her and pointing out the approaching stranger to her notice, he saw an immediate paleness spread over her face, and her countenance became agitated by the powerful and contending emotions which were suddenly excited by his presence. As the stranger drew nearer, and his figure and features gradually became more distinctly visible through the evening gloom and the dim religious light of the cathedral, the lady's distress was evidently increased.

Alarmed by the agitation which he witnessed, but wholly ignorant of the cause, and supposing her to be suffering from some violent and sudden indisposition, Mr. B. L. called to entreat the assistance of her sister. The figure in the naval uniform was now immediately before them : the eyes of the lady were fixed upon it with a gaze of silent and motionless surprise, and a painful intensity of feeling; her lips were colourless and apart, and her breath passed heavily from her full and overburthened heart. The form was close upon them—it approached her side—it paused for an

but while the sheets were passing through the press, a friend of the party stated to the original publisher that making public the names would distress the feelings of more than one individual; for that only they were withheld.

instant—when, as quick as thought, a low and scarcely audible voice whispered in her ear, "There is a future state!" and the figure moved onward through the retiring aisle of the minster.

The father of the lady now arrived to the assistance of his daughter, and Mr. B. L. consigning her to his protection, hastened in pursuit of the mysterious visitor. He searched on every side; no such form was to be seen in the long perspective of the path by which the ill-omened stranger had departed. He listened with the most earnest attentiveness, but no sound of retreating footsteps was to be heard on the echoing pavement of the cathedral.

Baffled in his attempt to discover the object whose presence had thus disturbed the tranquillity of the time, Mr. B. L. re-sought his friends. The lady entreated the party to continue their examination of the building, and to leave her again to the protection of her former companion. The request was granted; and no sooner had she thus possessed herself of an opportunity of confidential communication than she implored him, with a quick and agitated voice, to conceal for a little while the occurrence of which he had been a witness. "We shall never be believed; besides, it were right that my poor dear father should be gradually prepared for the misery that he is distined to undergo. I have seen the spirit, and I have heard the voice, of a brother who exists no longer; he has perished at sea. We had agreed that the one who died the first should re-appear to the survivor, if it were possible, to clear up or to confirm the religious doubts which existed in both our minds."

In due time the account of the event arrived to verify the spiritual intimation; the brother was indeed no more. His death had happened on the very day and hour in which his form was seen by Mr. B. L. and his companion in the north aisle of York Cathedral.

The preceding narrative exhibits no symptoms of a hurried or heated imagination, but on the contrary, is at once cool, collected, and circumstantially perspicuous, so as to set the question of probability almost entirely at rest.—*From H. Welby.*

LIII.

An Awful Admonition.

Aubrey in his Miscellanies, narrates the following awful admonition of a departed friend, to a surviving friend:—

Two ladies of fortune, both not being long since deceased, were intimate acquaintances, and loved each other sincerely. It so fell out that one of them fell sick of the small-pox, and desired mightily to see the other, who would not come fearing the catching the distemper; the afflicted lady at last died of them. She had not been buried long before she appeared at the other's house in the dress of a widow, and asked for her friend who was then at cards; she sent down her woman to know her business, the answer was that she must impart it to none but her lady, who, after she had received this message bid her woman introduce her into a room, and desire her to stay till the game was done, and she would then wait on her. The game being finished, she went down stairs to the apparition, to know her business, "Madam" (said the ghost, turning up her veil, and her face appearing full of the small-pox), "you know very well that you and I loved entirely. Though I took it very ill of you that you was not so kind as to come and see me, yet I could not rest till I had seen you. Believe me, my dear, I am not come to frighten you; but only out of regard to your eternal happiness, to forewarn you of your approaching end, which I am sorry to say will be very miserable, if you do not prepare for it; you have led a very unthinking giddy life many years. I cannot stay, I am going; my time is just spent; prepare to die; and remember this, that when you make the thirtieth at a ball, you have but a few days to live." She then vanished. To conclude, she was at a ball where she made the thirtieth in number; and was afterwards asked by the brother of the deceased, whether his sister did appear to her as was reported; she made him no answer, but fell a weeping, and died in a little time after.

LIV.

Apparitions recorded in Boswell's Life of Johnson.

Talking of ghosts, Dr. Johnson said he knew one friend, who was an honest man, who had told him he had seen a ghost; old Mr. Edward Cave, the printer, at St. John's Gate. He said Mr. Cave did not like to talk of it, and seemed to be in great horror whenever it was mentioned. Boswell said, "Pray, sir, what did he say was the appearance." Johnson—"Why, sir, something of a shadowy being. Goldsmith told us he was assured by his brother that he also had seen one. General Oglethorpe told us that Pendergast, an officer in the Duke of Marlborough's army, had mentioned to many of his friends that he should die on a particular day; that upon that day a battle took place with the French; that, after it was over and Pendergast was still alive, his brother officers, while they were yet in the field, jestingly asked him where was his prophecy now? Pendergast gravely answered, 'I shall die, notwithstanding what you see.' Soon afterwards there came a shot from a French battery, to which the orders for a cessation of arms had not reached, and he was killed upon the spot. Colonel Cecil, who took possession of his effects, found in his pocket-book the following solemn entry:—(here the date.) 'Dreamt or was told by an apparition Sir John Friend meets me—(here the very day on which he was killed was mentioned.) Pendergast had been connected with Sir John Friend, who was executed for high treason. General Oglethorpe said he was with Colonel Cecil when Pope came and inquired into the truth of his story, which made a great noise at the time, and was then confirmed by the colonel. *Boswell* —Was there not a story of the ghost of Parson Ford having appeared? *Johnson*—Sir, it was believed. A waiter at the Hummums, in which Ford died, had been absent for some time, and returned, not knowing Ford was dead; going down to the cellar, according to the story, he met him; going down again, he met him a second time. When he came up he asked some of the people of the house what Ford could be doing there? They told him Ford was dead. The waiter took a fever in which he lay some time; when he recovered, he said he had a message to deliver to some women from Ford, but he was not to tell what, or to whom. He walked out; he was followed, but somewhere about St. Paul's they lost him; he came back, and said he had delivered the message, and the women exclaimed, 'Then we are all undone!' Dr. Pellet, who was not a credulous man, inquired into the truth of this story, and said the evidence was irresistible. My wife went to the Hummums (it is a place where people get themselves cupped); I believe she went with the intention to hear about this story of Ford. At first they were unwilling to tell her; but, after they had talked to her, she came away satisfied that it was true. To be sure the man had a fever, and this vision may have been the beginning of it; but if the message to the women and their behaviour upon hearing it were true, as related, there was something supernatural; that rests upon his word, and there it remains."

LV.

Ann Taylor of Tiverton.

The case of this unfortunate girl excited considerable interest throughout the whole of the west of England in the year 1814. She was the daughter of a respectable yeoman, living in the parish of Tiverton; and being ill, she lay six days in a state of insensibility, and to all appearance dead, doubtless one of those cases of suspended animation of which there have been many instances. Whilst lying in this state she had a dream, which the family called a trance, the printed account of which they widely circulated. Her request on awaking from her trance, and the extraordinary circumstances which happened after her decease, are thus related by her father:—

"When she recovered from her stupor, she requested some one would write down all she had to unfold, and I charged the person who did it, as she might be put on her oath, not to add or diminish a word, nor to ask her a question, which I know was duly attended to. Then she earnestly requested all might be printed, and desired I would get it done; I endeavoured to evade it by putting some papers in the room, merely to satisfy her mind, but she soon discovered it was not the thing; she then said if it were not printed my sins would never be forgiven; as she continued urging me to it, I went for that purpose the next day, and even went so far as the printer's door, but was ashamed to go in, as I was convinced the world would ridicule it. I returned to my home, and she renewing her inquiries, I told her it was not yet done, but that it should; she replied, 'but *too late.*' The next day, notwithstanding it was Sunday, I was obliged to go and request that some might be printed early the following morning. I returned and told her, but she again said '*it will be too late.*' She died the same evening at seven o'clock. The next morning her voice was distinctly and *repeatedly* heard (in a shrill tone) by the person who wrote the relation, making her former inquiry. Between ten and twelve the men came to put her in the coffin; and when performed, the whole family assembled to dinner, but, wonderful to relate, her voice was again heard, saying, '*Father, it is not printed.*' Had I been alone, I should have considered it was my agitated mind that deceived me, but all present heard it, and the men became as if they were thunderstruck."

This was heard and solemnly attested by no less than six witnesses, all of whom concurred in one testimony, and were considered as persons of veracity.

After her death, a sermon was preached by a dissenting minister named Vowles, at Steps Meeting, Tiverton, in which much presumption and high-toned dogmatism were adduced, to prove the fraud of the whole story. Mr. Vowles's sermon obtained considerable circulation, and two large editions were sold; but it is a question whether the high authorities adduced by him as having credited supernatural voices, &c., did not tend to support the theory in a stronger proportion, than his arguments were calculated to weaken it.

LVI.

Apparition seen by Lady Pennyman and Mrs. Atkins.

At the commencement of the French revolution, Lady Pennyman and her two daughters retired to Lisle, where they hired a large and handsome house at a trifling rent. During their residence there, the lady received from her husband, Sir John Pennyman, a draft for a considerable sum, which she carried to the banker of the town and requested to have cashed. The man, as is often the case on the continent, gave her a large portion of silver in exchange. As Lady Pennyman was proceeding to pay some visits, she requested that the banker would send the money to her house, of which she described the situation. The parcel was instantly committed to the care of a porter; and, on the lady's enquiring of him whether he understood, from her directions, the place to which his charge was to be conveyed, the man replied that he was perfectly aware of the place designated, and that it was called the "Haunted House." The latter part of this answer was addressed to the banker in a low tone of voice, but was overheard by Lady Pennyman; she paid, however, no attention to the words, and naturally supposed that the report connected with her habitation was one of those which are raised by the imagination of the ignorant respecting every dwelling which is long untenanted, or remarkable for its antiquity.

A few weeks afterwards, the words were recalled to her recollection in a manner that surprised her: the housekeeper, with many apologies for being obliged to mention any thing that might appear so idle and absurd, came to the apartment in which her mistress was sitting, and said that two of the servants who had accompanied her ladyship from England had that morning given warning, and expressed the determination of quitting her ladyship's service, on account of the mysterious noises by which they had been, night after night, disturbed and terrified. "I trust, Carter," replied Lady Pennyman, "that you have too much good sense to be alarmed on your own account by any of these superstitious and visionary fears; and pray exert yourself in endeavouring to tranquillize the apprehensions of others, and persuade them to continue in their places." The persuasion of Carter was ineffectual: the servants insisted that the noises which had alarmed them were not the operation of any earthly beings, and persevered in their resolution of returning to their native country.

The room from which the sounds were supposed to have proceeded was at a distance from Lady Pennyman's apartments, and immediately over those which were occupied by the two female servants who had been terrified by them, and whose report had spread a general panic throughout the family. To quiet the alarm, Lady Pennyman resolved on leaving her own chamber for a time and establishing herself in the one which had been lately occupied by the domestics.

The room above was a long spacious apartment, which appeared to have been for a length of time deserted. In the centre of the chamber was a large iron cage: it was an extraordinary piece of furniture to find in any mansion, but the legend which the servants had collected respecting it appeared to be still more extraordinary. It was said that a late proprietor of the house, a young man of enormous property, had in his minority been confined in that apartment by his uncle and guardian, and there hastened to a premature death by the privations and cruelties to which he was exposed; those cruelties having been practised under the pretence of necessary correction. The savage purpose of murdering the boy, under the pretence of a strict attention to his interest or his improvement, was successful; the lad was declared to be incorrigible, there was a feigned necessity for the severest correction, and he was sentenced to a term of captivity and privation. On his uncle's arriving, with the show of an hypocritical leniency, an hour previous to the appointed time to deliver him from the residue of his punishment, it was found that death had anticipated the false mercy, and had for ever emancipated the innocent sufferer from the hands of the oppressor.

The wealth was won, but it was an unprofitable acquisition. The wrongful possessor was haunted by an active conscience that would not be silenced; the form of the dead and inoffensive boy was constantly before him. His dreams represented to his view the playful and beautiful looks that won all eyes towards him, while his parents were yet alive to cheer and to delight him: and then the vision of his sleep would change, and he would see his calm suffering and his silent tears, his patient endurance and his indefatigable exertions in attempting the accomplishment of difficult exactions; his pale cheek, wasted limbs, and spiritless countenance; and then, at last, there was the rigid, bony, and distorted form, the glazed open eye, the mouth violently compressed, and the clenched hands, on which his view had rested for a moment, when all his wicked hopes had attained their most sanguine consummation and he surveyed the corpse of his murdered relative. These recollections banished him from his home, the mansion was left tenantless; and, till Lady Pennyman had inadvertently engaged it, all had dreaded to become the inmates of a dwelling which been fatal to one possessor and shunned as destructive to the tranquillity of his heir.

During the first night or two of Lady Pennyman's occupation of her new apartment she met with no interruptions; nor was her sleep in the least disturbed by any of those mysterious noises in the Cage Chamber (for so it was commonly called in the family) which she had been induced to expect by the representations of the departed servants. This quiet, however, was of very short duration; one night she was awakened from her sleep by the sound of a slow and measured step that appeared to be pacing the chamber overhead; it continued to move backwards and forwards with nearly the same constant and regular motion for rather more than an hour—perhaps Lady Pennyman's agitation might have deceived her and induced her to think the time longer than it really was. It at length ceased: morn dawned upon her, and she went down to breakfast, after forming a resolution not to mention the event.

Lady Pennyman and her daughters had nearly completed their breakfast before her son, a young man who had lately returned from sea, descended from his apartment. "My dear Charles," said his mother, "I wonder you are not ashamed of your indolence and your want of gallantry, to suffer your sisters and myself to finish breakfast before you are ready to join us." "Indeed, madam," he replied, "it is not my fault if I am late; I have not had any sleep all night. There have been people knocking at my door and peeping into my room every half hour since I went up stairs to bed: I presume they wanted to see if my candle was extinguished. It has been really very distressing, as I certainly never gave you any occasion to suspect I should be careless in taking so necessary a precaution; and it is not pleasant to be represented in such a light to the domestics." "Indeed, my dear, the interruption has taken place entirely without my knowledge. I assure you it is not by any order of mine that your room has been looked into: I cannot think what could induce any servant of mine to be guilty of such a liberty. Are you certain that you have not mistaken the nature and origin of the sound by which your sleep has been disturbed?" "Oh, no; there could have been no mistake: I was perfectly awake when the interruption first took place, and afterwards it was so frequently repeated as to prevent the possibility of my sleeping."

More complaints from the housekeeper; no servant would remain; every individual of the family had his tale of terror to increase the apprehensions of the rest; Lady Pennyman began to be herself alarmed. Mrs. Atkins, a woman devoid of every kind of superstitious fear, and of tried courage, understanding, and resolution, determined at once to silence all the stories that had been fabricated respecting the Cage Room, and to allay their terrors by adopting that apartment for her own bedchamber during the remainder of her residence at Lisle. A bed was accordingly placed in the apartment. The Cage Room was rendered as comfortable as possible on so short a notice; and Mrs. Atkins retired to rest, attended by her favourite spaniel.

Mrs. Atkins now examined her chamber in every direction: she sounded every panel of the wainscot to prove that there was no hollowness which might argue a concealed passage, and having bolted the door of the Cage Room, retired to rest. Her assurance was doomed to be shortlived: she had only been a few minutes asleep when her dog, which lay by the bedside, leaped, howling and terrified, upon the bed; the door of the chamber slowly opened, and a pale, thin, sickly youth came in, cast his eyes mildly towards her, walked up to the iron cage in the middle of the room, and then leaned in the melancholy attitude of one revolving in his mind the sorrows of a cheerless and unblest existence; after a while he withdrew, and retired by the way he entered.

Mrs. Atkins, on witnessing his departure, felt the return of her resolution; she persuaded herself to believe the figure the work of some skilful impostor, and she determined on following its footsteps: she took up her chamber lamp, and hastened to put her design into execution. On reaching the door, to her infinite surprise, she discovered it to be fastened, as she had herself left it on retiring to her bed. Withdrawing the bolt and opening the door, she saw the back of the youth descending the staircase; she followed, till, on reaching the foot of the stairs, the form appeared to sink into the earth. It was in vain to attempt to conceal the occurrences of this night ; her voice, her manner, the impossibility of sleeping a second time in the evil chamber would necessarily betray that something of a painful and mysterious nature had occurred.

The event was related to Lady Pennyman : she determined to remain no longer in her present habitation. The man of whom the house had been engaged was spoken to on the subject : he became extremely violent—said it was no time for the English to indulge their imaginations, insinuated something of the guillotine, and bade her, at her peril, drop a single expression to the injury of his property. While she remained in France not a word was uttered upon the subject ; she framed an excuse for her abrupt departure : another residence was offered in the vicinity of Lisle, which she engaged on the pretext of its being better calculated to the size of her family ; and at once relinquished her habitation and with it every preternatural occasion of anxiety.

Although the preceding story "smells of the cloister," is somewhat tinctured with romance, and has been enlarged upon by successsive narrators, the facts are authenticated and accredited by the parties to whom they occurred. An old deserted house at Lisle would probably be an object of terror to weak minds, but not to the understandings of the well educated heads of a family, as well as the other several members of a large establishment.—*From H. Welby.*

LVII.

The Midnight Storm.

(FROM THE FRENCH.)

―――"Of shapes that walk
At dead of night, and clank their chains, and wave
The torch of hell around the murderer's bed."

Pleasures of Imagination.

On the evening of the 12th June, ――――, a joyous party was assembled at Monsieur de Montbrun's chateau to celebrate the marriage of his nephew, who had in the morn of that day led to the altar the long-sought object of his fond attachment. The mansion which was on this occasion the scene of merriment, was situated in the province of Gascony, at no very great distance from the town of ――――.

It was a venerable building, erected during the war of the League, and consequently discovered in its exterior some traces of that style of architecture which endeavoured to unite strength and massiveness with domestic comfort. Situated in a romantic but thinly-peopled district, the family of Monsieur de Montbrun was compelled principally to rely on itself for amusement and society. This family consisted of the chevalier, an old soldier of blunt but hospitable manners; his nephew, the bridegroom, whom (having no male children) he had adopted as his son, and Mademoiselle Emily, his only daughter: the latter was amiable, frank, and generous; warm in her attachments but rather romantic in forming them. Employed in rural sports and occupations, and particularly attached to botany, for which the country around afforded an inexhaustible field, the chevalier and his inmates had not much cultivated the intimacy of the few families which disgust of the world, or other remote motives, had planted in this retired spot. Occasional visits exchanged with the nearest of their neighbours, sometimes enlivened their small circle; but with the greater part of those who lived at a distance they were scarcely acquainted even by name.

The approaching nuptials, however of Theodore (Monsieur de Montbrun's adopted son), excited considerable conversation in the adjacent district: and the wedding of her cousin, it was determined by Emily, should not pass off unaccompanied by every festivity which the nature of their position and the joyfulness of the event would allow. On this occasion, therefore, inquiries were made as to all the neighbouring gentry within a considerable distance around; and there were none of the least note neglected in the invitations, which were scattered in all directions. Many persons were consequently present with whose persons and character the host and his family were totally unacquainted: some also accepted the summons who were strangers to them even by name.

Emily was attentive and courteous to all; but to one lady in particular she attached herself during the entertainment with most sedulous regard. Madame de Nunez, the immediate object of Emily's care, had lately settled in the neighbourhood, and had hitherto studied to shun society. It was supposed that she was the widow of a Spanish officer of the Walloon guards, to whom she had been fondly attached; indeed so much so, that, notwithstanding he had been dead several years the lady never appeared but in deep mourning. She had only lately settled in Gascony; but her motives for retiring from Spain and fixing on the French side of the Pyrenees, were not known, and but slightly conjectured. Isabella de Nunez was about twenty-eight years of age, tall and well-formed: her countenance was striking, nay even handsome, but a nice physiognomist would have traced in her features evidence of the stronger passions of human nature. He would have seen pride softened by distress; and would have fancied, at times, that the effects of some concealed crime were still evident in her knit brow and retiring eye, when she became the object of marked scrutiny.

She had never before entered the chateau de Montbrun, and her person had hitherto been unnoticed by Emily; but now that she had once seen her she devoted herself with all the ardour of a warm and impulsive nature to her new friend. The lady received the attentions of her amiable hostess with grateful but dignified reserve.

The morning had been extremely sultry, and an oppressive sensation in the atmosphere as the day closed threw an air of gloom over the company ill suited to the occasion of their meeting. Madame de Nunez appeared more than any one else to feel the effects of the half-stifling closeness; the occasional sparks of gaiety which she had discovered gradually disappeared, and before the day had entirely closed she seemed at times perfectly abstracted and at other times to start with causeless apprehension. In order to divert or dispel this increasing uneasiness, which threatened to interfere seriously with the pleasure of the festival, dancing was proposed, and the enlivening sounds of the music in a short time dissipated the temporary gloom. The dancing had not however long continued when the expected storm burst in all its fury on the chateau; the thunder, with its continued roar, reverberated by the adjoining mountains, caused the utmost alarm amongst the fair visitors; the torrents of rain which fell might almost be said to have swelled the waters of the neighbouring Garonne, whilst sheets of lightning reflected on its broad waves gave a deeper horror to the pitchy darkness which succeeded. The continuance of the storm gradually increased the apprehensions of the greater part of the females to horror; and they took refuge in the arched vaults and long subterranean passages which branched beneath the chateau, from the vivid glare of the lightning, although unable to shut their ears to the reiterated claps of thunder which seemed to shake the building to its foundations.

In this general scene of horror, Isabella alone appeared unappalled. The alternate abstraction and alarm which before seemed to harass her mind had now vanished, and had given place to an appearance of resignation which might almost be considered as bordering on apathy. While the younger females yielded without resistance to the increasing horrors of the tempest, and by frequent shrieks and exclamations of dread bore testimony to the terror excited in their bosoms by the aggravated circumstances of the scene, she suffered no symptom of apprehension to be visible in her now unvarying features. Agitation had yielded to quiet; she sat ostensibly placid: but her apparent inattention was not the effect of tranquility, but the result of persevering exertion.

The hour was approaching towards midnight; and the storm, instead of blowing over, having increased in violence, the hospitable owner of the mansion proposed to his guests that they should abandon the idea of returning home through the torrents of rain—which had already deluged the country and rendered the roads in the vicinity impassable—but should accommodate themselves, with mutual concessions to circumstances, to the only plan now to be devised—that of making themselves easy during the remainder of this dismal night. Although his mansion was not extensive, yet he proposed, with the aid of temporary couches, and putting the ladies to the inconvenience of sleeping two in each room, to render the party as comfortable as the means at his disposal would allow, and which would at all events be more agreeable than braving abroad the horrors of the tempest.

Reasonable as such a plan was in itself, it was still more strongly recommended by the circumstance that the carriages which were expected to convey the parties to their respective abodes had not arrived; and from the state of the roads, and the continuance of the still pitiless storm, it seemed hopeless to expect them.

The party, therefore, yielded without regret to the arrangement, save but one dissenting voice. The fair Spaniard alone positively declined the offered accommodation. Argument in vain was used for a considerable space of time to detain her; she positively insisted on returning home; and would have faced the storm in defiance of all appeal, had not an obstacle which appeared invincible militated against her resolve —her carriage and servants were not arrived, and from the representation of Monsieur de Montbrun's domestics (some of whom had been detached to examine the condition of the neighbouring roads), it was perfectly clear that with that part of the district in which she resided no communication could for several hours take place. Madame de Nunez, therefore, at length yielded to necessity, although the pertinacity of her resistance had already excited much surprise, and called forth innumerable conjectures.

The arrangements between the respective parties were soon made, and the greater part of the ladies gladly retired to seek repose from the harassing events of the day. Emily, who had not relaxed in her marked attention to her interesting friend, warmly pressed her to share her own room in which a sofa had been prepared as a couch, to which she herself insisted on retiring, while Madame de Nunez should take possession of the bed. The latter, however, again strenuously objected to this plan, asserting that she should prefer remaining all night in one of the sitting-rooms, with no other companion than a book. She appeared obstinately to adhere to this resolution, until Emily politely, yet positively, declared, that were such the intention of her new friend she would also join her in the saloon and pass the time in conversation until the day should break, or until Madame's servants should arrive. This proposition, or rather determination, was received by the frowning Isabella with an air of visible chagrin and disappointment not altogether polite. She expressed her unwillingness that Mademoiselle should be inconvenienced, with some peevishness; but this, however, soon gave place to her former air of good breeding.

She now appeared anxious to hurry to her room; and the rest of the party having some time retired, she was escorted thither by the ever attentive Emily. No sooner had they reached the chamber, than Isabella sunk into a chair; and after struggling for some time in evident emotion for utterance, at length exclaimed:—

"Why, dearest Emily, would you insist on sharing with me the horrors of this night? To me the punishment is a merited one: but to you——"

"What, my dearest madam, do you say?" replied Emily affectionately—"The terrors of the night are over, the thunder appears retiring, and the lightning is less vivid; and see in the west (she added as she went to the window) there are still some remains of the summer twilight. Do not any longer, then, suffer the apprehensions of the storm which has passed over us to disturb the repose which you will, I hope, so shortly enjoy."

"Talk you of repose!" said Madame de Nunez, in a voice almost choked with agitation. "Know you not, then, that on the anniversary of this horrid night — but what am I saying!—to you, at present, all this is mystery; too soon your own feelings will add conviction to the terrible experience which six revolving years have afforded me, and which, even now but to think on harrows up my soul. But no more."

Then darting suddenly towards the door, which had hitherto remained ajar, she closed it with violence; and locking it, withdrew the key, which she placed in her own pocket. Emily had scarcely time to express her surprise at this action and the apparent distraction which accompanied it, ere Madame de Nunez seized both her hands with more than female strength, and with a maddening voice, and eyes straining on vacancy, exclaimed:—

"Bear witness, ye powers of terror! that I imposed not this dreadful scene on the female whose oath must now secure her silence."

Then staring wildly on Mademoiselle de Montbrun, she continued:—

"Why, foolish girl, wouldst thou insist on my partaking thy bed? the viper might have coiled in thy bosom; the midnight assassin might have aimed his dagger at thy breast: but the poison of the one would have been less fatal, and the apprehension of instant annihilation from the other would have been less oppressive, than the harrowing scene which thou art doomed this night to witness—doomed, I say; for all the powers of hell, whose orgies you must behold, cannot release you from the spectacle which you have voluntarily sought."

"To what am I doomed!" cried Emily, whose fears for herself were lessened in the dread she felt for her friend's intellect, which she supposed was suddenly become affected by illness, or the exciting incidents of the past day.

Isabella, after a silence of several minutes, during which she endeavoured to recover some degree of composure, in a softened but determined voice, added:—

"Think not my friend (if I may use that endearing expression to one whose early prospects and happier

slow rolling of a carriage was heard in the paved court-yard; at the noise of which, Madame de Nunez started from the posture in which she had continued at the feet of Emily, and rushed towards the door, which she had previously locked. Emily now heard heavy footsteps ascending the oaken staircase; and before she could recall her recollection, which so singular a circumstance had bewildered, the door of the room in which they were sitting, spite of its fastening, slowly moved on its hinges; and in the next minute Emily sunk on the earth in a state of stupefaction.

It is well for the human frame, that when assailed by circumstances too powerful to support, it seeks shelter in oblivion. The mind recoils from the horrors which it cannot meet, and is driven into insensibility.

At an early hour of the ensuing morning Madame de Nunez quitted Monsieur de Montbrun's chateau, accompanied by her servants, whom the retiring torrents had permitted to await their mistress's commands. She took a hasty farewell of the master of the mansion, and without making any inquiries as to the rest of the party, departed.

At the usual hour of breakfast, Emily did not appear; and her father at length went to her room door, and receiving no answer to his inquiries, went in. Judge his horror when he discovered his daughter lying on the bed in the clothes she had worn the preceding day, but in a state of apparent insensibility. Immediate medical assistance was procured, and she at length discovered symptoms of returning life; but no sooner had she recovered her recollection, than, looking with horror and affright around her, she relapsed into a state of insensibility. Repeated cordials being administered, she was again restored to life; but only to become the victim of a brain fever, which in a few days put a period to her existence. In a short interval of recollection, in the early part of her illness, she confided to her father what we have here related; but conscientiously kept from his knowledge what she was bound by her oath to conceal. The very remembrance of what she had witnessed on that fatal night hurried her into deliriums, and she fell a victim to the force of recollection.

Madame de Nunez did not long survive her; but expired under circumstances of unexampled horror.—*From H. Welby.*

LVIII.

Apparition seen by Mr. Walker, Curate of Warblington, in Hampshire.

The following letter from Mr. Caswell, the mathematician, was found among Dr. Bentley's papers:—

"SIR,—When I was in London, April last, I fully intended to have waited upon you again, as I said, but cold and lameness seized me next day: the cold took away my voice, and the other my power of walking; so I presently took coach for Oxford. I am much your debtor; and in particular for your good intentions in relation to Mr. D. though that, as it has proved, would not have turned to my advantage: however, I am obliged to you upon that and other accounts, and if I had opportunity to show it, you should find how much I am your faithful servant. I have sent you enclosed a relation of an apparition. The story I had from two persons, who each had it from the author, and yet their accounts somewhat varied, and passing through more mouths, has varied still more. Threefore I got a friend to bring me to the author's, at a chamber, where I wrote it down from the author's mouth, after which I read it to him, and gave him another copy. He said he could swear to the truth of it, as far as he is concerned. He is curate of Warblington, bachelor of arts of Trinity College in Oxford, about six years standing in the university. I hear no ill report of his behaviour here; he is now gone to his curacy. He has promised to send up the accounts of the tenant and his man, who is a smith by trade, and the farmer's men, as far as they are concerned. Mr. Brinton, the rector, would have him say nothing of the story; for that he can get no tenant, although he has offered the house for ten pounds a-year less. Mr. P., the former incumbent, whom the apparition represented, was a man of a very ill report, supposed to have seduced his servant-maid, and to have murdered the offspring; but I advised the curate to say nothing himself of this last part of P. but leave that to the parishioners who knew him. Those who knew this P. say he had exactly such a gown, and that he used to whistle.—Yours,

"J. CASWELL."

Enclosed in this letter is the following circumstantial and perspicuous narrative :—

At Warblington, near Havant, in Hampshire, within six miles of Portsmouth, in the parsonage-house, dwelt Thomas Perse, the tenant, with his wife and a child, a man-servant, Thomas, and a maid-servant. About the beginning of August, 1695, on a Monday, about nine or ten at night, all being in bed except the maid with the child, the maid being in the kitchen and having raked up the fire, took a candle in one hand and the child in the other arm, and turning about, saw one in a black gown walk through the room, and thence out of the door into the orchard. Upon this the maid cried out; the master and the mistress ran down stairs, found the candle in her hand, while she grasped the child firmly with the other arm: she told them the reason of her crying out. She would not sleep that night in the house, but removed to another belonging to one Henry Salter, farmer, and she could not be persuaded to go any more to the house on any terms.

On the morrow (Tuesday), the tenant's wife came to me, lodging then at Havant, to desire my advice, and consult with some friends about it; I told her I thought it was a flam, and that they had a mind to abuse Mr. Brereton, the rector, whose house it was. She desired I would come up. I told her I would come up, and either sit up or sleep there as she pleased; for then, as to all stories of ghosts or apparitions, I was an infidel. I went thither, and sat up the Tuesday night with the tenant and his man-servant. About twelve or one o'clock I searched all the rooms in the house, to see if anybody was hidden there to impose upon me. At last we came into a lumber room, where I, smiling, told the tenant that was with me that I would call for the apparation, and oblige him to come. The tenant then seemed to be afraid, but I told him I would defend him from harm; and then I repeated, "*Barbara, celarent Darii,*" &c.; on this the tenant's countenance changed, so that he was ready to drop down with fear; and I told him I perceived he was afraid, and I would prevent its coming, and repeated, "*Baralipton,*" &c.; then he recovered his spirits pretty well, and we left the room and went down into the kitchen, where we were before, and sat up there the remaining part of the night, and had no farther disturbance. Thursday night the tenant and I slept in the same room, and the man in another room; and he saw something glide along in a black gown and place itself against a window; stand there for some time, and then walk off. Friday morning, the man relating this, I asked him why he did not call me, and I told him I thought that it was a trick or a flam; he told me the reason why he did not call me was, that he was not able to speak or move. Friday night we slept as before, and experienced no disturbance either of the nights.

Sunday night I occupied one room alone (apart from that in which the man saw the apparition) and the tenant and the man were in one bed in another room; and betwixt twelve and two the man heard something walk in their room at the bed's foot, and whistling very well; and at last it came to the bedside, drew the curtain, and looked on them; after some time it moved off. Then the man called to me, desired me to come, for that there was something in the room going about whistling. I asked him whether he had any light, or could strike one; he told me, no. Then I leaped out of bed, and not staying to put on my clothes, went out of my room and along a gallery to the door, which I found locked or bolted. I desired him to unlock the door, as that I could not get in; he then got out of bed and opened the door, which was near, and went immediately again to bed. I went in three or four steps; and it being a moonlight night, I saw the apparation move from the bedside, and up against the wall that divided their room and mine. I went and stood directly against it, within my arm's length of it, and asked it in the name of God what it was that made it come disturbing us. I stood some time expecting an answer, and receiving none, and thinking it might be some fellow hidden in the room to frighten me, I put out my arm to feel it, and my hand seemingly went through the body of it, and felt no manner of substance till it came to the wall; then I drew back my hand, and still it was in the same place. Till now I had not the least fear, and even now had very little. Then I adjured it to tell me what it was. When I had said those words, it, keeping its back against the wall, moved gently along towards the door; I followed, and going out at the door, it turned its back towards me; went a little along the gallery and disappeared where there was no corner for it to turn, and before it came to the end of the gallery where were the stairs. Then

I found myself very cold from my feet as high as my hips, though I was not in great fear. I went into the bed betwixt the tenant and his man, and they complained of my being exceeding cold.

The tenant's man leaned over his master in the bed, and saw me stretch out my hand towards the apparition, and heard me speak the words; the tenant also heard the words.

The apparition seemed to have on a morning gown of a darkish colour, no hat nor cap, short black hair, a thin meagre visage of a pale swarthy colour; appeared to be of a middle stature, and about five and forty or fifty years old; the eyes were half shut, the arms hanging down, the hands visible beneath the sleeve. I related this description to Mr. John Lardner rector of Havant, and to Major Batten of Langstone, in Havant parish; they both said the description accorded with Mr. P., a former rector of the place, who had been dead above twenty years. Upon this the tenant and his wife left the house, which has remained void ever since.

The Monday after last Michaelmas day a man of Chodson, in Warwickshire, having been at Havant fair, passed by the aforesaid parsonage house about nine or ten at night, and saw a light in most of the rooms of the house. His pathway being close by the house, he, wondering at the light, looked into the kitchen window, and saw only a light; but, turning himself to go away, he saw the appearance of a man in a long gown: he made haste away; the apparition followed him over a piece of glebe land of several acres, to a lane which he crossed, and over a little meadow; then over another lane to some pales, which belong to farmer Henry Salter, my landlord, near a barn, in which were some of the farmer's men and some others. This man went into the barn, and told them how he had been frightened and followed from the parsonage-house by an apparition, which they might see standing against the pales if they went out: they went out, and saw it scratch against the pales, and heard a hideous noise; it stood there some time, and then disappeared: their description agreed with what I saw.

This last account I had from the man himself, and also from the farmer's men.

THOMAS WILKINS,
Curate of Warburton.

December 11, 1695, Oxon.

LIX.

Lord Orrery and the Butler.

A gentleman in Ireland, residing near the Earl of Orrery, sent his butler one afternoon to buy some cards. As he passed along, he saw a company of people sitting round a table with good cheer before them, in the midst of a field. On approaching them they all arose and saluted him, and desired him to sit down with them; but one of them whispered these words in his ear, "Do nothing this company invites you to do." Hereupon he refused to sit down at the table, and immediately table and all that belonged disappeared; and the company began dancing and playing upon musical instruments. The butler being asked to join them, he refused; and they not being able to prevail upon him to accompany them in working, any more than in feasting or dancing, they all disappeared, and the butler was left alone. Instead of going forward, he returned home as fast as he could in great consternation; and had no sooner entered his master's door, than he fell down, and lay some time senseless; but recovering himself, he related to his master what had passed.

The night following there came one of this company to his bedside, and told him, that if he offered to stir out of doors the next day he would be carried away. Hereupon he kept at home; but towards the evening he ventured to put one foot over the threshold (several persons standing by), which he had no sooner done, than a rope was thrown about his middle, and the poor man was hurried away with great swiftness; the spectators followed him as fast as they could, but could not overtake him. At length they espied a horseman coming towards him, and made signs to him to stop the man, whom he saw approaching him; he could also see both ends of the rope but nobody drawing it. When they met he laid hold on one end of the rope, and immediately had a smart blow given him over the arm with the other end; but by this means the man was stopped, and the horseman brought him back with him.

The Earl of Orrery hearing these strange reports, requested that the man might be sent to his house the morning following, or quickly after; when he told the Earl that his spectre had been with him again, and assured him that that day he should most certainly be carried away, and that no endeavours would avail to save him; upon this he was kept in a large room with a considerable number of persons to guard him, among whom was the famous Mr. Greatrakes, who was a neighbour. There were, besides other persons of quality, two bishops in the house at the same time, who were consulting concerning the use of a medicine which the spectre prescribed; but they determined on the negative.

Up to the middle of the afternoon all was quiet, but at length he was perceived to rise from the ground, whereupon Mr. Greatrakes and another lusty man placed their arms over his shoulders, one of them before him, and the other behind him, and weighed him down with all their strength; but he was forcibly taken up from them, and for a considerable time he was carried in the air to and fro over their heads, several of the company still running under him to prevent his receiving injury if he should fall. At length he fell, and was caught before he came to the ground, and by that means was not hurt.

All being quiet till bedtime, Lord Orrery ordered two of his servants to lie with him; and the next morning he told his Lordship that his spectre was again with him, and brought a wooden dish, with grey liquor in it, and bid him drink it off. At the first sight of the spectre, he said he endeavoured to wake his bed-fellows, but it told him that such endeavour should be in vain; and that he had no cause to fear him, he being his friend, and he that at first gave him the good advice in the field, which, had he not followed, he would have been before now perfectly in the power of the company he saw there. He added, that he concluded it was impossible that he should escape being carried away the day before, there was so strong a combination against him; but now he could assure him that there would be no more attempts of that nature, and knowing that he was troubled with two kinds of fits, he had brought that liquor to cure him, and bade him drink it. He peremptorily refused, when the spectre upbraided him, but told him, however, if he would take plantain juice he should be cured of one sort of fits, but he should carry the other to his grave.

The spectre now asked him whether he did not know him? He answered, no. It replied, I am———; the man answered, "he has been long dead." "I have been dead," said the spectre, "seven years, and you know that I lived a loose life, and ever since I died I have been hurried up and down in a restless condition with the company you saw, and shall be to the day of judgment."—*From H. Welby.*

LX.

Apparition of Lord Tyrone to Lady Beresford.

Lord Tyrone and Miss —— were born in Ireland, and were left orphans in their infancy to the care of the same person, by whom they were both educated in the principles of deism.

Their guardian dying when they were each of them about fourteen years of age, they fell into very indifferent hands. Though separated from each other, their friendship was unalterable, and they continued to regard each other with a sincere and fraternal affection. After some years had elapsed, and both were grown up, they made a solemn promise to each other that whichever should die first, would, if permitted, appear to the other, to declare what religion was most approved by the Supreme Being. Miss —— was shortly after addressed by Sir Martin Beresford, to whom she was after a few years married, but a change of condition had no power to alter their friendship. The families visited each other, and often spent some weeks together. A short time after one of these visits, Sir Martin remarked when his lady came down to breakfast, that her countenance was disturbed, and inquired of her health. She assured him she was quite well. He then asked her if she had hurt her wrist; "Have you sprained it?" said he, observing a black ribbon round it. She answered in the negative, and added, "Let me conjure you, Sir Martin, never to inquire the cause of my wearing this ribbon; you will never see me without it. If it concerned you as a husband to know, I would not for a moment conceal it; I never in my life denied you a request, but of this I entreat you to forgive me the refusal, and never to urge me farther on the subject." "Very well," said he, smiling, "since you beg me so earnestly, I will inquire no more." The conversation here ended; but breakfast was scarce over when Lady Beresford eagerly inquired if the post was come in; she was told it was not. In a few minutes she rang again and repeated the inquiry. She was again answered as at first. "Do you expect letters?" said Sir Martin, "that you are so anxious for the arrival of the post?" "I do," she answered, "I expect to hear that Lord Tyrone is dead; he died last Tuesday at four o'clock." "I never in my life," said Sir Martin, "believed your superstitions; some idle dream has surely thus alarmed you." At that instant the servant entered and delivered to them a letter sealed with black. "It is as I expected," exclaimed Lady Beresford, "Lord Tyrone is dead." Sir Martin open the letter; it came from Lord Tyrone's stewart, and contained the melancholy intelligence of his master's death, and on the very day and hour Lady Beresford had before specified. Sir Martin begged Lady Beresford to compose herself, and she assured him she felt much easier than she had done for a long time; and added, "I can communicate intelligence to you which I know will prove welcome; I can assure you, beyond the possibility of a doubt, that I shall in some months present you with a son." Sir Martin received this news with the greatest joy. After some months, Lady Beresford was delivered of a son (she had before been the mother of two daughters). Sir Martin survived the birth of his son little more than four years. After his decease, his widow seldom left home; she visited no family but that of a clergyman who resided in the same village; with them she frequently passed a few hours every day; the rest of her time was spent in solitude, and she appeared determined for ever to banish all other society. The clergyman's family consisted of himself, his wife, and one son, who at the time of Sir Martin's death, was quite a youth; to this son, however, she was, after a few years married, notwithstanding the disparity of years and the manifest imprudence of a connection so unequal in every point of view. Lady Beresford was treated by her young husband with contempt and cruelty, while at the same time his conduct evinced the most abandoned libertinism, utterly destitute of every principle of virtue and humanity. By this, her second husband, she had two daughters; after which such was the baseness of his conduct that she insisted on a separation. They parted for a few years, when so great was the contrition he expressed for his former conduct, that, won over by his supplications, promises, and entreaties, she was induced to pardon and once more to reside with him, and was in time the mother of a son.

The day on which she had lain-in a month, being the anniversary of her birthday, she sent for Lady Betty Cobb (of whose friendship she had long been possessed) and a few other friends, to request them to spend the day with her. About seven the clergyman by whom she had been christened and with whom she had all her life been intimate, came into the room to inquire after her health. She told him she was perfectly well, and requested him to spend the day with them; for, said she, "This is my birthday. I am forty-eight to-day." "No, madam," answered the clergyman, "you are mistaken; your mother and myself have had many disputes concerning your age, and I have at last discovered that I was right. I happened to go last week into the parish where you were born; I was resolved to put an end to the dispute; I searched the register, and find that you are but forty-seven this day." "You have signed my death warrant," she exclaimed, "I have then but a few hours to live. I must therefore entreat you to leave me immediately, as I have something of importance to settle before I die." When the clergyman left her, Lady Beresford sent to forbid the company coming, and at the same time to request Lady Betty Cobb and her son (of whom Sir Martin was the father, and who was then about twenty-two years of age), to come to her apartment immediately.

Upon their arrival, having ordered the attendants to quit the room, 'I have something,' she said, 'of the greatest importance to communicate to you both before I die, a period which is not far distant. You, Lady Betty, are no stranger to the friendship which subsisted between Lord Tyrone and myself; we were educated under the same roof, and in the same principles of deism. When the friends, into whose hands we afterwards fell, endeavoured to persuade us to embrace revealed religion, their arguments, though insufficient to convince, were powerful enough to stagger our former feelings, and to leave us wavering between the two opinions; in this perplexing state of doubt and uncertainty, we made a solemn promise to each other, that whichever died first should (if permitted) appear to the other, and declare what religion was most acceptable to God; accordingly, one night, while Sir Martin and myself were in bed, I suddenly awoke and discovered Lord Tyrone sitting by my bedside. I screamed out and endeavoured to awake Sir Martin; "For Heaven's sake," I exclaimed, "Lord Tyrone, by what means or for what reason came you hither at this time of night." "Have you then forgotten our promise?" said he, "I died last Tuesday at four o'clock, and have been permitted by the Supreme Being to appear to you, to assure you that the revealed religion is the true, and the only religion by which we can be saved. I am further suffered to inform you that you will soon produce a son, which it is decreed will marry my daughter; not many years after his birth Sir Martin will die, and you will marry again, and to a man by whose ill-treatment you will be rendered miserable: you will have two daughters, and afterwards a son, and you will die in the forty-seventh year of your age." "Just Heavens!" I exclaimed, "and cannot I prevent this?" "Undoubtedly you may," returned the spectre; "you are a free agent, and may prevent it all by resisting every temptation to a second marriage; but your passions are strong, you know not their power; hitherto you have had no trials. More I am not permitted to reveal, but, if after this warning you persist in your infidelity, your lot in another world will be miserable indeed!" "May I not ask," said I, "if you are happy?" "Had I been otherwise," he replied, "I should not have been permitted to appear to you." "I may then infer that you are happy?" He smiled. "But how," said I, "when morning comes, shall I know that your appearance to me has been real, and not the mere representation of my own imagination?" "Will not the news of my death be sufficient to convince you?" "No," I returned, "I might have had such a dream, and that dream accidentally come to pass. I will have some strong proofs of its reality." "You shall," said he, and waving his hand, the bed-curtains, which were crimson velvet were instantly drawn through a large iron hoop by which the tester of the bed was suspended. "In that," said he, "you cannot be mistaken; no mortal arm could have performed this." "True," said I, "but sleeping we are often possessed of far more strength than when awake; though waking I could not have done it, asleep I might; and shall still doubt." "Here is a pocket-book, in this," said he, "I will write my name: you know my handwriting." I replied, "Yes." He wrote with a pencil on one side of the leaves. "Still," said I, "in the morning I may doubt; though waking I could not imitate your hand, asleep I might." "You are hard of belief," said he: "were I to touch you it would injure you irreparably; it is not for spirits to touch mortal flesh." "I do not," said I, "regard a slight blemish." "You are a woman of courage," replied he, "Hold out your hand." I did so: he struck my wrist, his hand was cold as marble, and in a moment the sinews shrunk up, every nerve withered. "Now," said he, "while you live let no mortal eye behold that wrist: to see it is sacrilege." He stopped; I turned to him again; he was gone. During the time I had conversed with him my thoughts were perfectly calm and collected, but the moment he was gone I felt chilled with horror, the very bed moved under me; I endeavoured, but in vain, to awake Sir Martin, all my attempts were ineffectual, and in this state of agitation and terror I lay for some time, when a shower of tears came to my relief, and I dropped asleep. In the morning, Sir Martin arose and dressed himself as usual without perceiving the state the curtains remained in.

'When I awoke I found Sir Martin gone down; I arose, and having put on my clothes, went to the gallery adjoining the apartment and took from thence a long broom (such as cornices are swept with), by the help of this I took down with some difficulty the curtains, as I imagined their extraordinary position might excite suspicion in the family. I then went to the bureau, took up my pocket-book, and bound a piece of black ribbon round my wrist. When I came down, the agitation of my mind had left an impression on my countenance too visible to pass unobserved by my husband. He instantly remarked it, and asked the cause; I informed him that Lord Tyrone was no more, that he died at the hour of four on the preceding Tuesday, and desired him never to question me more respecting the black ribbon; which he kindly desisted from after. You, my son, as had been foretold, I afterwards brought into the world, and in little more than four years after your birth, your lamented father expired in my arms.

'After this melancholy event, I determined, as the only probable chance to avoid the sequel of the prediction, for ever to abandon all society; to give up every pleasure resulting from it, and to pass the rest of my days in solitude and retirement. But few can long endure to exist in a state of perfect sequestration: I began an intimacy with a family, and one alone; nor could I then forsee the fatal consequences which afterwards resulted from it. Little did I think their son, their only son, then a mere youth, would form the person destined by fate to prove my destruction. In a very few years I ceased to regard him with indifference. I endeavoured by every possible way to conquer a passion, the fatal effects of which I too well knew. I had fondly imagined I had overcome its influence, when the evening of one fatal day terminated my fortitude, and plunged me in a moment down that abyss I had so long been meditating to shun. He had often solicited his parents for leave to go into the army, and at last obtained permission, and came to bid me adieu before his departure. The instant he entered the room he fell upon his knees at my feet, told me he was miserable, and that I alone was the cause. At that moment my fortitude forsook me, I gave myself up for lost, and regarding my fate as inevitable, without farther hesitation consented to a union, the immediate result of which I knew to be misery, and its end death. The conduct of my husband, after a few years, amply justified a separation, and I hoped by this means to avoid the fatal sequel of the prophecy; but won over by his reiterated entreaties, I was prevailed upon to pardon, and once more reside with him, though not till after I had, as I thought, passed my forty-seventh year.

'But alas! I have this day heard from indisputable

authority, that I have hitherto lain under a mistake with regard to my age, and that I am but forty-seven to-day. Of the near approach of my death then I entertain not the slightest doubt.

'When I am dead, as the necessity of concealment closes with my life, I could wish that you, Lady Betty, would unbind my wrist, take from thence the black ribbon, and let my son with yourself behold it.' Lady Beresford here paused for some time, but resuming the conversation, she entreated her son would behave himself so as to merit the high honour he would in future receive from a union with the daughter of Lord Tyrone.

Lady B. then expressed a wish to lay down on the bed and endeavoured to compose herself to sleep. Lady Betty Cobb and her son immediately called her domestics and quitted the room, having first desired them to watch their mistress attentively, and if they observed the smallest change in her to call instantly.

An hour passed, and all was quiet in the room. They listened at the door, and everything remained still, but in half an hour more a bell rang violently; they flew to her apartment, but before they reached the door, they heard the servant exclaim, "Oh, she is dead!" Lady Betty then bade the servants for a few minutes to quit the room, and herself with Lady Beresford's son approached the bed of his mother; they knelt down by the side of it; Lady Betty then lifted up her hand and untied the ribbon; the wrist was found exactly as Lady Beresford had described it, every sinew shrunk, every nerve withered.

Lady Beresford's son, as had been predicted, is since married to Lord Tyrone's daughter. The black ribbon and pocket-book were formerly in the possession of Lady Betty Cobb, Marlborough Buildings, Bath, who during her life was ever ready to attest the truth of this narration, as also the whole of the Tyrone and Beresford families.—*From H. Welby.*

LXI.

Two Apparitions to Mr. William Lilly.

THE FOLLOWING AFFAIR EXCITED CONSIDERABLE INTEREST IN THE NORTH ABOUT THE MIDDLE OF THE LAST CENTURY.

On the first Sunday in the year 1749, Mr. Thomas Lilly, the son of a farmer in the parish of Kelso in Roxburghshire, a young man intended for the Church of Scotland, remained at home to keep the house in company with a shepherd's boy, all the rest of the family, except a maid-servant, being at church. The young student and the boy being by the fire whilst the girl was gone to the well for water, a venerable old gentleman, clad in an antique garb, presented himself, and after some little ceremony, desired the student to take up the family bible which lay on a table, and turn over to a certain chapter and verse in the Second Book of Kings. The student did so, and read—"there is death in the pot."

On this the old man, with much apparent agitation, pointed to the great family pot boiling on the fire, declaring that the maid had cast a great quantity of arsenic into it with an intent to poison the whole family, to the end she might rob the house of the hundred guineas which she knew her master had lately taken for sheep and grain which he had sold. Just as he was so saying the maid came to the door. The old gentleman said to the student, "remember my warning and save the lives of the family!" and that instant disappeared.

The maid entered with a smiling countenance, emptied her pail, and returned to the well for a fresh supply. Meanwhile young Lilly put some oatmeal into a wooden dish, skimmed the pot of the fat and mixed it for what is called brose or croudy, and when the maid returned, he with the boy appeared busily employed in eating the mixture. "Come, Peggy," said the student, "here is enough left for you; are not you fond of croudy?" She smiled, took up the dish, and reaching a horn spoon, withdrew to the back room. The shepherd's dog followed her, unseen by the boy, and the poor animal, on the croudy being put down by the maid, fell a victim to his voracious appetite; for before the return of the family from church it was enormously swelled, and expired in great agony.

The student enjoined the boy to remain quite passive for the present; meanwhile he attempted to shew his ingenuity by resolving the cause of the sudden death of the dog into insanity, in order to keep the girl in countenance till a fit opportunity of discovering the plot should present itself.

Soon after his father and family with the other servants returned from church.

The table was instantly replenished with wooden bowls and trenchers, while a heap of barley bannocks graced the top. The kail or broth, infused with leeks or winter-cabbages, was poured forth in plenty; and Peggy, with a prodigal hand, filled all the dishes with the homely dainties of Teviotdale. The master began grace, and all hats and bonnets were instantly off; "O Lord," prayed the farmer, "we have been hearing thy word, from the mouth of thy aged servant Mr. Ramsay; we have been alarmed by the awful famine in Samaria, and of death being in the pot!" Here the young scholar interrupted his father, by exclaiming—"Yes sir, there is death in the pot now here, as well as there was once in Israel! Touch not! taste not! see the dog dead by the poisoned pot!"

"What!" cried the farmer, "have you been raising the devil by your conjuration? Is this the effect of your study, sir?" "No, father," said the student, "I pretend to no such arts of magic or necromancy, but this day, as the boy can testifiy, I had a solemn warning from one whom I take to be no demon, but a good angel. To him we all owe our lives. As to Peggy, according to his intimation, she has put poison into the pot for the purpose of destroying the whole family." Here the girl fell into a fit, from which being with some trouble recovered, she confessed the whole of her deadly design, and was suffered to quit the family and her native country. She was soon after executed at Newcastle-upon-Tyne for the murder of her illegitimate child, again making ample confession of the above diabolical design.

In 1750, the same young Lilly was one day reading the 20th chapter of the Revelation of John the Divine; just as he was entering upon that part which describes the angel binding the devil a thousand years, "after which he was to be loosed a little;" a very venerable personage appeared at his elbow. The young man fell on the floor, but quickly arose, and in the name of the Lord demanded who he was and the nature of his business. Upon this the following colloquy ensued:—

Lilly.—Shall I call thee Satan, the crooked serpent, the Devil, Beelzebub, or Lucifer son of the morning.

Appar.—I am a messenger from the dead, to see or to cause justice to be done to thee and thy father. I am the spirit of one of thy ancestors!

Lilly.—Art thou the soul of my grandfather, who, amidst immense riches, perished for want of food?

Appar.—Thou art right. Money was my deity, and Mammon my master: I heaped up gold, but did not enjoy it.

Lilly.—I have frequently heard my father mention you as a sordid, avaricious, miserable man. How did you dispose of the immense riches which you are said to have accumulated?

Appar.—It is, for the most part, hidden in a field in the farm of your father, and I intend that you, his son, should be the sole possessor of it, without suffering your father to know from whence you riches originated. Do not you recognize my face since the beginning of the last year?

Lilly.—Are you the old gentleman whose timely intelligence saved the lives of all our family?

Appar.—I am. Therefore think not your father ill rewarded already.

Lilly.—How can I account to him for the immediate accumulation of so much money as you seem to intimate?

Appar.—Twenty thousand pounds sterling money!

Lilly.—You seem even now in your disembodied state to feel much emotion at the mention of so much money.

Appar.—But now I cannot touch the money of mortals. But I cannot stay: follow me to the field, and I will point out the precise place where you are to dig.

Here the apparition stalked forth round the barn yard, and Lilly followed him, till he came to a field about three furlongs from his father's door, when the apparition stood still on a certain spot, wheeled thrice round, and vanished into air.

This proved to be the precise place which young Lilly and his companions had often devoted to pastime, being a hollow whence stone had formerly been dug. He lost but little time in consideration, and having procured a pick-axe and a spade, he set to work and discovered the treasure. His immense wealth enabled him to perform many acts of charity in that country, as many can testify to this day.

The pots in which the money, consisting of large pieces of gold and silver, were deposited, have often been shewn as curiosities hardly to be equalled in the south of Scotland.—*World of Spirits*, 1796.

LXII.

Apparition of Mr. Thomkins to the Rev. Mr. Warren.

Mr. John Warren, minister of Hatfield-Broadoak, in Essex, a worthy and pious man, was one day in his garden reading Bunyan's "Publican and Pharisee," when he was accosted by a neighbour, who entered into discourse with him upon the words, "Shall a man be more righteous than his Maker?" Mr. Warren's discourse in general ran upon the promises, while Mr. Thomkins, his neighbour, chiefly urged the threatenings of God. At length Mr. Warren's servant came and informed him the dinner was ready and his mistress waited for him: he asked his neighbour Thomkins to dine with him, which the latter, with tears in his eyes, refused, saying, "my time is come, and I must away."

Mr. Warren was proceeding to expostulate with his friend Thomkins, when the servant repeated the mesage, urging that a neighbour had sent for him to go immediately to a case of great inportance and imminent danger. Mr. Warren withdrawing towards the house, still continued the discourse upon the former subject, comforting his friend till he arrived at the door, when entering first, he left the door open that Mr. Thomkins might follow; but nobody coming in he went directly and sought him all over his garden, but found him not, which much disturbed his mind then, and much more soon afterwards, when he found that his neighbour and friend Thomkins was just expired, and had not been out of his house, according to every testimony, that day. Mr. Warren's servant testified seeing her master in conversation with a person in the garden, and telling her mistress so, who wondered she had seen nobody go through the house, as there was no other way into the garden. Mr. Warren, a pious and sensible divine, often related this to Mr. Goodman, who recites it in his work, entitled "Winter-Evening Conferences between Neighbours."—*World of Spirits.*

LXIII.

Strange Experiences of the Wesley Family at Epworth.

FROM THE NARRATIVE PREPARED BY THE REV. JOHN WESLEY.

"When I was very young, I heard several letters read, wrote to my elder brother by my father, giving an account of strange disturbances which were in his house at Epworth, in Lincolnshire.

"When I went down thither in the year 1720, I carefully inquired into the particulars. I spoke to each of the persons who were then in the house, and took down what each could testify of his or her own knowledge. The sum of which was this:

"On December 2, 1716, while Rober tBrown, my father's servant, was sitting with one of the maids a little before ten at night in the dining-room, which opened into the garden, they both heard one knocking at the door. Robert rose and opened it, but could see nobody. Quickly it knocked again, and groaned. "It is Mr. Turpine," said Robert; "he has the stone and used to groan so." He opened the door again twice or thrice, the knocking being twice or thrice repeated. But still seeing nothing, and being a little startled, they rose and went up to their bedrooms. When Robert came to the top of the garret stairs, he saw a hand mill, which was at a distance, whirled about very swiftly. When he related this, he said, "Nought vexed me, but that it was empty. I thought if it had but been full of malt he might have ground his heart out for me." When he was in bed, he heard as it were the gobbling of a turkey-cock close to the bed-side; and soon after the sound of one stumbling over his shoes and boots, but there were none there; he had left them below. The next day, he and the maid related these things to the other maid, who laughed heartily and said, "What a couple of fools you are! I defy anything to frighten me." After churning in the evening, she put the butter in the tray, and had no sooner carried it into the dairy, than she heard a knocking on the shelf where several puncheons of milk stood, first above the shelf, then below; she took the candle and searched both above and below; but being unable to find anything, threw down butter, tray, and all, and ran away as for her life.

"The next evening between five and six o'clock, my sister Molly, then about twenty years of age, sitting in the dining-room reading, heard as if it were the door that led into the hall open, and a person walking in, that seemed to have on a silk night-gown, rustling and trailing along. It seemed to walk round her, then to the door, then round again: but she could see nothing. She thought, "it signifies nothing to run away; for whatever it is, it can run faster than me." So she rose, put her book under her arm, and walked slowly away. After supper, she was sitting with my sister Suky (about a year older than her), in one of the chambers, and telling her what had happened; she quite made light of it, telling her, "I wonder you are so easily frighted; I would fain see what would fright me." Presently a knocking began under the table. She took the candle and looked, but could find nothing. Then the iron casement began to clatter, and the lid of a warming pan. Next the latch of the door moved up and down without ceasing. She started up, leaped into bed without undressing, pulled the bed clothes over her head, and never ventured to look up till next morning.

"A night or two after, my sister Hetty, a year

younger than my sister Molly, was waiting as usual between nine and ten, to take away my father's candle, when she heard one coming down the garret stairs, walking slowly by her, then going down the best stairs, then up the back stairs, and up the garret stairs. And at every step it seemed the house shook from top to bottom. Just then my father knocked. She went in, took his candle, and got to bed as fast as possible. In the morning she told this to my eldest sister, who told her, "You know, I believe none of these things. Pray let me take away the candle to-night and I will find out the trick." She accordingly took my sister Hetty's place, and had no sooner taken away the candle, than she heard a noise below. She hastened down stairs to the hall where the noise was. But it was then in the kitchen. She ran into the kitchen, where it was drumming on the inside of the screen. When she went round it was drumming on the outside, and so always on the side opposite to her. Then she heard a knocking at the back kitchen door. She ran to it, unlocked it softly, and when the knocking was repeated, suddenly opened it; but nothing was to be seen. As soon as she had shut it, the knocking began again; she opened it again, but could see nothing; when she went to shut the door it was violently thrust against her; she let it fly open, but nothing appeared. She went again to shut it, and it was again thrust against her; but she set her knee and her shoulder to the door, forced it to, and turned the key. Then the knocking began again; but she let it go on, and went up to bed. However, from that time she was thoroughly convinced that there was no imposture in the affair.

"The next morning, my sister telling my mother what had happened, she said, "If I hear anything myself, I shall know how to judge." Soon after, she begged her to come into the nursery. She did, and heard in the corner of the room, as it were the violent rocking of a cradle; but no cradle had been there for some years. She was convinced it was preternatural, and earnestly prayed it might not disturb her in her own chamber at the hours of retirement; and it never did. She now thought it was proper to tell my father. But he was extremely angry, and said, "Suky, I am ashamed of you; these boys and girls fright one another, but you are a woman of sense and should know better. Let me hear of it no more." At six in the evening, he had family prayers as usual. When he began the prayer for the King, a knocking began all round the room, and a thundering knock attended the Amen. The same was heard from this time every morning and evening, while prayers for the King was repeated. As both my father and mother are now at rest, and incapable of being pained thereby, I think it is my duty to furnish the serious reader with a key to this circumstance.

"The year before King William died, my father observed my mother did not say Amen to the prayer for the King. She said she could not; for she did not believe the Prince of Orange was King. He vowed he never would cohabit with her till she did. He then took his horse and rode away, nor did she hear anything of him for a twelvemonth. He then came back and lived with her as before. But I fear his vow was not forgotten before God.

"Being informed that Mr. Hoole, the vicar of Haxey (an eminently pious and sensible man), could give me some farther information, I walked over to him. He said, "Robert Brown came over to me and told me your father desired my company. When I came, he gave me an account of all that had happened, particularly the knocking during family prayer. But that evening (to my great satisfaction) we had no knocking at all. But between nine and ten, a servant came in and said, 'Old Jefferies is coming' (that was the name of one that died in the house), 'for I hear the signal.' This they informed me was heard every night about a quarter before ten. It was toward the top of the house on the outside, at the north-east corner, resembling the loud creaking of a saw, or rather that of a windmill, when the body of it is turned about, in order to shift the sails to the wind. We then heard a knocking over our heads, and Mr. Wesley catching up a candle, said, 'Come, sir, now you shall hear for yourself.' We went up stairs; he with much hope, and I (to say the truth) with much fear. When we came into the nursery, it was knocking in the next room; when we were there, it was knocking in the nursery. And there it continued to knock, though we came in, particularly at the head of the bed (which was of wood) in which Miss Hetty and two of her younger sisters lay. Mr. Wesley, observing that they were much affected though asleep, sweating, and trembling exceedingly, was very angry, and pulling out a pistol, was going to fire at the place from whence the sound came. But I catched him by the arm, and said, 'Sir, you are convinced this is something supernatural. If so, you cannot hurt it; but you give it power to hurt you.' He then went close to the place and said sternly, 'Thou deaf and dumb devil, why dost though fright these children? Come to me in my study that am a man!' Instantly it knocked his knock (the particular knock which he always used at the gate) as if it would shiver the boards in pieces, and we heard nothing more that night." Till this time my father had never heard the least disturbances in his study. But the next evening as he attempted to go into his study (of which none had any key but himself), when he opened the door, it was thrown back with such violence, as had like to have thrown him down. However, he thrust the door open and went in. Presently there was knocking first on one side, then on the other; and after a time in the next room, wherein my sister Nancy was. He went into that room, and (the noise continuing) adjured it to speak; but in vain. He then said, " These spirits love darkness : put out the candle, and perhaps it will speak;" she did so, and he repeated his adjuration; but still there was only knocking, and no articulate sound. Upon this he said, " Nancy, two Christians are an overmatch for the devil. Go all of you down stairs; it may be, when I am alone, he will have the courage to speak." When she was gone, a thought came in, and he said, " If thou art the spirit of my son Samuel, I pray knock three knocks and no more." Immediately all was silence, and there was no more knocking at all that night. I asked my sister Nancy (then about fifteen years old) whether she was not afraid, when my father used that adjuration? She answered, she. was sadly afraid it would speak when she put out the candle; but she was not at all afraid in the day time when it walked after her as she swept the chambers, as it constantly did, and seemed to sweep after her; only she thought he might have done it for her, and saved her the trouble. By this time all my sisters were so accustomed to these noises, that they gave them little disturbance. A gentle tapping at their bed's head usually began between nine and ten at night. They then commonly said to each other, " Jeffery is coming; it is time to go to sleep." And if they heard a noise in the day, and said to my youngest sister, " Hark, Kezzy, Jeffery is knocking above," she would run up stairs and pursue it from room to room, saying, she desired no better diversion.

"A few nights after, my father and mother were just gone to bed, and the candle was not taken away, when they heard three blows, and a second and a third three, as it were with a large oaken staff, struck upon a chest which stood by the bedside. My father immediately arose, put on his night-gown, and hearing great noises below, took the candle and went down: my mother walked by his side. As they went down the broad stairs, they heard as if a vessel full of silver was poured upon my mother's breast, and ran jingling down to her feet. Quickly after there was a sound, as if a large iron ball was thrown among many bottles under the stairs; but nothing was hurt. Soon after, our large mastiff dog came and ran to shelter himself between them. While the disturbances continued, he used to bark and leap, and snap on one side and the other; and that frequently before any person in the room heard any noise at all. But after two or three days, he used to tremble, and creep away before the noise began. And by this, the family knew it was at hand; nor did the observation ever fail. A little before my father and mother came into the hall, it seemed as if a very large coal was violently thrown upon the floor and dashed all in pieces; but nothing was seen. My father then cried out, "Suky, do you not hear? All the pewter is thrown about the kitchen." But when they looked, all the pewter stood in its place. There then was a loud knocking at the back door. My father opened it, but saw nothing. It was then at the fore-door. He opened that: but it was still lost labour. After opening first the one, then the other several times, he turned and went up to bed. But the noises were so violent all over the house, that he could not sleep till four in the morning.

"Several gentlemen and clergymen now earnestly advised my father to quit the house, but he constantly answered, " No ; let the devil flee from me ; I will never flee from the devil." But he wrote to my eldest brother at London to come down. He was preparing so to do, when another letter came, informing him the disturbances were over, after they had continued (the latter part of the time day and night) from the second of December to the end of January."

An author who in this age relates such a story, and treats it as not utterly incredible and absurd, must expect to be ridiculed, and very justly; but the testimony upon which it rests is far too strong to be set aside because of the strangeness of the relation. The letters which passed at the time between Samuel Wesley and the family at Epworth, the journal which Mr. Wesley kept of these remarkable transactions, and the evidence concerning them which John afterwards collected, fell into the hands of Dr. Priestley, and were published by him as being "perhaps the best authenticated and best told story of the kind that is anywhere extant." He observes in favour of the story, "that all the parties seem to have been sufficiently void of fear, and also free from credulity, except the general belief that such things were supernatural."

We give the most important and circumstantial of the family letters relating to this subject. The MS. is the handwriting of Mr. S. Wesley. The titles of the letters, denoting the writers and the persons to whom they were written, are only added.

To Mr. Samuel Wesley, from his Mother.

JANUARY 12, 1716-7.

DEAR SAM,—This evening we were agreeably surprised with your pacquet, which brought the welcome news of your being alive, after we had been in the greatest panic imaginable, almost a month, thinking either you was dead, or one of your brothers by some misfortune been killed.

The reason of our fears is as follows. On the first of December our maid heard at the door of the dining-room several dismal groans, like a person in extremes, at the point of death. We gave little heed to her relation, and endeavoured to laugh her out of her fears. Some nights (two or three) after, several of the family heard a strange knocking in divers places, usually three or four knocks at a time, and then stayed a little. This continued every night for a fortnight; sometimes it was in the garret, but most commonly in the nursery or green chamber. We all heard it but your father, and I was not willing he should be informed of it, lest he should fancy it was against his own death, which, indeed, we all apprehended. But when it began to be so troublesome both day and night, that few or none of the family durst be alone, I resolved to tell him of it, being minded he should speak to it. At first he would not believe but somebody did it to alarm us; but the night after, as soon as he was in bed, it knocked loudly nine times, just by his bed-side. He rose, and went to see if he could find out what it was, but could see nothing. Afterwards he heard it as the rest.

One night it made such a noise in the room over our heads as if several people were walking, then run up and down stairs, and was so outrageous that we thought the children would be frighted, so your father and I rose, and went down in the dark to light a candle. Just as we came to the bottom of the broad stairs, having hold of each other, on my side there seemed as if sombody had emptied a bag of money at my feet; and on his, as if all the bottles under the stairs (which were many) had been dashed in a thousand pieces. We passed through the hall into the kitchen and got a candle, and went to see the children, whom we found asleep.

The next night your father would get Mr. Hoole to lie at our house, and we all sat together till one or two o'clock in the morning, and heard the knocking as usual. Sometimes it would make a noise like the winding up of a jack, at other times, as that night Mr. Hoole was with us, like a carpenter planing deals; but most commonly it knocked thrice and stopped, and then thrice again, and so many hours together. We persuaded your father to speak, and try if any voice would be heard. One night about six o'clock he went into the nursery in the dark, and at first heard several deep groans, then knocking. He adjured it to speak if it had the power, and tell him why it troubled his house, but no voice was heard, but it knocked thrice aloud. Then he questioned it if it were Sammy, and bid it, if it were and could not speak, knock again, but it knocked no more that night, which made us hope it was not against your death.

Thus it continued till the 28th of December, when it loudly knocked (as your father used to do at the gate) in the nursery, and departed. We have various conjectures what this may mean. For my own part, I fear nothing now you are safe at London hitherto, and I hope God will still preserve you. Though sometimes I am inclined to think my brother is dead. Let me know your thoughts on it. S. W.

From Miss Susannah Wesley to her Brother Samuel.

EPWORTH, Jan. 24.

DEAR BROTHER,—About the first of December, a most terrible and astonishing noise was heard by a maid-servant, as at the dining-room door, which caused the up-starting of her hair, and made her ears prick forth at an unusual rate. She said it was like the groans of one expiring. These so frighted her, that for a great while she durst not go out of one room into another, after it began to get dark, without company. But, to lay aside jesting, which should not be done in serious matters, I assure you that from the first to the last of a lunar month, the groans, squeaks, tinglings, and knockings, were frightful enough.

Though it is needless for me to send you any account of what we all heard, my father himself having a larger account of the matter than I am able to give, which he designs to send you; yet in compliance with your desire, I will tell you as briefly as I can, what I heard of it. The first night I ever heard it, my sister Nancy and I were sitting in the dining-room. We heard something rush on the outside of the doors that opened into the garden, then three loud knocks immediately after other three, and in half a minute the same number over our head. We enquired whether any body had been in the garden, or in the room above us, but there was nobody. Soon after, my sister Molly and I were up after all the family were a-bed (except my sister Nancy) about some business. We heard three bouncing thumps under our feet, which soon made us throw away our work, and tumble into bed. Afterwards the tingling of the latch and warming pan, and so it took its leave that night.

Soon after the above mentioned, we heard a noise as if a great piece of sounding metal was thrown down on the outside of our chamber. We, lying in the quietest part of the house, heard less than the rest for a pretty while, but the latter end of the night that Mr. Hoole sat up on, I lay in the nursery, where it was very violent. I then heard frequent knocks over and under the room where I lay, and at the children's bed head, which was made of boards. It seemed to rap against it very hard and loud, so that the bed shook under them. I heard something walk by my bedside, like a man in a long night-gown. The knocks were so loud that Mr. Hoole came out of their chamber to us. It still continued. My father spoke, but nothing answered. It ended that night with my father's particular knock, very fierce.

It is now pretty quiet, only at our repeating the

prayers for the king and prince, when it usually begins, especially when my father says, "Our most gracious Sovereign Lord," &c. This my father is angry at, and designs to say three instead of two for the royal family. We all heard the same noise, and at the same time, and as coming from the same place. To conclude this, it now makes its personal appearance: but of this more hereafter. Do not say one word of this to our folk, nor give the least hint.

I am,
Your sincere friend and affectionate Sister,
SUSANNAH WESLEY.

From Miss Emily Wesley to her Brother Samuel.

DEAR BROTHER,—I thank you for your last, and shall give you what satisfaction is in my power, concerning what has happened in our family. I am so far from being superstitious, that I was too much inclined to infidelity; so that I heartily rejoice at having such an opportunity of convincing myself past doubt or scruple, of the existence of some beings besides those we see. A whole month was sufficient to convince any body of the reality of the thing, and to try all ways of discovering any trick, had it been possible for any such to have been used. I shall only tell you what I myself heard, and leave the rest to others.

My sisters in the paper chamber had heard noises, and told me of them, but I did not much believe, till one night, about a week after the first groans were heard, which was the beginning, just after the clock had struck ten, I went down stairs to lock the doors, which I always do. Scarce had I got up the best stairs, when I heard a noise, like a person throwing down a vast coal in the middle of the fore kitchen, and all the splinters seemed to fly about from it. I was not much frightened, but went to my sister Suky, and we together went all over the low rooms, but there was nothing out of order.

Our dog was fast asleep, and our only cat in the other end of the house. No sooner was I got up stairs, and undressing for bed, but I heard a noise among many bottles that stand under the best stairs, just like the throwing of a great stone among them, which had broken them all to pieces. This made me hasten to bed; but my sister Hetty, who sits always to wait on my father going to bed, was still sitting on the lowest step on the garret stairs, the door being shut at her back, when soon after there came down the stairs behind her something like a man, in a loose night-gown trailing after him, which made her fly rather than run to me in the nursery.

All this time we never told our father of it, but soon after we did. He smiled, and gave no answer, but was more careful than usual, from that time, to see us in bed, imagining it to be some of us young women that sat up late and made a noise. His incredulity, and especially his imputing it to us or our lovers, made me, I own, desirous of its continuance till he was convinced. As for my mother, she firmly believed it to be rats, and sent for a horn to blow them away. I laughed to think how wisely they were employed, who were striving half a day to fright away Jeffery, for that name I gave it, with a horn.

But whatever it was, I perceived it could be made angry; for from that time it was so outrageous there was no quiet for us after ten at night. I heard frequently between ten and eleven something like the quick winding up of a jack, at the corner of the room by my bed's head, just like the running of the wheels and the creaking of the ironwork. This was the common signal of its coming. Then it would knock on the floor three times, then at my sister's bed's head, in the same room, almost always three together, and then stay. The sound was hollow and loud, so as none of us could ever imitate.

It would answer to my mother if she stamped on the floor and bid it. It would knock when I was putting the children to bed, just under me where I sat. One time little Kesy, pretending to scare Patty as I was undressing them, stamped with her foot on the floor, and immediately it answered with three knocks just in the same place. It was more loud and fierce if any one said it was rats, or anything natural.

I could tell you abundance more of it, but the rest will write, and therefore it would be needless. I was not much frighted at first, and very little at last; but it was never near me, except two or three times, and never followed me, as it did my sister Hetty. I have been with her when it has knocked under her, and when she has removed has followed, and still kept just under her feet, which was enough to terrify a stouter person.

If you would know my opinion of the reason of this, I shall briefly tell you. I believe it to be witchcraft, for these reasons. About a year since there was a disturbance at a town near us that was undoubtedly witches; and if so near, why may they not reach us? Then my father had for several Sundays before its coming preached warmly against consulting those that are called cunning men, which our people are given to; and it had a particular spite at my father.

Besides, something was thrice seen. The first time by my mother, under my sister's bed, like a badger, only without any head that was discernible. The same creature was sat by the dining-room fire one evening: when our man went into the room, it run by him, through the hall under the stairs. He followed with a candle, and searched, but it was departed. The last time he saw it in the kitchen, like a white rabbit,

which seems likely to be some witch; and I do so really believe it to be one, that I would venture to fire a pistol at it if I saw it long enough. It has been heard by me and others since December. I have filled up all my room, and have only time to tell you, I am,
           Your loving sister,
                     EMILY WESLEY.

Addenda to (and from) my Father's Diary.

Friday, December 21.—Knocking I heard first, I think, this night: to which disturbance I hope God will in his good time put an end.

Sunday, December 23.—Not much disturbed with the noises that are now grown customary to me.

Wednesday, December 26.—Sat up to hear noises. Strange! spoke to it, knocked off.

Friday, 28.—The noises very boisterous and disturbing this night.

Saturday, 29.—Not frighted with the continued disturbance of my family.

Tuesday, January 1, 1717.—My family have had no disturbance since I went.

Of the General Circumstances which follow, most, if not all the family were frequent Witnesses.

1. Presently after any noise was heard, the wind commonly rose, and whistled very loud round the house, and increased with it.

2. The signal was given, which my father likens to the turning round of a windmill when the wind changes: Mr. Hoole (Rector of Haxey) to the planing of deal boards; my sister to the swift winding up of a jack. It commonly began at the corner of the top of the nursery.

3. Before it came into any room, the latches were

frequently lifted up, the windows clattered, and whatever iron or brass was about the chamber, rung and jarred exceedingly.

4. When it was in any room, let them make what noise they would, as they sometimes did on purpose, its dead hollow note would be clearly heard above them all.

5. It constantly knocked when the prayers for the King and Prince were being repeated, and was plainly heard by all in the room, but my father, and sometimes by him, as were also the thundering knocks at the Amen.

6. The sound very often seemed in the air in the middle of a room, nor could they ever make any such themselves by any contrivance.

7. Though it seemed to rattle down the pewter, to clap the doors, draw the curtains, kick the man's shoes up and down, &c., yet it never moved anything except the latches, otherwise than making it tremble; unless once, when it threw open the nursery door.

8. The mastiff, though he barked violently at it the first day he came, yet whenever it came after that, nay, sometimes before the family perceived it, he ran whining, or quite silent, to shelter himself behind some of the company.

9. It never came by day, till my mother ordered the horn to be blown.

10. After that time scarce anyone could go from one room into another but the latch of the room they went to was lifted up before they touched it.

11. It never came once into my father's study, till he talked to it sharply, called it deaf and dumb devil, and bid it cease to disturb the innocent children, and come to him in his study, if it had anything to say to him.

12. From the time of my mother's desiring it not to disturb her from five to six, it was never heard in her

chamber from five till she came down stairs, nor at any other time, when she was employed in devotion.

13. Whether our clock went right or wrong, it always came, as near as could be guessed, when by the night it wanted a quarter of ten.

The Rev. Mr. Hoole's Account.

SEPT. 10.

As soon as I came to Epworth, Mr. Wesley telling me he sent for me to conjure, I knew not what he meant, till some of your sisters told me what had happened, and that I was sent for to sit up. I expected every hour, it being then about noon, to hear something extraordinary, but to no purpose. At supper, too, and at prayers, all was silent, contrary to custom; but soon after, one of the maids who went up to sheet a bed, brought the alarm that Jeffery was come above stairs. We all went up, and as we were standing round the fire in the east chamber, something began knocking just on the other side of the wall, on the chimney-piece, as with a key. Presently the knocking was under our feet, Mr. Wesley and I went down, he with great a deal of hope, and I with fear. As soon as we were in the kitchen, the sound was above us, in the room we had left. We returned up the narrow stairs, and heard at the broad stairs head some one slaring with their feet (all the family being now in bed beside us) and then trailing, as it were, and rustling with a silk night-gown. Quickly it was in the nursery at the bed's head, knocking as it had done at first, three by three. Mr. Wesley spoke to it, and said he believed it was the devil, and soon after it knocked at the window, and changed its sound into one like the planing of boards. From thence it went on the outward south-side of the house, sounding fainter and fainter, till it was heard no more.

I was no other time than this during the noises at Epworth, and do not now remember any more circumstances than these.—*See Southey's Life of Wesley.*

LXIV.

Dr. Pitcairne's Dream.

Doctor Pitcairne is said never to have related this story without some emotion of spirit. His friend Mr. Lindesey upon reading with the doctor, when very young, the known story of the two platonic philosophers who promised to one another that whoever died first should return a visit to his surviving companion, entered into the same engagement with him. Some years after, Pitcairne at his father's house in Fife dreamed one morning that Lindesey, who was then at Paris, came to him and told him that he was not dead as was commonly reported, but still alive, and living in a very pleasant place, to which he could not as yet carry him. By the next post news came of Lindesey's death, which happened very suddenly on the morning of the dream.—*From H. Welby.*

LXV.

Apparition of Ficinus to Michael Mercato.
RELATED BY BARONIUS.

Ficinus and Mercato, after a long discourse on the nature of the soul, had agreed that whoever of the two should die first, should if possible appear to his surviving friend, and inform him of his condition in the other world.

A short time afterwards, says Baronius*, it happened

---

* Baronii Annales.—This story was told to Baronius by the grandson of Mercato, who was prothonotary of the Church, and a man of the greatest probity as well as of general knowledge.

that while Michael Mercarto the elder was studying philosophy, early one morning he suddenly heard the noise of a horse galloping in the street, which stopped at his door, when the voice of his friend Ficinus was heard exclaiming—"O Michael! O Michael! those things are true." Astonished at his address, Mercato rose and looked out of the window, where he saw the back of his friend, who was dressed in white, and galloping away on a white horse. He called after him, and followed him with his eyes till the appearance vanished. Upon inquiry he learned that Ficinus had died at Florence at the very time when the vision was presented to Mercato, at a considerable distance.
—*From H. Welby.*

LXVI.

Apparitions seen at Portnedown Bridge after the Irish Massacre;

BEING COPIES OF THE EVIDENCE PRODUCED BY SIR JOHN TEMPLE.

1. James Shaw, of Market Hill in the County of Armagh, innkeeper, deposeth, that many of the Irish rebels in the time of this deponent's restraint, and while he was staying among them, told him very often, and it was a common report, that all those who lived about the Bridge of Portnedown were so affrighted with the cries and noise made there of some spirits or visions demanding revenge, as that they durst not stay, but fled away thence affrighted to Market Hill, saying they durst not return thither for fear of those cries and spirits, but took grounds and made creachs, in or near the parish of Mulabrac.

Jurat, August 14, 1642.

2. Joan, the relict of Gabriel Constable, late of Durmant, in the County of Armagh, gent., deposeth and

saith, that she often heard the rebels, Owen O'Farren, Patrick O'Connellan, and divers others of the rebels at Durmant, earnestly say, protest, and tell one another, that the blood of some of those that were knocked on the head and afterwards drowned at Portnedown Bridge still remained on the bridge, and would not be washed away; and that often there appeared visions or apparitions, sometimes of men, sometimes of women, breast-high above the water, at or near Portnedown, which did most extremely and fearfully screech and cry out for vengeance against the Irish that had murdered their bodies there: and that their cries and screeches did so terrify the Irish thereabouts, that none durst stay or live longer there, but fled and removed farther into the country; that this was common report amongst the rebels there, and that it passed for a truth amongst them, for any thing she could ever observe to the contrary,

Jurat, Jannary 1, 1643.

3. Katherine, the relict of William Coke, late of the County of Armagh, carpenter, sworn and examined, saith that, about the twentieth of December, 1641, a great number of rebels in that county did most barbarously drown at that time one hundred and eighty Protestants, men, women, and children, in that river, at the Bridge of Portnedown; and that, about nine days afterwards, she saw a vision or spirit in the shape of a man as she apprehended, standing in that river, in the place of the drowning, bolt upright, heart high, with hands lifted up, where it remained until the latter end of Lent next following; about which time some of the English army marching in those parts, whereof her husband was one (as he and they confidently affirmed to the deponent), saw that same spirit or vision standing upright in the posture aforementioned; but after that time the said spirit or vision vanished,

and appeared no more that she knoweth. And she heard, but saw not, that there were other visions and apparitions, and much screeching and strange noises heard in that river at times afterwards.

Jurat, February 24, 1643.

4. Elizabeth, the wife of Captain Rice Price, of Armagh, deposeth and saith that she and other women, whose husbands were murderers, hearing of divers apparitions and visions that were seen near Portnedown Bridge, since the drowning of her children and the rest of the Protestants there, went unto the aforesaid bridge about twilight in the evening; then there appeared unto them, upon a sudden, a vision or spirit in the shape of a woman standing waist high upright in the water, naked, with elevated and closed hands, her hair hanging down very white, her eyes seeming to twinkle, and her skin as white as snow; which spirit seemed to stand straight up in the water, and often repeated the words, " Revenge, Revenge, Revenge !" whereat this deponent and the rest, being put into a strong amazement, and affrighted, walked from the place.

Jurat, January 29, 1642.

5. Arthur Azlum, of Clowargher, in the County of Cavan, esquire, deposeth that he was credibly informed by some that were present there, that there were thirty women and young children, and seven men flung into the river of Belturbet; and when some of them offered to swim for their lives, they were by the rebels followed in carts, and knocked upon the head with poles. The same day they hanged two women at Turbet; and this deponent doth verily believe that Rutmore O'Reby, the then sheriff, had a hand in commanding the murder of those said persons; for that he saw him write two notes, which he sent to Turbet by Bryan O'Reby, upon whose coming their murders were com-

mitted: and those persons who were present also affirmed that the bodies of those thirty persons drowned did not appear on the water till about six weeks past; as the said Reby came to the town all the bodies came floating up to the very bridge; and those persons were all formerly retained in the town by his protection, when the rest of their neighbours in town went away.
—*History of the Irish Rebellion, by Sir John Temple.*

LXVII.

Apparition of Major Blomberg to the Governor of Dominica.

Early in the American war, Major Blomberg, the father of Dr. Blomberg, was expected to join his regiment, which was at the time on service in the Island of Dominica. His period of absence had expired, and his brother officers eagerly anticipating his return, as vessel after vessel arrived from England without conveying the-looked-for passenger declared one to another, "well, at all events, he must come in the next." His presence in the island now became indispensible; and the governor, impatient of so long an absence, was on the point of writing a remonstrance on the subject to the authorities in England, when, as he was sitting at night in his study with his secretary, and remarking on the conduct of the absentee with no very favourable or lenient expressions, a step was heard to ascend the stairs, and walk along the passage without. "Who can it be?" exclaimed the governor, "intruding at so late an hour." "It is Blomberg's step," replied the secretary. "The very man himself," said the governor; for, as he spoke, the door opened, and Major Blomberg stood before them. The major advanced towards the table at which the gentlemen were sitting, and flung himself into a chair opposite the governor. There was something hurried in his manner; a forgetfulness of all the ordinary forms of greeting; and abruptly saying: " I must converse with you alone:" he gave a sign for the secretary to retreat. The sign was obeyed. There was an air of conscious superiority about the manner of the visitor that admitted no dispute. " On your return to England," he continued, as soon as the apartment was cleared of the objectionable witness, " on your return to England you will go to a farm house, near the village of ———, in Dorsetshire; you will there find two children; they are mine; the offspring and the orphans of my secret marriage. Be a guardian to those parentless infants. To prove their legitimacy, and their consequent right to my property, you must demand of the woman, with whom they are placed at nurse, the red morocco case which was committed to her charge. Open it; it contains the necessary papers. Adieu! you will see me no more." Major Blomberg instantly withdrew. The governor of Dominica, surprised at the commission, at the abrupt entrance, and the abrupt departure, rang the bell to desire some of his household to follow the major and request his return. None had seen him enter: none had witnessed his exit. It was strange! it was passing strange! There soon after arrived intelligence that Major Blomberg had embarked on board a vessel for Dominica, which had been dismasted in a storm at sea and was supposed to have subsequently sunk about the time in which the figure had appeared to the governor and his secretary, as she was never more heard of.

All that Major Blomberg had communicated was carefully stamped in the memory of his friend. On his return to England, which occurred in a few months after the apparition above described had been seen by the governor, he immediately hastened to the village in Dorsetshire, and to the house in which the children were resident.

He found them; he asked for the case; it was immediately surrendered. The legitimacy and the claims of the orphans of Blomberg were established, and they were admitted to the enjoyment of their rights without any controversy or dispute.

This tale was related to the late Queen Charlotte, and so deeply interested her, that she immediately adopted the son as the object of her peculiar care and favour. He was brought to Windsor, and educated with her eldest son, afterwards George IV., of whom he was through life the favourite, the companion, and the friend.—*From H. Welby.*

LXVIII.

The Abbey Vault.

In convivial circles, the weakness of mankind too frequently becomes the idle and sportive jest of the passing hour. Among hypochondriacs the same subject often feeds the distempered imagination with airy nothings, until the soul becomes frozen and horrified at the bare narration of the most simple and accountable facts. Belonging to both classes is the celebrated relation of a frolicsome visit to Westminster Abbey, which is said to have arisen at a jovial party, where mirth had reigned so long that it was thought prudent to shift the scene to the grave and serious.

The purpose of this story is evidently to subvert the whole theory of apparitions and a future state; but we cannot for a moment be so weak as to imagine it feasible that this question, which has been disputed by the wisest men in all ages, should be settled by a circle of topers, whose wits were quickened by the potent influences of wine and mirth.

The narrative is given by Sinclair, in his *Invisible World*, and we quote it in his own words :—

"Five or six gentlemen, who had dined together at a tavern were drawn to visit the Royal Vault in King Henry's Chapel in Westminster Abbey. As they looked down the steep descent, by which so many monarchs had been carried to their last resting place one cried, 'tis hellish dark ;—another stooped his nostrils, and exclaimed against the noisome vapour that ascended from it. All had their different sayings, but as it is natural for such spectacles to excite some moral reflections even in the most gay and giddy, they all returned with countenances more serious than those with which they had entered.

"Having agreed, however, to pass the evening together, they all returned to the place where they had dined, and the conversation turning on a future state and apparitions, one among them, who was an infidel in these matters especially as to spirits becoming visible, took upon himself to rally the others, who seemed rather inclined to the contrary opinion.

"At length, to end the contest, they proposed him a wager of twenty guineas, that, great hero as he pretended or really imagined himself to be, he had not the courage enough to go alone, at midnight, into the vault of Henry the Seventh's chapel. This he readily accepted, and was quite elated with the prospect of success.

"The money on both sides was deposited in the hands of the landlord of the house ; and one of the vergers of the Abbey was sent for, whom they engaged to attend the adventurous gentleman to the gate of the cathedral, then to shut him in and wait his return.

"Every thing being thus settled, the clock no sooner struck twelve than they all set out together ; those who laid the wager being resolved not to be imposed upon by his tampering with the verger. Another scruple arose; which was, that though they saw him enter the chapel, how should they be convinced that he went as far as the vault; but he instantly removed it by pulling out a penknife he had in his pocket:— 'This,' said he, 'will I stick into the earth and leave there, and if you do not find it in the inside of the vault, I will own the wager lost.'

"These words left them nothing to suspect, and they agreed to wait for him at the door, beginning now to believe he had no less resolution than he had pretended.

"Every step he took was echoed by the hollow ground, and though it was not altogether dark, the verger having left a lamp burning just before the door that led to the chapel, yet the faint glimmering it gave rather added to, than diminished, the solemnity of the scene.

"At length, sometimes groping his way and sometimes directed by the distant lamp, he reached the entrance of the vault :—his inward tremor increased, yet determined not to be overpowered by it he descended, and having reached the last stair, stooped forward, and stuck his penknife into the earth; but as he was rising to turn back and leave the vault, he felt something, as he thought, suddenly catch hold of him and pluck him forward; he lost in an instant everything that could support him, and fell into a swoon, with his head in the vault, and part of his body on the stairs.

"His friends waited patiently till one o'clock, when not making his appearance, they debated among themselves what they should do in the affair; the verger they found, though accustomed to the place, did not care to go alone; therefore they resolved to accompany him, and accordingly, preceded by a torch, which a footman belonging to one of the company had with him, they went into the abbey, calling loudly for him as they proceeded.

"No answer, however, being returned, they moved on till they came to the stairs of the vault, where looking down they saw the condition he was in;— they immediately ran to him, rubbed his temples, and did every thing they could think of to restore him, but all in vain, till they got out of the abbey, when the fresh air recovered him.

"After two or three deep groans, he cried, 'Heaven help me; Lord have mercy upon me,' which surprised his friends; but imagining he was not yet perfectly come to his senses, they forbore saying any thing to him til. they had got him into a tavern, where, having placed him in a chair by the fire side, they began to enquire into his situation, on which he acquainted them with the apprehensions he was seized with immediately after he had left them, and that having stuck his penknife into the floor of the vault, according to his agreement, he was about to return with all possible haste when something plucked him forward into the vault; but he added that he had neither seen nor heard any thing but that his reason might easily account for, and should have returned with the same sentiments he went, had not this unseen hand convinced him of the injustice of his unbelief.

One of the company now saw the penknife sticking through the fore lappet of his coat, on which presently conjecturing the truth, and finding how deeply affected his friend was by his mistake, as indeed were all the rest, not doubting but his return had been impeded by a supernatural hand, he plucked out the penknife before them all, and said, 'here is the mystery discovered; in the attitude of stooping to stick this into the ground, I happened, as you see, to pass through the coat, and on your attempting to rise, the terror you were in magnified this little obstruction into an imaginary impossibility of withdrawing yourself.'

"His friends now ridiculed his credulity, but the singularity of this accident did not shake his faith."

[The foregoing story (from Welby) is worth including in such a collection as the present, although its individual merit is small. The obvious moral of it is that if you force yourself into the midst of unnatural circumstances, and thus deliberately bring a great and unnecesssary pressure to bear upon your nerves, they may refuse to be so trifled with and let you down. And serve you right.—ED.]

LXIX.

The Disobedient Son.

About the year 1796, a young gentleman of good birth and fortune, having a great inclination to see the world, resolved to go into the army. His father was dead, and had left him a good estate, besides his mother's jointure, which at her death would consequently fall to him.

His mother earnestly intreated him not to go into the army, but persuaded him rather to travel, by which means the calamities and hazards of war might be avoided. He however slighted her entreaties, and at length mortgaged part of his estate to purchase a company in the first regiment of guards, which he effected.

The night before he signed the agreement for the company, being in bed and fast asleep, he saw in a dream his father approach him in his gown, and with a great fur cap on, such as he was accustomed to wear; calling him by his name, he said, what is the reason that you will not listen to the entreaties of your mother to relinquish all ideas of the army. I assure you, that if you resolve to take this commission, you will not enjoy it three years.

He seemed to slight the admonition, and said it was too late to retract. "Too late! too late!" said the old man, repeating those words; "then go on, and repent too late." He was not much affected with this apparition when he waked and found it was but a dream; but bought the commission.

A few days afterwards the father appeared to his mother in a dream as to her son, and noticing his obstinacy, added, "Young heads are wilful; Robert will go into the army; but tell him from me he shall never come back."

These notices were of no avail with the son; two battalions of his regiment went into the field that summer, of which his company was one, and he was ordered into Flanders.

He acquitted himself bravely in several warm actions. One day, in the third year of his service, the army being drawn out in order of battle, the General had received advice that the enemy were about to attack them. As he stood at the head of his company he was suddenly seized with a cold shivering fit, which was so violent, as to be noticed by some officers who were near him. It continued about a quarter of an hour, and the enemy did come on as was expected; but the fight began upon the left, at a good distance from them, so that the whole left wing was engaged before they began.

While this lasted, the lieutenant called to him "captain, how are you? I hope your shivering fit is over." "No," said the captain, "it is not over, but it is somewhat better." "It will be all right presently," said the lieutenant.

"Ay, so it will," said the capain: "I am very easy, I know what it was now." He then called the lieutenant, to whom he said, "I know now what ailed me, I am very easy, I have seen my father; I shall be killed the first volley; let my mother know I told you this."

In a few minutes after this, a body of the enemy advanced, and the first volley the regiment received was the fire of five platoons of grenadiers, by which the captain and several other officers, besides private men, were killed, and the whole brigade was soon after thrown into confusion; though, being supported by some regiments of the second line, they rallied again soon after. The captain's body was presently recovered; but he was dead, having received a shot in the face.—*From H. Welby.*

LXX.

The Yatton Demoniac.

In the year 1788 considerable interest was excited throughout the County of Somerset by the extraordinary case of one George Lukins, who was said to have been possessed of evil spirits for nearly eighteen years. The subject was at first treated as an impostor, but much controversy and sceptical dispute arising, several illiberal ex-parte statements appeared in the *Bristol Gazette* and *Bath Chronicle.* At length the evidence and circumstances were collected by the Rev. Joseph Easterbrook, the Vicar of Temple Church, Bristol, of which the following narrative is the substance:—

"On Saturday, May 31st, 1788, Mrs. Sarah Baber called on me, acquainting me that she had just returned from a visit to Yatton, in the County of Somerset, where she had found a poor man afflicted with an extraordinary malady. She said his name was George Lukins; that he had fits daily during her stay at Yatton, in which he sang and screamed in various sounds, some of which did not resemble the modifications of a human voice; that he cursed and swore in a most tremendous manner while in his fits, and declared that doctors could do him no service. She likewise said that she could take upon her to affirm that he had been subject to fits of a very uncommon nature for the last eighteen years, for the cure of which he had been placed for a considerable time under the care of Mr. Smith, an eminent surgeon of Wrington, who administered all the assistance in his power, without effect. Many other medical gentlemen, she said, had in like manner tried to help him, but in vain. Most of the people about Yatton then conceived him to be bewitched; but latterly he had himself declared that he was possessed of seven devils, and that nothing would avail but the united prayers of seven clergymen, who could ask deliverance for him in faith; but seven could not be procured in that neighbourhood to meet his ideas, and try the experiment: she therefore earnestly requested me to go to Yatton to see him.

* * * * * * *

"I consented that George Lukins should be brought to me; little expecting that an attention to his pitiable case would have produced such a torrent of opposition and illiberal abuse upon the parties concerned in his relief.

"In compliance with my promise to Mrs. Baber, I applied to such of the clergy of the established church as I conceived to be most cordial in co-operating in benevolent acts, namely, to the Rev. Mr. Symes, rector of St. Werburgh's; the Rev. Dr. Robins, precentor of the Cathedral; and the Rev. Mr. Brown, rector of Portishead; requesting that these gentlemen would with me attend a meeting for prayer in behalf of this object of commiseration; but though they acknowledged it as their opinion that his was a supernatural affliction, I could not prevail upon them to join with me in this attempt to relieve him. And as these gentlemen rejected my application, it appeared to me that there was no rational ground of hope for more success with those of my brethren who were less disposed to admit the doctrine of the influence of good and evil spirits.

The more frequently I saw and heard of the misery which George Lukins experienced, the more I pitied him, and being unwilling to dismiss him from Bristol till some effort had been made for his recovery, I next desired certain persons in connection with the Rev. Mr. Wesley to attend a prayer meeting on his account, to which request they readily acceded. Accordingly a meeting was appointed for Friday morning the 13th of June, at eleven o'clock. And as the most horrible noises usually proceeded from him in his fits, it was suggested that the vestry-room of Temple Church, which is bounded by the churchyard, was the most retired place that could be found in Temple parish; and for that reason that situation was preferred to any other, it being our design to conduct this business with as much secrecy as possible. But we soon found that our design in this respect was rendered abortive; for on Wednesday evening, the 11th of June, there was published in the *Bristol Gazette*, an ingenious letter from the *Bath Chronicle*, from which the following is an extract:

"About eighteen years ago George Lukins, going about the neighbourhood with other young fellows, acting Christmas plays or mummeries, suddenly fell down senseless, and was with great difficulty recovered. When he came to himself, the account that he gave was, that he seemed at the moment of his fall to have received a violent blow from the hand of some person who, as he thought, was allowed thus to punish him for acting a part in the play. From that moment he has been subject, at uncertain and different periods, to fits of a most singular and dreadful nature. The first symptom is a powerful agitation of the right hand, to which succeed terrible distortions of the countenance. The influence of the fit has then commenced. He declares in a roaring voice that he is the devil, who with many horrid execrations summons about him certain persons devoted to his will, and commands them to torture this unhappy patient with all the diobolical means in their power. The supposed demon then directs his servants to sing. Accordingly the patient sings in a different voice a jovial hunting song, which, having received the approbation of the foul fiend, is succeeded by a song in a female voice, very delicately expressed, and this is followed, at the particular injunction of the demon, by a pastoral song in the form of a dialogue, sung by, and in the real character of, the patient himself. After a pause, and more violent distortions, he again personates the demon, and sings in a hoarse, frightful voice, another hunting song. But in all these songs, whenever any expression of goodness, benevolence, or innocence, occurs in the original, it is regularly changed to another of its opposite meaning; neither can the patient bear to hear any good words whatever, nor any expression relating to the church, during the influence of his fit, but is exasperated by them into blasphemy and outrage. Neither can he speak or write any expressions of this tendency whilst the subsequent weakness of his fits is upon him, but is driven to madness by their mention. Having performed the songs, he continues to personate the demon, and derides the attempts which the patient has been making to get out of his power, that he will persecute and torment him more and more to the end of his life, and that all the efforts of parsons and physicians shall prove fruitless. An *inverted Te Deum* is then sung in the alternate voices of a man and woman, who with much profaneness thank the demon for having given them power over the patient, which they will continue to exercise as long as he lives. The demon then concludes the ceremony by declaring his unalterable resolution to punish him for ever; and after barking fiercely, and interspersing many assertions of his own diabolical dignity, the fit subsides into the same strong agitation of the hand that introduced it, and the patient recovers from its influence, utterly weakened and exhausted. At certain periods of the fit, he is so violent, that an assistant is always obliged to be at hand to restrain him from committing some injury on himself, though to the spectators he is perfectly harmless. He understands all that is said and done during his fits, and will even reply sometimes to questions asked him. He is under the influence of these paroxysms generally near an hour, during which time his eyes are fast closed. Sometimes he fancies himself changed into the form of an animal, when he assumes all the motions and sounds that are peculiar to it. From the execrations he utters it may be presumed that he is or was of an abandoned and profligate character, but the reverse is the truth; he was ever of a remarkably innocent and inoffensive disposition. Every method that the variety of persons who have come to see him have suggested, every effort of some very ingenious gentlemen of the faculty who applied their serious attention to his case, has been long ago and recently exerted without success; and some years ago he was sent to St. George's Hospital, where he remained about twenty weeks, and was pronounced incurable. The emaciated and exhausted figure that he presents, the number of years that he has been subject to this malady, and the prospect of want and distress that lies before him, through being thus disabled from following his business, all preclude the suspicion of imposture. His life is become a series of intense anxieties."

WRINGTON, Jan. 5, 1788.   W. R. W.

This letter attracted the notice of the citizens ; and it having been made known that a prayer meeting on Friday morning was to be held in the vestry-room of Temple Church, for the man who was the subject of that letter, a considerable number of people planted themselves upon the walls of the vestry-room and heard part of the prayers, the singings, the conversation, and the wonderful sounds which proceeded from George Lukins, and carried some account of these circumstances to a printer, who instantly dispatched papers upon the subject through the streets of Bristol and its vicinage. Similar papers were shortly carried through the streets of Bath and London, and through many other parts of the country; so that contrary to our design the affair was in this manner brought before the public.

On Friday morning, June 13, fourteen gentlemen, accompanied by George Lukins, met at the vestry-room at Temple Church at eleven o'clock, to pray for the relief of this afflicted man, when the following ceremony took place :—

1. They began singing an hymn, on which the man was immediately thrown into strange agitations (very different from his usual seizures), his face was variously distorted, and his whole body strongly convulsed. His right hand and arm then began to shake with violence, and after some violent throes, he spake in a deep, hoarse, hollow voice, *personating an invisible agent*, calling the man to an account, and upbraiding him as a fool for bringing that silly company together : said it was to no purpose, and swore "by his infernal den" that he would never quit his hold of him, but would torment him a thousand times worse for making this vain attempt.

2. He then began to sing in his usual manner (*still personating some invisible agent*), blaspheming, boasted of his power, and vowed eternal vengeance on the

miserable object, and on those present for daring to oppose him; and commanded his " faithful and obedient servants" to appear and take their stations.

3. He then spoke in a female voice, expressive of scorn and derision, and demanded to know why the fool had brought such a company there? And swore " by the devil" that he would not quit his hold of him, and bid defiance to, and cursed all, who should attempt to rescue the miserable object from him. He then sung, in the same female voice, a love song, at the conclusion of which he was violently tortured, and repeated most horrid imprecations.

4. Another invisible agent came forth, assuming a different voice, but his manner was much the same as the preceding one. A kind of dialogue was then sung in a hoarse and soft voice alternately, at the conclusion of which, as before, the man was thrown into violent agonies, and blasphemed in a manner too dreadful to be expressed.

5. He then personated, and said, " I am the great devil;" and after much boasting of his power, and bidding defiance to all his opposers, sung a kind of hunting song, at the conclusion of which he was most violently tortured, so that it was with difficulty that two strong men could hold him (though he is but a small man, and very weak in constitution); sometimes he would set up a hideous laugh, at other times bark in a manner indescribably horrid.

6. After this he summoned all the infernals to appear, and drive the company away. And while the ministers were engaged in fervent prayer, he sung a *Te Deum* to the devil in different voices, saying, " We praise thee, O devil; we acknowledge thee to be the supreme governor, &c. &c."

7. When the noise was so great as to obstruct the company proceeding in prayer, they sang together an hymn suitable to the occasion. Whilst they were in

prayer, the voice which personated the great devil bid defiance, cursing and vowing dreadful vengeance on all present. One in the company commanded him in the name of the great Jehovah to declare his name? To which he replied, "I am the devil." The same person then charged him in the name of Jehovah to declare why he tormented the man? To which he made answer, "That I may shew my power amongst men."

8. The poor man still remained in great agonies and torture, and prayer was continued for his deliverance. A clergyman present desired him to endeavour to speak the name of "Jesus," and several times repeated it to him, at all of which he replied "devil." During this attempt a small faint voice was heard saying, "Why don't you adjure?" On which the clergyman commanded, in the name of Jesus, and in the name of the Father, the Son, and the Holy Ghost, I command thee, evil spirit, to depart from this man; which he repeated several times, when a voice was heard to say, "Must I give up my power?" and this was followed by dreadful howlings. Soon after another voice, as with astonishment, said, "Our master has deceived us." The clergyman still continuing to repeat the adjuration, a voice was heard to say, "Where shall we go?" and the reply was, "To hell, thine own infernal den, and return no more to torment this man." On this the man's agitations and distortions were stronger than ever, attended with the most dreadful howlings that can be conceived. But as soon as this conflict was over, he said, in his own natural voice, "Blessed Jesus!" became quite serene, immediately praised God for his deliverance, and, kneeling down, said the Lord's Prayer, and returned his most devout thanks to all who were present.

The meeting broke up a little before one o'clock, having lasted nearly two hours, and the man went away entirely delivered, and has had no return of the disorder since.

(*Mr. Easterbrook then proceeds to give a variety of well-authenticated documents substantiating the whole of the above circumstantial narrative.*)

Lukins was visited by several persons of distinction, all of whom bore testimony to the foregoing circumstances. The extravagance of his language, and his blasphemous ravings were appalling.

Several pamphlets were published on the subject, but the narrative of Mr. Easterbrook is in every respect supported by authorities of unquestionable veracity, and recommended by its perspicuous and intelligible details.

LXX.

Sword Signs.

A young nobleman, of high hopes and fortune, chanced to lose his way in the town which he inhabited, the capital of a German province; he accidentally involved himself among the narrow winding streets of a suburb, inhabited by the lowest order of the people, and an approaching thunder shower determined him to ask a short refuge in the most decent habitation that was near him. He knocked at the door, which was opened by a tall man, of a grisly and ferocious aspect, and sordid dress. The stranger was readily ushered to a chamber, where swords, scourges, and machines, which seemed to be implements of torture, were suspended on the wall. One of these swords dropped from its scabbard, as the nobleman, after a moment's hesitation, crossed the threshold. His host immediately stared at him with such marked expression, that the young man could not help demanding his name and business, and the meaning of his looking at him so fixedly. "I am," answered the man, "the public executioner of this city; and the incident you have observed is a sure augury that I shall, in discharge of my duty, one day cut off your head with the weapon which has just now spontaneously unsheathed itself." The nobleman lost no time in leaving his place of refuge; but engaging in some plots of the period, was very shortly after decapitated by that very man and instrument.

Lord Lovat is said, by the author of letters from Scotland, to have affirmed that a number of swords that hung up in the hall of the mansion-house, leaped of themselves out of the scabbard at the instant he was born. This story passed current among his clan, and like that of the story just quoted, proved an unfortunate omen.—*From H. Welby.*

LXXI.

Apparition to Lady Fanshaw.

"Supernatural intimation of approaching fate," says Sir Walter Scott, "are not, I believe, confined to highland families. Howel mentions having seen at a lapidary's in 1632, a monumental stone prepared for four persons of the name of Oxenham, before the death of each of whom, the inscription stated, a white bird to have appeared and fluttered round the bed while the patient was in the last agony." (*Familiar Letters*, Edit. 1726, p. 247.) Glanville mentions one family, the members of which received this solemn sign by music, the sound of which floated from the family residence and seemed to die in a neighbouring wood; another, that of Captain Wood of Bampton, to whom the signal was given by knocking.

But the most remarkable instance of presentiment of death occurs in the MS. memoirs of Lady Fanshaw, so exemplary for her conjugal affection. Her husband,

Sir Richard, and she, chanced, during their abode in Ireland, to visit a friend, the head of a sept, who resided in his ancient baronial castle surrounded with a moat. At midnight she was awakened by a ghastly and supernatural scream, and looking out of bed, beheld by the moonlight a female face and part of the form hovering at the window. The distance from the ground, as well as the circumstance of the moat, excluded the possibility that what she beheld was of this world. The face was that of a young and rather handsome woman, but pale, and the hair, which was of a reddish colour, loose and dishevelled. The dress, which Lady Fanshaw's terror did not prevent her remarking accurately, was that of the ancient Irish. This apparition continued to exhibit itself for some time, and then vanished with two shrieks similar to the one which had first excited Lady Fanshaw's attention. In the morning, with infinite terror, she communicated to her host what she had witnessed, and found him prepared not only to credit but to account for the apparition. "A near relative of my family," said he, "expired last night in the castle. We disguised our certain expectation of the event from you, lest it should throw a cloud over the cheerful reception which was your due. Now, before such an event happens in this family and castle, the female spectre which you have seen is always visible. She is believed to be the spirit of a woman of inferior rank, whom one of my ancestors degraded himself by marrying, and whom afterwards, to expiate the dishonour done to his family, he caused to be drowned in the castle moat."—*From H. Welby.*

LXXII.

Apparition to Philip Melancthon.

The name of Melancthon, as the intimate friend and distinguished coadjutor of Martin Luther in the glorious work of the Reformation, must be dear to every enlightened Protestant; and his labours as a reformer and scholar rank him among the brightest ornaments of religion and literature.

The merits of this good and great man have been set forth in a work of considerable worth, by F. A. Cox, A.M. In the course of his interesting biographical narrative, he gives the following relation of an incident which occurred at the second Diet of Spires, convened in the year 1529.

"A curious circumstance," says Mr. Cox, " occurred at this convocation, which Melancthon relates in his commentary on the angelic appearance mentioned in the tenth chapter of Daniel, and which he affirms was but one out of many of a similar nature which he could fully authenticate. The case was briefly this: Simon Grynæus, a very intimate friend of his, and at this period a Greek professor in the University of Heidelberg, who combined profound erudition with zealous piety, came over unexpectedly to see him at Spires. He ventured to encounter Faber, the Catholic Bishop of Vienna, and to urge him closely on some topics in discussion between the Catholics and the Reformers. The bishop, who was plausible but shallow, fearful of engaging in argument, but cruelly ready to use the sword, pretended that private business with the king required his attention at that moment, but that he felt extremely desirous of the friendship of Grynæus and of another opportunity of discussing the controverted points. No dissembler himself, Grynæus returned to his friends without suspicion of the wily courtier's intentions; nor could any of them have known it but for what Melancthon deemed a supernatural interference. They were just sitting down to supper, and Grynæus had related part of the conversation between himself and the bishop, when Melancthon was suddenly called out of the room to an old man whom he had never seen nor heard of, or could afterwards discover; he was characterized by a most observable peculiarity of manner and dress, and said, that persons by the king's authority would soon arrive to seize Grynæus and put him in prison, Faber having influenced him to this persecuting measure. He enjoined that instant means should be adopted to secure the departure of Grynæus to a place of safety, and urged that there should not be a moment's delay. Upon communicating this information he immediately withdrew. Melancthon and his friends instantly bestirred themselves, and saw him safe across the Rhine. It afterwards appeared that the king's messengers were in the house almost as soon as they had left it, but Grynæus was out of the reach of danger; a danger, as Melancthon remarks, easily imagined by those who were acquainted with Faber's cruelty. He says, they were all of opinion that this was a divine interposition, so singular was the appearance of the old man, and so rapid the movements of the instruments of vengeance, from whose power Grynæus scarcely escaped."

Such is the narrative which the reader is put in possession of without note or comment. Some will think it supernatural, others will exclaim, *Credat Judæus Apella*, and many perhaps will consider it, though remarkable, capable of explanation, without allowing it to have been miraculous. The use Melancthon makes of the statement must be admitted to be worthy of his exalted piety; " Let us," says he, " be grateful to God who sends his angels to be our protectors, and let us with increased tranquility of mind, fulfil the duties assigned us."—*Cox's Life of Melancthon.*

It should be added that no subsequent discovery was made of the identity of the old man, who thus preserved the Reformer and his fellow-labourers; nor did circumstances in the slightest degree tend to invalidate the above conclusion.

LXXIII.

Apparition of Mrs. Bargrave to Mrs. Veal, at Canterbury.

The credit of the following narrative has been much depreciated by those who have erroneously considered it as a mere fable prefixed to Drelincourt's Treatise on Death,* owing to the circumstance of that book being preferred by Mrs. Veal, one of the parties. The publisher, to promote the sale of Drelincourt's work, printed an incorrect and garbled edition of this narrative, with irreconcileable inconsistencies, which has made the affair pass as a mere stratagem of trade. These imperfections will be evident on a comparison of the following original statement with that prefixed to Drelincourt's work. Thus, it is illiberal and unjust

---

* The motives of the author in this work are unquestionably those of a sincere Christian who has the interest of his fellow-creatures at heart. We now see it in the cottages of the labouring poor; but its influence is neither restrained to the noble, the opulent, or the needy; since by placing DEATH, or a *temporary cessation or suspension of existence*, in a proper point of view, it encourages and supports man in his severest trials. The character and eccentricities of the late Duke of Norfolk are well-known. His life was one round of gaiety and pleasurable licence, by which means he shortened his career and thus deprived mankind of the benefit of his useful talents. He died in St. James's Square, December, 1815; but remorse overtook him ere he left his darling world; and it is a well-authenticated fact, that only a few hours previous to his death, he requested that his servant might be despatched to his booksellers in Pall Mall to procure a copy of Drelincourt's Treatise on Death.

to decide on its credibility, merely because it has been printed with interested motives.*

Mrs. Margaret Veal and Mrs. Mary Bargrave (before her marriage called Lodowick) had contracted an affectionate intimacy in their younger years, at which time the father of one was customer, and that of the other minister of Dover.

This friendship, being true and faithful, was of use to Mrs Veal in one particular, for when her father by his extravagance had reduced his family, she found a seasonable relief from it in her necessity.

Besides this, Mrs. Bargrave was instrumental to her better fortune, for by her interest with a gentleman, one Mr. Boyce, her relation, Mrs. Veal's brother, was recommended to Archbishop Tillotson, by whom he was introduced to Queen Mary; and her Majesty, for his relation by the mother to the Hyde family, gave him the post of comptroller of the customs at Dover, which place he enjoyed to his death.

Time and change of circumstances on both sides had interrupted their friendship for some years; and Mrs. Bargrave being half a year in London, and afterwards settling at Canterbury, had neither seen nor heard from Mrs. Veal for a year and a half.

Mrs. Veal, some time before her death, received the addresses of a gentleman of the army, Major-General Sibourg (a natural son of the Duke of Scomberg), killed in the battle of Mons, and was engaged so far that her brother's not consenting to it is believed to have brought on those fits which were the cause of her death. She died at Dover, on Friday, in the month of September, 1705.

On Saturday, a little before twelve in the morning, Mrs. Bargrave being by herself in her own house at Canterbury, as she was taking her work in her hand

* This story was fabricated by De Foe, the ingenious author of *Robinson Crusoe.*

heard somebody knock at the door, and going out, to her astonishment, found it to be her old friend Mrs. Veal.

After expressing her surprise to see so great a stranger, she offered to salute her, which the other declined as it were, by hanging down her head and saying she was not well, on which Mrs. Bargrave desired her to walk in and sit down, which she did.

She was dressed in a silk dove-coloured riding gown, with French night-clothes; she appeared expressly the same as in her lifetime, and Mrs. Bargrave remembered to have heard her steps distinctly as she walked in.

Mrs. Bargrave began by asking where she was going in that dress? She answered she was going her journey, which the other concluded to be to Tunbridge, where she went every year for the benefit of her health; and said, you are going to the old place.

Mrs. Veal being never trusted abroad without attendance, on account of her fits, she asked how she came alone from her uncle's (meaning one Captain Watson in Canterbury, with whom she always lodged). She replied, she had given them the slip to see her. She then asked how she came to find her out in such a house, being reduced by her husband's extravagance to take up with a much smaller one than she had been accustomed to? To which the other made answer, she should find her out anywhere.

Mrs. Bargrave's husband was a barrister, who dissipated his money in excesses; and, as he was the worst of husbands, his wife had gone through a long course of ill-usage which was in a great measure unknown to the world. The use of this is to show one end of Mrs. Veal's visit, which seems to be to give her the relief they had often communicated to each other in the course of their friendship.

Mrs. Veal then began with Mrs. Bargrave by asking

her what was the matter with her, that she looked so ill? She replied, she had been thinking on her misfortunes. "I must now act the part you did to me under my misfortunes," said Mrs. Veal, " I must comfort you as you used to do me. I would have you by no means think that God Almighty is displeased with you; but that his intention is only to try and perfect you, for God does not afflict willingly, nor grieve the children of men. Besides, one moment's happiness of the other world will be more than a reward for all your sufferings, when as upon a hill you shall be above all the storms and dangers of a troublesome world." She proceeded in this manner with unusual vehemence, and striking her hand often on her knees, she cried, " you must believe it."

Mrs. Bargrave being so earnestly pressed, asked if she did not think she believed it? To which she replied, "no doubt you do; but you must believe it thoroughly."

Mrs. Bargrave, moved with the discourse, chanced by a turn of the chair to throw down from a shelf Drelincourt's Treatise of the Christian Defence against the Fears of Death, which they had so often read together. "I see," said Mrs. Veal, "you keep on your old way of reading, which, if you continue to do, will not fail to bring you to the happy condition he speaks of." The other mentioning Dr. Sherlock and some others on that subject, she said, "Drelincourt had the clearest notion of death," and that neither Dr. Sherlock nor any other on that subject are to be compared with him to understanding.* "Dear Mrs. Bargrave," said she, " if the eyes of our faith were but open as the eyes of our bodily senses, we should see innumerable angels about us for our guard; but our notions of

* This partial allusion to Drelincourt's book, has suggested the fabricated statements which have tended to invalidate the report of the narrative.

heaven are nothing like what it is, as Drelincourt says. Believe me, my dear friend, one moment of future happiness will be more than amends for all your suffering; nor yet can I believe that God will suffer you to spend all your days in this afflicted condition, but be assured your sufferings will leave you, or you them, in a short time, therefore be comforted under them, and be assured that God Almighty has a particular regard for you; that they are marks of his favour, and when they have done the business they were sent for, they will be removed. Mrs. Bargrave, saying how dark such a condition as hers was, that had no ease at present, Mrs. Veal assured her that the worst storms would be recompensed by the reception she would meet with in her Father's house, and quoted from Isaiah lvii., "that God would not content for ever, nor be always wrath, for the spirit should fall before him, and the souls which he had made." Mrs. Bargrave's husband dying about two years after that event, made her reflect on this part of her discourse as pointing to her deliverance.

In the course of conversation, Mrs. Veal entered upon the subject of friendship, and saying there was now little friendship in the world, the other replied, she hoped she herself had no reason to complain of every one being a friend to the rich; "I mean," said Mrs. Veal, "such friendship as you and I had to improve one another in what is useful. What did you think of my friendship, which I am sure has not at all repaid what I owe you? If you can forgive me, you are the best-hearted creature in the world." Mrs. Bargrave replied, "Do not mention such a thing, I have not had an uneasy thought about it; I can forgive you." "But what do you think of me?" urged Mrs. Veal. "I thought," replied Mrs. Bargrave, "that, like the rest of the world, prosperity had altered you." "I have been," said Mrs. Veal, "the most ungrateful wretch in the world," and then recounted many of the kindnesses she had received from her in her adversity, saying, she wished her brother knew how she was troubled about it. Being asked why she did not acquaint her brother of it, if it was such a trouble to her, she said she did not think of it till she came away.

To divert the discourse, Mrs. Bargrave asked her if she had seen a copy of some verses by Mr. Norris on Friendship, in a dialogue between Damon and Pythias. She said that she had seen other parts of his works, but not that. Mrs. Bargrave said, "I have them of my own writing," and the other desiring to see them, she went upstairs and brought them to her to read; but Mrs. Veal said, "it is your own scrawl, pray read it yourself, holding down my head will make it ache." Mrs. Bargrave then read them. There was a passage, "that friendship survives even death," which the other desired to have repeated, and said, "Mrs. Bargrave, those poets call heaven by a strange name, that is Elysium;" and then assured her, with particular emphasis, that their friendship should have no end in a future world.

Mrs. Veal asked her what was become of her husband, and being told he was abroad, said she wished he might not come home while she was there, for though he always treated her with respect, yet she had sometimes been frightened with his frolics.

At last, she said, she had great apprehensions of her fits, and, in case that she should die of them, desired Mrs. Bargrave to write to her brother and tell him she wished him to make certain arrangements for her, viz., give her best clothes to her uncle Watson's daughter, as also two small pieces of gold laid up in a cabinet in a purse; certain pieces to another person, two rings to Mr. Bretton, commissioner of the customs, a ring to Major-General Sibourg (of which Mrs. Bargrave sent him a letter), and further desired her to charge her brother not to take any interest of such a certain person whose plate she had in security.

As she often pressed this message, the other as often declined it; saying it would be disagreeable to trouble such a young gentleman as her brother was, with their conversation, that he would wonder at her impertinence, and that she had better do it herself. To this she replied that though it might seem impertinent now, she would see the reason of it hereafter; that her brother, though a sober man, and free from other vices, was yet vain, which she desired her to tell him; as also of their discourse, and to give her credit, she told her some secret of consequence between him and herself. Seeing her so importunate, Mrs. Bargrave fetched pen and ink, upon which the other said, "let it alone till I am gone, but be sure that you do it."

This discourse gave Mrs. Bargrave apprehension of her fits, so that she drew her chair close to her to prevent her from falling, during which she several times took hold of the sleeve of her gown, which Mrs. B. admired. Mrs. Veal said she had better take it for herself; the other answered you are going a journey, how will you do without it? She said, "as well as you, who have often taken off your gown from your back for me."

Towards the end of this discourse, she told Mrs. Bargrave that she had received a pension of ten pounds a year from Mr. Bretton, commissioner of the customs, who, she said, had been her great friend and benefactor.

She asked Mrs. Bargrave if she knew her sister, Mrs. Haslewood, who, she said, was coming to see her as she was taking her journey? The other asked again how she came to order matters so strangely? She said the house was ready for them. It proved that Mrs. Haslewood and her husband came to her house just as she was dying.

By this time she began to look disordered, and forgetful of what she had said, as if the fits were coming upon her. As this visit seemed in a great measure designed in gratitude to a friend, without giving any apprehensions, so the several parts of her discourse that related to Mr. Bretton's pension, her sister Haslewood, her gown, the quantity of gold in the purse, the rings and the plate in pawn, were designed as credentials to her brother and the world.

At last she asked Mrs. Bargrave, "where is Molly?" meaning her daughter; she replied, " she is at school, but if you wish to see her, I will send for her;" to which the other agreeing, she went to a neighbour's house to send for her, and at her return found Mrs. Veal without the door of the house, about to leave.

Mrs. Veal asked if she would not go with her? which the other took to be to Captain Watson's in Canterbury, and replied, "you know it is as much as my life is worth ; but I will see you to-morrow in the afternoon, after sermon. But why are you in such haste ?" Mrs. Veal then said, "in case you should not come, or should not see me, you will remember what I have said to you." She saw her walk off till she came to the turning of a corner, and then lost sight of her. It was market-day, and immediately after the clock had struck two.

Mrs. Bargrave at that instant told a neighbour of Mrs. Veal's visit, and of their conversation ; and a neighbour's servant, from a yard near her window, heard some of their discourse, and being asked by her mistress if Mr. Bargrave was talking with his wife? answered that they never talked of anything so good as what she overhead.

At night her husband came home in a frolicsome humour, and taking her by the hand, said, " Molly, you are hot, you want to be cooled," and so opening the door to the garden, put her out there, where she continued all night.

During Sunday she kept her bed, being in a high fever; and on Monday morning sent to Mrs. Watson's to enquire after Mrs. Veal, and as she could gain nothing satisfactory, went herself, but found as little. They were surprised at her enquiring for Mrs. Veal, and said they were sure by their not seeing her that she could not have been at Canterbury; but when Mrs. Bargrave persisted that she was, and described her dress, saying, she had on a scoured silk of such a colour, Mrs. Watson's daughter said that she must indeed have seen her, for none knew of the gown's being scoured but themselves, and that her mother assisted in making it up. In the meantime Captain Watson came in and told them that preparations was making in town for the funeral of some person of note in Dover. This quickly raised apprehensions in Mrs. Bargrave's mind, who went away directly to the undertaker's, and was no sooner informed it was for Mrs. Veal who was dead, than she fainted away in the street.

For a long time Mrs. Bargrave was visited by crowds of people who came to gratify their curiosity; consisting chiefly of the most sceptical and the most superstitious; and during her husband's lifetime she was exposed to his unsparing raillery.—*From H. Welby.*

LXXIV.

Mr. Booty and the Ship's Crew.

No circumstances connected with supernatural appearances has occasioned more altercation and controversy than the under-mentioned. The narrative certainly has an air of over-strained credulity; nevertheless, the affair is curious, and the coincidence very remarkable, especially as it was a *salvo* for Captain Barnaby. The former part of this narrative is transcribed from Captain Spink's journal, or log book, and the latter from the King's Bench Records for the time being.

"Tuesday, May the 12th, this day the wind S.S.W., and a little before four in the afternoon we anchored in Manser Road, where lay Captains Bristo, Brian, and Barnaby, all of them bound to Lucera to load. Wednesday, May the 13th, we weighed anchor, and in the afternoon I went on board of Captain Barnaby, and about two o'clock we sailed all of us for the island of Lucera, wind W.S.W. and bitter weather. Thursday the 14th, about two o'clock we saw the island, and all came to anchor in twelve fathoms of water, the wind W.S.W., and on the 15th May, we had an observation of Mr. Booty in the following manner:—Captains Bristo, Brian, and Barnaby went on shore shooting colues off Stromboli: when we had done we called our men together, about fourteen minutes after three in the afternoon, when, to our great surprise, we saw two men run by us with amazing swiftness. Captain Barnaby said, 'Lord bless me, the foremost man looks like my next-door neighbour, old Booty,' but he added that he did not know the one that was behind him. Booty was dressed in grey clothes, and the one behind him in black. We saw them run into the burning mountain in the midst of the flames, on which we heard a terrible noise, too horrible to be described. Captain Barnaby then desired us to look at our watches, pen the time down in our pocket-books and enter it in our journals, which we accordingly did.

"When we were laden, we all sailed for England, and arrived at Gravesend on the 6th of October, 1687. Mrs. Barnaby and Mrs. Brian came to congratulate us upon our safe arrival, and after some discourse,

Captain Barnaby's wife said, 'My dear, I have got some news to tell you, old Booty is dead.' He swore an oath and said, 'we all saw him run into hell.' Some time afterwards Mrs. Barnaby met with a lady of her acquaintance in London, and told her what her husband had seen concerning Mr. Booty. It came to Mrs. Booty's ears, she brought an action against Captain Barnaby, assessing £1000 damages. He gave bail, and it came to trial at the Court of King's Bench, where Mr. Booty's clothes were brought into court. The sexton of the parish and the people that were with him when he died, swore to the time when he died, and we swore to our journals, and they agreed within two minutes. Twelve of our men swore that the buttons of his coat were covered with the same grey cloth as his coat, and it appeared to be so; the jury asked Mr. Spink if he knew Mr. Booty in his lifetime; he said he never saw him till he saw him run by him into the burning mountain. The judge then said, " Lord, grant that I may never see the sight you have seen : one, two, or three, may be mistaken, but twenty or thirty cannot;" so the widow lost the cause.

N.B.—It is now in the Records at Westminster.

JAMES II., 1687.
HERBERT, *Chief-Justice.*
WYTHENS,
HOLLOWAY, and } *Justices.*
WRIGHT,

LXXV.

Remarkable Dream of the Rev Joseph Wilkins.

The late Rev. Joseph Wilkins, dissenting minister at Weymouth, dreamt in the early part of his life a very remarkable dream, which he carefully preserved in writing as follows:—" One night, soon after I was in bed, I fell asleep, and dreamt I was going to London. I thought it would not be much out of my way to go through Gloucestershire and call upon my friends there. Accordingly I set out, but remembered nothing that happened by the way till I came to my father's house; when I went to the front door and tried to open it, but found it fast; then I went to the backdoor which I opened and went in; but finding all the family had gone to bed, I went across the rooms up stairs, and entered the chamber where my father and mother were in bed. I went by the side of the bed on which my father lay and found him asleep, or thought he was so: then I went to the other side, and found my mother awake, to whom I said these words, 'Mother, I am going a long journey, and am come to bid you good-bye;' upon which she answered me in a fright, 'O dear son, thou art dead!' With this I awoke, and took no notice of it, more than a common dream, except that it appeared to me very perfect.

"In a few days after, as soon as a letter could reach me, I received one by post from my father, upon the receipt of which I was a little surprised, and concluded something extraordinary must have happened, as it was but a short time before I had a letter from my friends, and all were well. Upon opening it I was more surprised still, for my father addressed me as though I was dead, desiring me if alive, or the person into whose hands the letter might fall, to write immediately; but if the letter should find me living, they concluded I should not live long, and gave this as the reason of their fears:—That on a certain night, naming it, after they were in bed, my father asleep and my mother awake, she heard something try to open the front door, but finding it fast it went to the back door, which it opened, came in, and passed directly through the rooms up stairs, and she perfectly knew it to be my step; that I came to her bedside and spoke to her these words :—' Mother, I am going a long journey, and am come to bid you good-bye :' upon which she answered me in a fright, 'O! dear son, thou art dead!' which were the very circumstances and words of my dream, but she heard nothing more, and saw nothing; neither did I in my dream.

" Upon this she awoke and told my father what had passed; but he endeavoured to appease her, persuading her it was only a dream : she insisted it was no dream, for that she was as perfectly awake as ever she was, and had not the least inclination to sleep since she had been in bed. From these circumstances I am apt to think it was at the very same instant when my dream happened, though the distance between us was about one hundred miles; but of this I cannot speak positively. This occurred while I was at the academy at Ottery, Devon, in the year 1754, and at this moment every circumstance is fresh upon my mind. I have since had frequent opportunities of talking over the affair with my mother, and the whole was as fresh upon her mind as it was upon mine. I have often thought that her sensations as to this matter were stronger than mine. What may appear strange is that I cannot remember anything remarkable happening hereupon. This is only a plain simple narrative of a matter of fact."

Mr. Wilkins died November 15th, 1800, in the 70th year of his age.—*From H. Welby.*

LXXVI.

Apparition of Desfontaines to Mr. Bezuel.

Mr. Bezuel, when a schoolboy of fifteen (in 1695) contracted an intimacy with a younger boy named Desfontaines. After talking together of the compacts which have been often made between friends, that in case of death the spirit of the deceased should revisit the survivor, they agreed to form such a compact together and signed it respectively in 1696. Soon after this transaction they were separated by Desfontaines' removal to Caen.

In July, 1697, Bezuel, while amusing himself in haymaking near a friend's house, was seized with a fainting fit, after which he had a restless night. Notwithstanding this attack, he returned to the meadow next day, but on the succeeding day he had a still more severe attack. Bezuel thus relates the subsequent circumstances himself in the *Journal de Trevouse*, in 1726—

"I fell into a swoon; I lost my senses; one of the footmen perceived me, and called out for help. They recovered me a little, but my mind was more disordered than it had been before. I was told that they asked me then what ailed me, and that I answered I have seen what I thought I should never see. But I neither remember the question nor the answer. However, it agrees with what I remember; I saw then a naked man in half length, but I knew him not. They helped me to go down the ladder. I held the steps fast; but because I saw Desfontaines, my schoofellow, at the bottom of the ladder, I had again a fainting fit; my head got between two steps, and I again lost my senses. They let me down, and set me upon a large beam, which served for a seat in the great Place de Capucins. I sat upon it, and then I no longer saw Mr. de Sortoville, nor his servants, though they were present. And perceiving Desfontaines near the foot of the ladder, who made me a sign to come to him, I went back upon my seat as it were to make room for him; and those who saw me, and whom I did not see though my eyes were open, observed that motion. Because he did not come I got up to go to him. He came up to me, took hold of my left arm with his right hand, and carried me thirty paces farther into a by-lane, holding me fast. The servants believing that I was recovered, went to their business, except a little footboy, who told Mr. de Sortoville that I was talking to myself. Mr. de Sortoville thought I was drunk. He came near me and heard me ask some questions and return some answers, as he afterwards told.

"I talked with Desfontaines nearly three quarters of an hour. 'I promised you,' said he, 'that if I died before you I would come and tell you so. I am now come to tell you I was drowned in the river of Caen yesterday about this hour. I was walking with some friends: it was hot weather, and we agreed to go into the water. I grew faint and sunk to the bottom of the river. The Abbe Menilgian, my schoolfellow, dived to take me up; I took hold of his foot, but whether he was afraid or had a mind to rise to the top of the water, he struck out his leg so violently that he gave me a blow on the breast, and threw me again to the bottom of the river, which is very deep."

He always appeared to me taller than I had seen him, and even taller than he was when he died. I always saw him in half length, naked and bareheaded, with his fine light hair, and a white paper upon his forehead, twisted in his hair, upon which there was a writing, but I could only read *In cælo quies.—From H. Welby.*

LXXVII.

Sir John and Lady Owen.

Sir John Owen was a person of note, and of well-known credit. His lady and one of her sons lived in London, and being of a gay and expensive disposition, it was thought she lived beyond what the Knight could afford, and that he was sensible of it and uneasy about it. She had a good house in London, and a country house or lodgings for the summer at Hampstead, and kept a splendid equipage.

It happened one day when Lady Owen was at her country lodgings, that a person well-dressed, in appearance a gentleman, called at her city house and asked the maid if there were any lodgings to be let there, and if her lady was at home? On the servant's evincing some anger at so rude a question—"Well," said he, "don't be displeased, your lady has had some thoughts of staying at her summer lodgings all the winter, and so would dispose of some apartments in town for the parliament season; and I am directed by herself to look at the rooms, and give my answer: let me but just see them, I shall do you no harm. He then entered, and as it were pushed by her, and going into the first parlour, sat down in an easy chair, his servant waiting at the door, and as the maid did not apprehend any mischief she followed.

When she came in he rose up, and looking about the room found fault with the furniture, and the disposition of it; all was too good, too rich, and far above the quality of the owner; and he further said that the lady did not know what she did, that it was an expense she could not support, and that such a mode of living would bring her and all the family to ruin and beggary.

The servant now conducted him into another parlour, where he found the same fault. He told her he was surprised that her lady lived at so extravagant a rate, as Sir John's estate could not maintain it, that it would run him into debt and ruin him; and thus he would be undone by her extravagance.

Upon this the maid retorted, and told him that this was foreign to what he came about; if the lodgings were too good for him, that was his business indeed, else he had nothing to do with her lady's conduct or the furniture of her house; that her master was a gentleman of great estate, and had large plantations in Jamaica ; that he constantly supplied her lady with money sufficient for her support, and for all her expenses, and she wondered that he should interfere.

The stranger now calmly entered into conversation about Lady Owen and her way of living, and told many of the secrets of the family, so that the servant began to be more courteous.

She tried several times to learn who he was, his rank, country, name, and address; but he always declined, only telling her he would go to Hampstead where Lady Owen lodged, and wait upon her himself; and, thanking the servant for her civility, he left the house, his servant following him.

The girl now became much alarmed at these curious coincidences and circumstances. At length she went to give her lady an account of what had happened. On reaching Hampstead, she found her mistress very ill. At first she was refused admittance, but she urged extraordinary business. "What extraordinary business can you have?" said the lady's maid, tauntingly, "if your business was from the devil, you can't speak with my lady just now, for she is very ill and in bed."

"From the devil," said Mary, "I don't know but it may, and I believe it is indeed ; so I must speak with my lady immediately."

"Nay," replied the woman, "here has been one messenger too many from the devil already, I think ; sure you don't come of his errand too, do ye?"

"I don't know whose errand I come of, but I am frightened out of my wits; let me speak with my lady presently, or I shall die before I deliver my message."

"Die!" said the woman, "I wish my lady may not die before she hears it; pry'thee, Mary, if it be anything to frighten her, don't tell it her just now, for she is almost frightened to death already."

"Why," said Mary, "has my lady seen anything?"

"Ay, ay! seen," said the woman, "she has seen and heard too; there has been a man who has brought her dreadful tidings."

They talked so loud that the lady heard the noise, and immediately rang the bell for her maid. When the woman went in, "Who is that below?" said the lady, talking so earnestly, "is anybody come from London?" "Yes, madam," said the woman, "here is Mary come to speak to your ladyship." "Mary come," said she, surprised, "what can be the matter? why, sure, has she seen something too? Mercy on me, what's the matter? what does she say?"

At length Mary entered the room, and the woman was ordered to withdraw.

As soon as the door was shut, the lady burst into tears. "Oh, Mary," said she, "I have had a dreadful visit this afternoon; your master has been here." "My master! why, madam, that's impossible." "Nay, it was your master, I am sure."

In a word, the apparition of her husband had told her his estate would not support her expensive way of living, and that she would bring herself to misery and poverty, and much more to the same purpose as he had said to Mary.

Mary immediately asked her ladyship in what manner he appeared; and by the description that her mistress gave, it was exactly the same that had appeared to her, and desired to see the lodgings; then Mary gave her ladyship a particular relation of what had happened to her also, and of the message she was charged to deliver.

The lady was ultimately reduced, and obliged to sell her splendid furniture and equipage. But the most remarkable incident is that, just at this juncture,

Sir John Owen, the lady's husband, died in the West Indies.

This relation is taken from a manuscript that was in the possession of Sir Owen Ap Owen, of Brecknockshire; and the circumstance happened in the beginning of the reign of Queen Anne.

LXXVIII.
Omen to Charles II.

According to a tract published in 1680, Elizabeth Freeman, of Bishop's Hatfield, Herts, was visited by an apparition several times, which commanded her to deliver a message to Charles the Second. She swore before Sir Joseph Jordon and Dr. Lee, that on Monday, January 24, she saw the apparition of a woman who said to her, " The fifteenth of May is appointed for the royal blood to be poisoned." Again the apparition desired her to tell King Charles not to remove his Parliament, and stand to his Council.

LXXIX.
A Hint to Judge Brograve.

As Mr. Brograve of Hamel, near Puckeridge, Herts, when a young man, was one day riding in a lane, he suddenly received a violent blow on the cheek. He looked back, and saw that nobody was near him; soon afterwards he received another blow. He turned back, and fell-to the study of the law; and hence became a judge. This account I had from Sir John Penruddock, of Compton, chamberlain (our neighbour), whose lady was Judge Brograve's niece.—*Aubrey's Miscellanies*

LXXX.

Death of Commissioner Fostree.

Mr. Fostree, one of the Commissioners of the Victualling Office, died in 1767. What is remarkable is that a Commissioner of the same Board having dreamed that one of their number had fallen down dead, and telling his dream next morning, the words were scarcely uttered when Mr. Fostree suddenly expired.—*Annual Register.*

LXXXI.

Lord Lyttleton.

The subject of this narrative was the son of George Lord Lyttleton, and was alike distinguished for the raciness of his wit and the profligacy of his manners. The latter trait of his character has induced many persons to suppose that the apparition which he asserted he had seen, to have been the effect of a conscience quickened with remorse for innumerable vices and misdoings. The probability of the narrative has, consequently, been much questioned ; but in our own acquaintance we chance to know two gentlemen, one of whom was at Pitt Place, the seat of Lord Lyttleton, and the other in the immediate neighbourhood at the time of his Lordship's death ; and these bear ample testimony to the veracity of the whole affair.

The several narratives correspond in material points ; and we shall now proceed to relate the most circumstantial particulars written by a gentleman who was on a visit to his lordship :—

"I was at Pitt Place, Epsom, when Lord Lyttleton died ; Lord Fortescue, Lady Flood, and the two Miss Amphletts, were also present. Lord Lyttleton had not long been returned from Ireland, and frequently had been seized with suffocating fits : he was attacked several times by them in the course of the preceding month, while he was at his house in Hill Street, Berkeley Square. It happened that he dreamt, three days before his death, that he saw a fluttering bird; and afterwards that a woman appeared to him in white apparel, and said to him, 'Prepare to die, you will not exist three days.'* His lordship was much alarmed, and called to a servant from a closet adjoining, who found him much agitated, and in a profuse perspiration: the circumstance had a considerable effect all the next day on his lordship's spirits. On the third day, while his lordship was at breakfast with the above personages, he said, " If I live over to-night, I shall have jockied the ghost, for this is the third day.' The whole party presently set

* According to the narrative of a relative of Lady Lyttleton, the following is the version of the circumstances as related by Lord Lyttleton :—

Two nights before, on his retiring to his bed, after his servant was dismissed and his light extinguished, he had heard a noise resembling the fluttering of a dove at his chamber window. This attracted his attention to the spot ; when, looking in the direction of the sound, he saw the figure of an unhappy female whom he had seduced and deserted, and who, when deserted, had put a violent end to her own existence, standing in the aperture of the window from which the fluttering sound had proceeded. The form approached the foot of the bed :—the room was preternaturally light ; the objects of the chamber were distinctly visible. Raising her hand and pointing to a dial which stood on the mantelpiece of the chimney, the figure, with a severe solemnity of voice and manner, announced to the appalled and conscience-stricken man, that, at that very hour, on the third day after the visitation, his life and his sins would be concluded, and nothing but their punishment remain, if he availed himself not of the warning to repentance which he had received. The eye of Lord Lyttleton glanced upon the dial ; the hand was on the stroke of twelve. Again the apartment was involved in total darkness : the warning spirit disappeared, and bore away at her departure all the lightness of heart and buoyancy of spirit, the ready wit, and vivacity of manner, which had formerly been the pride and ornament of the unhappy being to whom she had delivered her tremendous summons.

off for Pitt Place, where they had not long arrived before his lordship was visited by one of his accustomed fits: after a short interval however he recovered. He dined at five o'clock that day, and went to bed at eleven, when his servant was about to give him rhubarb and mint-water; but his lordship, perceiving him stir it with a tooth-pick, called him a slovenly dog, and bid him go and fetch a tea-spoon. On the man's return, he found his master in a fit, and the pillow being placed high, his chin bore hard upon his neck. But the servant, instead of relieving his lordship on the instant from his perilous situation, ran, in his fright, and called out for help, but on his return he found his lordship dead."

In explanation of this strange tale, it is said that Lord Lyttleton acknowledged previously to his death, that the woman he had seen in his dream was the mother of the two Miss Amphletts mentioned above, whom, together with a third sister then in Ireland, his lordship had seduced and prevailed on to leave their parent, who resided near his country residence in Shropshire. It is further stated that Mrs. Amphlett died of grief through the desertion of her children, at the precise time when the female vision appeared to his lordship; and that, about the period of his dissolution, a personage answering to his description visited the bed-side of the late Miles Peter Andrews, Esq. (who had been the friend and companion of Lord Lyttleton in his revels), and suddenly throwing open the curtains, desired Mr. Andrews to come to him. The latter, not knowing that his lordship had returned from Ireland, suddenly got up, when the phantom disappeared! Mr. Andrews frequently declared that the alarm caused him to have a short fit of illness; and in his subsequent visits to Pitt Place, no solicitations could ever prevail on him to take a bed there; but he would invariably return, however late, to the Spread Eagle Inn at Epsom for the night.

Sir Nathaniel Wraxall, in his Memoirs, has the following passage :—

"Dining at Pitt Place, about four years after the death of Lord Lyttleton, in the year 1783, I had the curiosity to visit the bedchamber, where the casement window, at which Lord Lyttleton asserted the dove appeared to flutter, was pointed out to me. At his stepmother's, the dowager Lady Lyttleton, in Portugal Street, Grosvenor Square, I have frequently seen a painting which she herself executed in 1780, expressly to commemorate the event : it hung in a conspicuous part of her drawing-room. There the dove appears at the window, while a female figure, habited in white, stands at the foot of the bed, announcing to Lord Lyttleton his dissolution. Every part of the picture was faithfully designed, after the description given to her by the valet de chambre who attended him, to whom his master related all the circumstances."

An engraving, copied from this picture, has been published, and is still frequently to be met with in the collections of printsellers. —*From H. Welby.*

LXXXII.

Apparition of Mr. Barlow's Huntsman.

Last Christmas Day in the morning, Mr. Barlow was visited by a person who had the appearance and dress of his huntsman, who opened his curtains and asked him whether he proposed going out with the hounds that morning. Mr. Barlow told him that he was not then very well, and did not care to go himself, but that he, the huntsman, might take the dogs and go to such a mountain, where he might find a fox ; upon which the person left him. Mrs. Barlow hearing this conversation, as she thought between the huntsman and her husband, for she lay in a room contiguous to his, came sometime after to him and expostulated with him against sending out the hounds that day; what answer he made her is not certain, but when he came down stairs he saw some of his favourite hounds about the house, which led him to an enquiry why the huntsman had left those hounds behind him. The servants protested the huntsman had not been there that morning, and that the dogs were all in the kennel; upon which a servant was sent to Narbeth, where the huntsman lived, to see whether he had been at Slebetch or not. The huntsman strenuously denied it, and said he was just got out of bed, and his wife affirmed the same. On being informed of what had happened to his master, both man and wife fell ill with the conceit; the man is since pretty well recovered, but the woman still continues in a state of distraction. Barlow himself has been greatly shocked about it; he insists on the reality of the appearance; and Mrs. Barlow affirms she heard the huntsman that morning talking with her husband.—*Gentleman's Magazine, July* 1812.

LXXXIII.

Evidence of an Apparition.

EXTRACTED FROM THE RECORDS OF THE COURT OF JUSTICIARY IN EDINBURGH.

Upon the 10th of June, 1754, Duncan Terig, alias Clarke, and Alexander Bain Macdonald, were tried at Edinburgh before the Court of Justiciary, for the murder of Arthur Davis, sergeant in General Guise's regiment of foot, on the 28th of September, 1749.

In the course of the proof for the crown, Alexander M'Pherson deposed that an apparation came one night when he was in bed, to his bed-side, and he supposing his visitor to be one Farquharson, his acquaintance, got up and followed it to the door, when it told him it was Sergeant Davies, and desired him to go to a place it pointed out to him in the Hill of Christie, where he would find its bones; it further requested that he should go to Farquharson, who would accompany him to the hill and assist him in burying them; that he went to the place pointed out, and there found a human body, of which the flesh was mostly consumed, but at that time he did not bury it. A few nights afterwards the ghost paid him a second visit, and reminded him of his promise to bury the bones; and upon his enquiring who was the murderer, the ghost told him they were D. Clarke and Alexander M'Donald. After this second apparition the witness and Farquharson went and buried the bones.

Another witness, Isabella M'Hardie, deposed that she was in the same house with M'Pherson, and that she saw a naked man come into the house and go towards M'Pherson's bed.

Donald Farquharson confirmed the testimony of M'Pherson, as to the finding of the body, and his assisting in burying it. He likewise deposed that M'Pherson told him of the ghost's visit, and also of its request to get him (Farquharson) to assist him in burying the body.

The prisoners were acquitted principally on account of the evidence of these witnesses, whose information from the ghost threw an air of discredit on the whole proof. The agent for the prisoners told the relator of this extraordinary story that as they were then both dead, he had no difficulty to declare that in his own opinion they were both guilty.—*From H. Welby.*

LXXXIV.
The Massacre of St. Bartholomew.

This atrocious affair, perhaps one of the most bloody tragedies with which the page of history is stained, is on good authority said to have been prognosticated in several ways, and even a considerable time before its perpetration.

Sinclair, in his *Invisible World* says, " The histories of the time are full of secret warnings and notices given by the apparitions of invisible agents in dreams. Admiral Coligni had no less than three particular notices given him by dreams that his life was in danger, and that he would be murdered if he stayed in Paris ; an express was sent him from the Count S——, at Saumur, to make his escape and flee for his life before it was too late : nay, it was even said that the King of Navarre, afterwards Henry IV. sent a private message to him to be gone, and if he staid one night longer he would find it impossible ; but it was all in vain, he was deaf and indolent to his own safety.

" Others who were more obedient to the heavenly vision, more touched with the sense of their danger, as the Count de Montgomery, the Vidame of Chartres, Ee Caversac ; and who had severally, and some of them jointly, timely warning of their danger, mounted their horses and fled the night before, and foiling the vigilance of their pursuers made their escape."

Henry IV. said many times in public, that after the massacre of St. Bartholomew a swarm of ravens flew upon the top of the Louvre, and that during seven nights, the king himself and all the courtiers heard groans and dreadful cries at the same hour. He related a yet more extraordinary circumstance ; he said, that a few days previous to the massacre, while playing at dice with the Duke of Alencono and the Duke of Guise, he saw drops of blood upon the table; that twice he ordered them to be wiped off, and twice they appeared again, after which he left the game struck with horror.

Mezeray in his *History of France* relates the following fact: a few years before the massacre of St. Bartholomew, the guardian of the Convent of the Cordeliers of Saints whose name was Michael Crellet, having been condemned to be hanged by Admiral Coligni, foretold him that he would die assassinated, that his body would be thrown out of the windows, and that afterwards he would be hanged himself, which happened to the Admiral at the massacre of St. Bartholomew.—*Voltaire—Notes to Henriade.*

LXXXV.
Death of Henry III. of France Prognosticated.

When Henry the Third, king of France, was assassinated at the siege of Paris by a monk of the order of St. Francis, whose name was Jacques Clement, it was publicly said, and believed by many, that this fanatical monster had received an order from heaven to destroy a king who was then fighting against the rebellious clergy. We read the following narrative in a book published by a jacobin friar, and printed at Troyes, in the province of Champaign, some time after the death of Henry the third; we translate it from the old French language:—

'So that God, hearing favourably the prayer of this faithful servant, whose name was brother Jacques Clement, one night while he was in bed sent to him his angel in a vision, who appearing with a great light to the monk, and showing him a naked sword, addressed him with these words:—

"'Brother Jacques, I am the messenger of God Almighty, who cometh to inform thee that by thee the tyrant of France must be put to death. Think thou therefore for thyself, and prepare thyself, as the crown of martyrdom is prepared for thee.' Having spoken thus, the vision disappeared and let him think on those words of truth."—*From H. Welby.*

LXXXVI.

Alexander Peden.

This extraordinary man was once imprisoned in the Bass, a stupendous crag in the Highlands of Scotland, used as a place of confinement for state and other prisoners.

"One Sabbath morning," says the narrator, "being in the public worship of God, a young girl about the age of fourteen years came to Peden's chamber-door mocking with loud laughter; he said, 'poor thing, thou laughest and mockest at the worship of God, but ere long God shall write such a surprising judgment on thee, that shall stay this laughing,' &c. Very shortly after that, as she was walking on the rock, a blast of wind swept her off to the sea, where she was lost."—*From H. Welby.*

LXXXVII.

Remarkable Dream of the Celebrated Miss Hutton.

This lady was the daughter of the late Dr. Charles Hutton, one of the first mathematicians of his time. A few days before her death, which took place in October 1794, she had a remarkable dream, which her friends thought so curious that they desired her to write it down, which she immediately did, literally in the following words:—

"I dreamed that I was dead, and that my soul had ascended into one of the stars; there I found several persons whom I had formerly known, and among them some of the nuns whom I was particularly attached to when in France.* They told me, when they received me, they were glad to see me, but hoped I should not stay with them long, the place being a kind of purgatory; and that all the stars were for the reception of different people's souls, a different star being allotted for every kind of bad temper and vice; all the sharp tempers went to one star, the sulky to another, the peevish to another; and so on. Everybody in each star being of the same temper, no one would give up to another, and there was nothing but dissension and quarrels among them. Some of those who received me, taking offence at the information my friends were giving to me, a child, it made a quarrel, which at length became so rude and noisy that it awoke me."—*Gentlemen's Magazine.*

LXXXVIII.
Conversion of Henry De Joyeuse.

Vicieux, penitent, Courtier, Solitaire,
It prit, quitta, reprit la cuirasse et la haire.—VOLTAIRE.

These lines admirably describe the character and fortune of Henry de Joyeuse Count of Bouchage, and second brother of the Duke of Joyeuse, who was killed at the battle of Contras. Voltaire relates the following fact concerning this individual:—

"One day, at four o'clock in the morning, passing by the convent of the Capuchin Friars at Paris after a night spent in debauchery, he fancied that he heard angels singing matins in the convent. Struck with

---

* She had been for two years educated as a nun there.

this thought, he became a capuchin friar, and took the name of Brother Angel. Afterwards he left the frock, and fought against Henry IV. The Duke of Mayenne appointed him Governor of Languedoc, and created him a duke and peer, and a marshal of France. At length he made his peace with the king, but one day, being with his Majesty on a balcony, under which a great crowd were assembled; 'Cousin,' said Henry IV. 'those people appear to me very pleased to see together an apostate and a renegade.' These words of the king induced Joyeuse to return to his convent, where he died."

LXXXIX.

*Apparition to Ninon de L'Enclos.**

In the year 1633, as the famous Mademoiselle Ninon de L'Enclos one day sat alone in her chamber, her servant announced the arrival of a stranger who desired to speak with her but refused to tell his name. The young lady made answer that she was engaged with company. "No, no," said the stranger to the lacquey, "I know well that Mademoiselle is by herself, and for that very reason call upon her at present. Go, tell her, I have secrets of the last moment to impart, and cannot take a refusal." This extraordinary message by exciting female curiosity procured the stranger admittance. He was of low stature, of an

---

* Ninon de L'Enclos was born at Paris, of a noble family, in 1615. Her mother was anxious to place her in a convent, but was prevented by her father, who was a man of gaiety. She lost her parents at the age of fifteen, and possessing the most fascinating personal beauty, she was followed by some of the first men of her time, but would never unite herself in marriage. She died at the age of ninety, and what is most singular, preserved her charms to the last. A remarkable circumstance is related of one of her sons, who having been bred without knowing his mother, conceived a desire for her, but having discovered the secret of his birth, he stabbed himself in her presence.

ungracious aspect, and his grey hairs bespoke age. He was dressed in black, without a sword, wore a *calotte* (a small leather cap which covered the tonsure) and had a large patch on his forehead: in his left hand he held a very slender cane; his features were expressive, and his eyes sparkled vivacity.

"Madam," said he, on entering the apartment, "please to make your waiting maid retire; my words are not for third persons to hear."

Mdlle L'Enclos was much alarmed at this preamble; but reflecting she had to do with a decrepit old man, mustered up some resolution, and dismissed her maid.

"Let not my visit alarm you, Madam," said the stranger. "It is true I do not honour all indiscriminately with my presence, but be assured you have nothing to fear. All I beg is, that you would hear me with confidence and attention. You see before you a man whom the earth obeys, and whom nature has invested with the power of dispensing her gifts. I presided at your birth; the lot of mortals depends upon my rod; and I have condescended to ask what lot you would wish for yourself; the present is but the dawn of your brilliant days. Soon you shall arrive at that period, when the gates of the world shall fly open to receive you; for it depends wholly upon yourself to be the most illustrious, and the most prosperous lady of your age. I submit to your choice supreme honours, immense riches, and eternal beauty. Take which you choose and depend upon it, there exists not a mortal who can make you the same ample offer."

"That I verily believe," replied the fair one in a fit of laughter, "your gifts are so very splendid."

"I hope, Madam, you have too much good sense to make sport of a stranger. Once more, I seriously make you the same offer, but decide instantly."

"Then truly, sir, since your are so good as to give me my choice, I hesitate not to fix upon eternal beauty;

but how, pray, am I to obtain such an inestimable prize?"

"Madam, all I ask is, that you should put down your name in my tablets, and swear inviolable secrecy."

Mademoiselle de L'Enclos instantly complied, and wrote her name upon a black memorandum book with red edges. The old man at the same time struck her gently upon the left shoulder with his wand.

"This now," resumed he, " is the whole ceremony; henceforth, rely upon eternal beauty, and the subjugation of every heart. I bestow on you unlimited powers of charming,—the most precious privilege a tenant of this nether orb can enjoy. During the six thousand years that I have perambulated this globe, I have only found four who were worthy of such rare felicity. They were Semiramis, Helen, Cleopatra, and Diana of Poitenx; you are the fifth, and I am determined you shall be the last. You shall be ever fresh and ever blooming: charms and adorations shall track your steps: whoever beholds you shall that instant be captivated, and they whom you love shall reciprocally love you; you shall enjoy uninterrupted health and longevity without appearing old. Some females seem born to bewitch the eye, and some the heart; but you alone are fated to unite these different qualities: you shall taste of pleasure at an age when others of your sex are beset with decrepitude; your name shall live while the world endures. I am aware, Madam, that all this will appear to you like enchantment, but ask me no questions, for I dare not answer a word. In the course of your life you shall see me once again, and that ere fourscore years be run. Tremble then! for three short days shall close your existence! Remember, my name is Night Walker." With these words he vanished, and left the possessor of eternal beauty shivering with fear.

This lady of amorous memory, the narrator adds,

had a second visit from the gentleman in black in the year 1706, as she lingered on her deathbed. In spite of the efforts of servants he had found his way into her apartment; he stood by her bed, opened the curtains, and gazed. The patient turned pale, and shrieked aloud. The unwelcome guest after reminding her that the third day would be that of her dissolution, exhibited her own signature, and disappeared, as he exclaimed with a hideous voice, "Tremble, for it is past, and you are to fall." The third day came, and de L'Enclos was no more.—*From H. Welby.*

XC.

Apparition to Miss Hepburn of Garleton, in the Scottish Highlands.

Rather more than fifty years ago, an old maiden lady, Miss Janet Hepburn, sister to Colonel Hepburn, of Luffness and Congalton, of good family, was the tenant of one of the now decayed wings of the mansion house of Garleton. She is described as a tall thin figure, who wore a black silk cloak and bonnet, and walked with a large cane ornamented with a gold chain and tassel. She also displayed a great deal of eccentricity in her conduct, for she often walked at dead of night and early dawn, till she was so wetted by the dews and the long dank grass that on her return home she had to shift her clothes or go to bed. Add to this that she had the misfortune to be a papist, and was very ostensible in her devotions, and we need not wonder that she was regarded by the superstitious of the neighbourhood with no small degree of terror and aversion.

Having sauntered out one morning before sunrise, she sat down on the craggy hill, when " an odd looking man," as she termed him, approached her. She waved her cane to keep off the intruder, who, after muttering something, went away. The lady immediately returned home; but during the day could not banish the unwelcome visitor from her thoughts. At night, after locking the outer door, and placing the key below her pillow, she went to bed as usual, at a late hour. In vain she endeavoured to compose herself to sleep, and to dissipate the troublesome thoughts that arose in her mind; at length she heard the outer door open, and a heavy foot come tramping up the creaking stairs; something opened the door and entered the room adjoining to her bed-closet; the door of the latter next opened, and she again beheld the unwelcome visitor —the spectre of the morning.

She was only able to articulate, "Who comes there?" when the stranger replied, "this is my native place, and I have a long history to tell you!" The lady thinking the intruder was a robber, pointed to a small box containing her keys, and bade him take what he wanted and be gone. The mysterious personage still wished to speak; but as she waved her hand, and inclined not to listen, he dissappeared. As he retired, she again heard the heavy foot tramping down the creaking stairs, till the slashing of the outer door announced his exit.

Although the lady passed a sleepless night, she was unwilling to disturb the inmates of her house, which consisted only of a maiden lady and a domestic. Next morning when the servant came for the key of the outer door she told her what had happened, and that she imagined robbers had been in the house. The maid had also the imperfect recollection of some voice; but it was like the voice of a dream. At her lady's desire she immediately went to the press where the family plate was deposited, but found it unmolested; the silver wine cup stood on the mantlepiece, below the crucifix, untouched, and the outer door remained fast; in short, every thing stood in its place as on the preceding evening.

It was the impression of the less superstitious part of the neighbourhood that the old lady was superannuated, and that the ghastly visitant was the creature of a dream. Be this as it may, on 'that day twelvemonth, the lady of Garleton was seized with a convulsive fit in the evening, and expired about the same hour at which she had twelvemonths before had an interview with the unwelcome visitor. I have only to add, that the person from whom I had the preceding story is of unquestionable veracity, and that she had often heard it from the lady's own lips.

The ruins of the mansion house still remain at the foot of Garleton hills, and are a fine miniature specimen of Highland scenery.—*From H. Welby.*

XCI.

Apparition to Mr. Weston, of old Swinford, Worcestershire.

In the summer of 1759, Mr. Weston was walking one evening in the beautiful park of Lord Lyttleton, at Hagley (characterised in "Thomson's Seasons," the British Tempe), when being overtaken by a shower of rain he ran into a grotto, and stood beneath a spreading oak, under the shade of which several cattle were grazing.

He had not been above ten minutes in that situation, before he saw the form of a man pass over the brook close to the shade. Supposing it to be a poor peasant who had long worked for him, he called him by name, but received no answer; and the apparition quickly disappearing, his mind was much agitated. Regardless of the storm, Mr. Weston withdrew from his retreat, and walked round a rising hill, to endeavour to discover the form which had presented itself to him. That, however, had not the effect desired; but one abundantly more satisfactory it certainly had, for just as he had gained the summit of a hill on his return to the grotto, a tremendous flash of lightning darted its forked fury on the venerable oak, shivered it to pieces, and killed two of the cattle under its boughs.

On Mr. Weston's return to Swinford, he found that the death of the labourer was just announced in the neighbourhood. He instantly related the circumstance to his friend. He had the body decently interred at his own expense; and afterwards contributed to the support of the widow, not only by remitting a year's rent for her cottage and piece of ground, but also by settling a small annuity upon her till she should marry again.—*From H. Welby.*

XCII.

Second Sight.

Superstition has been universally attributed to the Scottish character, and it forms a prominent feature in its history. The author of Waverley has availed himself of their most popular Northern legends, and on them he may be said to have laid the basis of his literary fame; and they may well be considered as adding a peculiar charm to Scottish literature.

Among these traditions none are better authenticated than those of "Second Sight," which subject has been specially treated by various authors at considerable length.

Martin gives the following account of it:—*

"The second sight is a singular faculty of seeing an otherwise invisible object, without any previous

---

* Description of the Western Islands of Scotland. 8vo. 1803.

means used by the person that uses it for that end; the vision makes such a lively impression upon the seers, that they neither see nor think of anything else except the vision, as long as it continues; and then they appear pensive or jovial, according to the object which was represented to them.

"The seer knows neither the object, time, nor place of a vision before it appears; and the same object is often seen by different persons, living at a considerable distance from one another. The true way of judging as to the time and circumstance of an object is by observation; for several persons of judgment, without this faculty, are more capable to judge of the design of a vision than a novice that is a seer. If an object appear in the day or night, it will come to pass sooner or later accordingly.

"If an object is seen early in a morning (which is not frequent), it will be accomplished in a few hours afterwards. If at noon, it will be commonly accomplished that very day. If in the evening, perhaps that night; if after candles be lighted it will be accomplished that night: the later always in accomplishment, by weeks, months, and sometimes years, according to the time of night the vision is seen.

"When a shroud is perceived about one, it is a sure prognostic of death; the time is judged according to the height of it about the person; for if it is seen above the middle, death is not expected for the space of a year, and perhaps some months longer; and as it is frequently seen to ascend higher towards the head, death is concluded to be at hand within a few days, if not hours, as daily experience confirms. Examples of this kind were shown me, when the persons of whom the observations were then made, enjoyed perfect health.

"One instance was lately foretold by a seer that was a novice, concerning the death of one of my acquaintance; this was communicated to a few only, and with great confidence: I being one of the number did not in the least regard it, until the death of the person about the time foretold did confirm me of the certainty of the prediction. The novice mentioned above, is now a skilful seer, as appears from many late instances; he lives in the parish of St. Mary, the most northern in Skye.

"If two or three women are seen at once, near a man's left hand, she that is next him will undoubtedly be his wife first, and so on, whether all three, or the man, be single or married at the time of the vision or not; of this there are several late instances among those of my acquaintance. It is an ordinary thing for them to see a man that is to come to the house shortly after; and if he is not of the seer's acquaintance, yet he gives such a lively description of his stature, complexion, habit, &c. that upon his arrival he answers the character given him in all respects.

"It is ordinary with them to see houses, gardens, and trees in places void of all three; and this in progress of time used to be accomplished: as at Mogshot, in the Isle of Skye, where there were but a few sorry cow-houses, thatched with straw, yet in a very few years after the vision, which appeared often, was accomplished, by the building of several good houses on the very spot represented by the seers, and by the planting of orchards there.

"To see a spark of fire fall upon one's arm or breast is a forerunner of a dead child to be seen in the arms of those persons; of which there are several fresh instances.

"To see a seat empty at the time of one's sitting in it is a presage of that person's death soon after.

"When a novice, or one that has lately obtained the second sight, sees a vision in the night-time without doors, and comes near a fire, he presently falls into a swoon.

"Some find themselves as it were in a crowd of people, having a corpse which they carry along with them; and after such visions the seers come in sweating, and describe the people that appeared: if there be any of their acquaintance among them, they give an account of their names, as also of the bearers, but they know nothing concerning the corpse."

Dr. Johnson, in his "Journey to the Hebrides," says: "The second sight is an impression made either by the mind upon the eye, or by the eye upon the mind, by which things distant or future are perceived and seen as if they were present. A man on a journey far from home, falls from his horse; another, who is perhaps at work about the house, sees him bleeding on the ground, commonly with a landscape of the place where the accident befalls him. Another seer, driving home his cattle, or wandering in idleness, or musing in the sunshine, is suddenly surprised by the appearance of a bridal ceremony, or funeral procession, and counts the mourners or attendants, of whom, if he knows them, he relates their names; if he knows them not, he can describe the dresses. Things distant are seen at the instant when they happen. Of things future I know not that there is any rule for determining the time between the sight and the event.

"By the term second sight seems to be meant a mode of seeing superadded to that which nature bestows. In the Earse it is called *Taisch;* which signifies, likewise, a spectre, or a vision. I know not, nor is it likely, that the Highlanders ever examined, whether by Taisch, used for the second sight, they mean the power of seeing, or the thing seen. I do not find it to be true, as it is reported, that to the second sight nothing is presented but phantoms of evil. Good seems to have the same proportion in those visionary scenes as it obtains in real life: almost all remarkable events have evil for their basis, and are either miseries incurred, or miseries escaped. Our sense is so much stronger of what we suffer, than of what we enjoy, that the ideas of pain predominate in almost every mind. What is recollection but a revival of vexations, or history but a record of wars, treasons, and calamities? Death, which is considered as the greatest evil, happens to all. The greatest good be it what it may, is the lot but of a part. That they should often see death is to be expected, because death is an event frequent and important. But they see likewise more pleasing incidents. A gentleman told me, that when he had once gone far from his own island, one of his labouring servants predicted his return, and described the livery of his attendants, which he had never worn at home; and which had been, without any previous design, occasionally given him."

We now proceed to quote a few instances of this remarkable faculty:—

I.

A gentleman travelling in the Highlands, in the year 1654, with a retinue of servants, ordered one of them to precede him, and bespeak accommodation for him at an inn in the neighbouring town. On entering the house the man suddenly stepped back, and fell by a stone, against which he struck his foot. On his master questioning him as to his fears, he said he must not lodge in that house. The master asked him the reason, when he replied, because a dead corpse would very shortly be carried out of it; and that several persons met him (in vision) at the door carrying the body, when he cried out. He conjured his master not to lodge in the house, which induced the latter to inquire if there was any sick person there, when he was answered in the negative. The landlord, a strong healthy Highlander, died the next day of an apoplectic fit.

II.

In January, 1652, Lieut.-Col. Munro was quartered in a public house in Ferrinlia, in Rosse. The Colonel and a friend were one evening seated by the fire, with a vacant chair on the left of the former. In the corner of a capacious chimney were two Highlanders who had arrived that evening. While one of them was in conversation with Monro's friend, the other looked strangely towards the Colonel: on being asked his meaning he desired him to rise from that chair, because it was an unlucky one. On being asked why, he said there was a dead man in the chair next to it. The Colonel replied, "Well, if he be in the chair next me, I may keep my own; but describe the man." The Highlander replied that he was a tall man, wearing a long grey coat, with boots, one of his legs hanging over the arm of the chair, his head hanging on the other side, and his arm hanging down as if broken. At that time there were some English troops quartered in the adjoining village. About two days afterwards four or five of these troops rode by the door of the inn, who, with the assistance of some servants, were carrying one of their comrades, who had his arm broken. They brought him into the hall, and set him in the chair which the Highlander had singularized to Colonel Monro a few days previous.

III.

A gentleman connected with the family of Dr. Ferrier, an officer in the army, in the middle of the eighteenth century, was quartered, early in life, near the castle of a gentleman in the north of Scotland who was supposed to possess the second sight. Strange rumours were afloat respecting the old chieftain: he had spoken to an apparition which ran along the battlements of the house, and had never been cheerful afterwards: his prophetic vision excited surprise, which was favoured by his retired habits. One day, while he was reading a play to the ladies of this family, the chief, who had been walking across the room, stopped suddenly, and assumed the look of a seer; he rang the bell, and ordered the groom to saddle a horse, to proceed immediately to a seat in the neighbourhood, and to enquire after the health of Lady ———; if the account were favourable, he then directed him to call at another castle, to ask after another lady whom he named. The reader immediately closed his book, and declared that he would not proceed till these abrupt orders were explained, as he was convinced they were produced by the second sight. The chief was very unwilling to explain himself, but at length he owned that the door had appeared to open, and that a little woman, without a head, had entered the room; that the apparition indicated the sudden death of some person of his acquaintance, and the only two persons who resembled the figure were those ladies after whose health he had sent to inquire.

A few hours afterwards the servant returned, with an account that one of the ladies had died of an apoplectic fit, about the time when the vision appeared.

Aubrey, Beaumont, Baxter, Glanvill, Scott, &c., abound with similar narratives, but contain none of less impeached veracity than the preceding.—*From H. Welby.*

XCIII.

Duel Prevented.

Thomas Horton, Esq., a gentleman of fortune, had

an intrigue with a lady, in which his younger brother was his rival. The lady was handsome, and of respectable fortune, but much inferior to the eldest son of the family, whose expectant fortune was near two thousand pounds per annum, after the death of his father, Sir George Horton.

The younger gentleman was really in love with the lady, and inclined to marry her, if he could bring his father to consent to it, and had two or three times spoken to the knight on the subject; nor was his father averse to it, except that he thought her fortune too small.

The rivalry between the two brothers continued for some time; several quarrels took place, when one evening, the younger brother received a challenge from the elder, appointing time and place to meet the next morning at five o'clock. The father, who was then living, could know nothing of what had passed between his sons, for he was at his seat in Wiltshire, sixty miles from London, when this affair took place.

On the morning appointed they accordingly met, when the younger brother seeing his antagonist at a distance said, "I am sure I am within time; don't be impatient, Tom, I'll be with you presently." He had not proceeded many steps, before he saw his brother (as he still thought him to be) advancing as if to meet him, with his drawn sword in his hand.

"You are very nimble with your sword," said he, "what, did you think I would not give you time to draw?" But how was he surprised when he came up to him and found it was not his brother, but his *father;* and that, instead of a sword in his hand, he had a small cane, such as the old knight generally walked with.

He was the more at a stand, because he supposed his father was, as is said above, at his seat in Wiltshire, above sixty miles off; however, he was out of doubt, when he not only saw him nearer at hand, but when his father spoke to him.

"Why how now, Jack," said the old gentleman, "what! challenge,* and draw upon your father?" "You may be sure, Sir," said he, "I did not suppose it was you. I make no doubt but you know whom I expected here; it is a poor cowardly shift for him first to challenge his brother, and then send you in his stead." "It is no time to talk now, Jack," said the father, "I have your challenge here, and I am come to fight you, therefore draw." "Draw!" says Jack, "what, upon my father! Heaven forbid! no, I'll be murdered first."

But his father advancing again, with a furious countenance, Jack pulled out his sword from the scabbard, and throwing it on the ground, cried out, "there, Sir, take it, kill me with it; what do you mean?" But his father running upon him, Jack turned from him, and seemed resolved to run: at which his father stooped, took up his sword, and stood still. The young gentleman, surprised and amazed at the rencounter, knew not what to do; but retiring, observed that his father was gone. He, however, resolved, though he had no sword, he would go to the place appointed, and see if his brother was come. Accordingly he returned to the place, and waited near two hours there, but heard nothing of his brother; but on coming away he found his sword lying in the place where it was thrown down. This surprised him still more, and at length he took up the sword, and went home wondering at the meaning of all this.

He had not been long at home, before his brother's servant came to his lodgings with a civil message, to ask him from his brother, if he had not met with something extraordinary that morning, and to tell him,

---

* When he thought he saw his brother with his sword in his hand, he laid his hand on his own sword.

that he (his brother) was very ill or he would have called on him. The oddness of this message added to his surprise; he called the messenger up stairs, and the following dialogue ensued :—

J. What's the matter, Will? how is my brother?

Will. My master gives his service to you, Sir, and sent me, to know how you are.

J. Indeed; I'm a little out of order; but how is your master, what's the matter?

Will. Why 'truly and't please you, Sir, I don't know what's the matter, I think my master has been frightened this morning.

J. Frightened, Will! with what, pr'ythee? your master is not easily frightened.

Will. Why no, and't it please you, I know he is not; but there has been something extraordinary; I dont know how it is, for I was not with my master; but they talk in the house, that he has seen his father, or seen an apparition in his father's shape.

J. Why so have I too, Will; now you frighten me indeed, for I made light of it before; why, it was my father to be sure.

Will. No, Sir, alas, your father! why, my old master was at Sarum, in Wiltshire, and very ill in his bed but last Friday; I came from him, my master sent me to him on an errand.

J. And did you see him yourself, Will?

Will. I'll take my oath I saw him, and spoke to him, in his bed and very ill he was; I hope your worship will believe I know my old master.

J. Yes, yes, you know him, no doubt, Will. I think you lived four years with him, did you not?

Will. I dressed and undressed him five years and a half, and't please you; I think I may say I know him in his clothes or out of them.

J. Well, William, and I hope you will allow that I

know my father too, or him I have called father these thirty years.

Will. Yes, to be sure, and't please you.

J. Well, then, tell my brother, it was either my father or the devil; I both saw him and spoke with him, and I am frightened out of my wits.

The servant returned with this message to his master who immediately went with Will to see his brother.

As soon as he came into the room to his brother, "dear Jack," said he, "we have both played the fool, but forgive me my part, and tell me what has happened." The servant had previously acquainted the elder brother with the appearance of his father to him that morning.

The other then related his story to the same purpose; that as he was coming to the place appointed, his father met him and asked him whither he was going; that he put him off, and told him he was going to Kensington to meet some gentlemen there, who were to go with him to Hampton Court. That upon this, his father seemed very angry; and said that he knew his errand as well he did himself; that he was going to murder his younger brother, and that he was come to satisfy his fury himself, and that he should murder him, not his brother.

The brothers now became reconciled; but Jack was uneasy about this being the real appearance of his father, and the words of his brother's man William ran in his mind all that night; for as to this first meeting, it was so taken up with the ecstacy of their reconciliation, that they had no time for any thing else; but the next morning the young gentleman went to see his brother to return his visit.

The young men were now very uneasy about one part of the story; accordingly they set off for their father's residence. They found him at home, and very ill, nor had he even been from home, but was greatly concerned for the safety of his sons, upon the following occasion :—

One night he was surprised in his sleep with a dream, or rather a vision, that his two sons had fallen out about a mistress; that they had quarrelled so as to challenge each other, and were gone into the fields to fight; but that somebody had given him notice of it, and he had got up in the morning at four o'clock to meet and prevent them. Upon this dream, he awaked in great disorder and terror; however, finding it but a dream he had composed his mind and gone to sleep again, but he dreamed it again. That in consequence of this dream he had sent a servant to ascertain if there had been any such breach; and earnestly to press them, if any breach had happened, that they would consent to let him mediate between them. This was the contents of a letter which arrived in town a few hours after they were set out. It should be here mentioned that the old gentleman could not have been in London, for he had scarce been a whole day from off his bed.—*Sinclair's Invisible World.*

XCIV.

The Sampford Ghost.

The narrative of the Sampford apparition is, we believe, the last of its kind on record, of authenticated character. It excited intense interest in the County of Devon, which was not a little increased by the circumstance of a clergyman of the established church, the Rev. C. C. Colton, publishing an account of the whole transaction. It took place at the house of one Mr. John Chave, in the village of Sampford Reverell, Devon, about five miles from Tiverton, in the year 1810.

As is usual on all such occasions a variety of wilful misrepresentations were propagated on the subject;

but the history published by Mr. Colton is certainly entitled to our preference, on account of the perspicuity which characterises its details, and with this we shall proceed forthwith.

Mr. Colton says, speaking in September 1810, the house became extremely troublesome, although long before that time some very unaccountable things had occasionally taken place in it. An apprentice boy had expressed himself often dreadfully alarmed by the apparition of a woman, and had heard some extraordinary sound in the night, but little or no attention was paid to it. But about April the inhabitants of the house were alarmed in the following manner: noises and blows by day were heard, extremely loud, in every apartment of the house. On going up stairs and stamping on any of the boards of the floor in any room, say five or six times, or more, corresponding blows, but generally louder and more in number, would be instantly returned; the vibrations of these boards caused by the violence of the blows would be sensibly felt through a shoe or boot on the sole of the foot, and the dust was thrown up from the boards that were beaten with such velocity as to affect the eyes of the spectators.

At mid-day the cause of these effects would announce its approach, by amazingly loud knocking in some apartment or other of the house, above stairs or below, as might happen, for at times more than a dozen witnesses have been present at once.

These noises would very often, and in repeated instances, absolutely follow the persons through any of the upper apartments, and faithfully answer the stamping of their feet wherever they went. And if persons were in different rooms, and one stamped with his foot in one room, the sound was in an instant repeated in another room, and these phenomena by day continued almost incessantly for about five weeks, when they gradually gave place to others still more curious and alarming. There were two apartments in this house, and all females who slept in either of these apartments (with the exception of one single instance), experienced, some of them all, and all of them some, of the following sensations: they were most dreadfully beaten, as bye-standers could hear and witness. I am quite certain I have myself heard more than two hundred blows given in the course of a night. The blows given can be compared to nothing but a very strong man striking with the greatest force he is master of, with a closed-fist on the bed; they left great soreness, and visible marks; I saw a swelling at least as big as a turkey's egg on the cheek of Ann Mills; she voluntarily made oath that she was alone in the bed when she received the blows from some invisible hand. Mrs. Dennis and Mary Woodbury have both sworn voluntarily before me and Mr. Sully the exciseman and Mr. Govett a surgeon, that they were so much beaten as to experience a peculiar kind of numbness, and were sore many days after; and that the shrieks he and Mr. Govett had heard, were so terrible that they could not be counterfeited.

Mr. Chave, the occupier of the house, deposed, that one night the two servants were so much agitated that they refused to sleep any longer in their apartment; Mr. Chave permitted them in the dead of the night to bring their bed and bed-clothes into the room where he and Mrs. Chave slept; after they had been quiet about half an hour, and the light put out, a large iron candle-stick began to move most rapidly over the whole room. He could hear no footsteps, but in the act of ringing the bell, the candlestick was violently thrown at his head, which it narrowly missed. Mr. Searle, late keeper of the county gaol, and a friend, watched one night; they saw a sword, placed by them on the foot of a bed with a large folio Testament placed on it, thrown violently against the wall, seven feet off. Mr. Taylor deposed that in going into the room in consequence of the shrieks of the women, the sword that was before lying on the floor, he saw clearly suspended in the centre of the room, with its point towards him: in about a minute it fell to the ground with a loud noise.

On September 14th, Ann Mills deposed on oath before Mr. Sully and myself, that one night while striking a light she received a very severe blow on the back, and the tinder-box was forcibly wrenched out of her hands and thrown into the centre of the room.

Mr. Sully the exciseman and his wife are ready to swear to the truth of what they have heard of these noises and thumpings, &c., James Dodds, cooper, voluntarily made oath, September 14th, that in his workshop adjoining Chave's house, he had constant opportunities of hearing these noises.

The Rev. Gentlemen said the names of the females that have suffered are as follows, Mary Dennis, sen., Mary Dennis, jun., Martha Woodbury, Ann Mills, Mrs. Pitts, and Sally Case.

"I have seen," he added, "a sword when placed in the hands of some of these women, repeatedly and violently wrested from them after a space of a few minutes, and thrown with a very loud noise sometimes into the middle of the room, sometimes still more violently against the wall. This sword I have heard taken up, and the bed beaten with it as if by shaking the handle in a particular manner; I have placed a large folio Greek Testament, weighing eight or nine pounds, on the bed; it has been repeatedly thrown into the centre of the room. Mr. Pullen, Mr. Betty, and himself have placed the Testament on the end of the bedstead, in such a manner that no part touched the bed-clothes, but it was thrown with a loud noise from the foot of the bed to the head." All this time the women were in bed, and he is sure they never moved, and he administered an oath to them the next morning in the presence of the same gentlemen. "I have often heard the curtains of the bed most violently agitated, accompanied with a loud and almost indescribable motion of the rings. These curtains, to prevent their motion, were often tied up, each one of them in one large knot (being four). Every curtain in that bed was agitated, and the knots thrown and whirled about with such rapidity, that it would have been unpleasant to have been in their vortex, or within the sphere of their action. Mr. Taylor, and Mr. Chave, of Mere (not related to the occupier), were witness to all this, and that it took up about two minutes, and concluded with a noise resembling the tearing of a person's shirt from top to bottom, but on examination, a rent was found across the grain of a strong new cotton curtain. I have heard in the presence of other witnesses footsteps walking by me, and round me, and have been conscious of candles burning, yet could see nothing. Mr. Quick heard it come down stairs like a man's foot in a slipper, and seem to pass through the wall. I have been in the act of opening a door, which was already half open, when a violent rapping was produced on the opposite of the same door; I paused a moment and the rapping continued; I suddenly opened the door with a candle in my hand, yet I can swear I could see nothing. I have been in one of the rooms that has a large modern window, when from the noises, knockings, blows on the bed, and rattling of the curtains, I did really begin to think the whole chamber was falling in. Mr. Taylor was sitting in the chair the whole time; the females were so terrified that large drops stood on their foreheads. When the act of beating has appeared from the sound of the blows near the foot of one bed, I have rushed to the spot, but it has instantly been heard near the head of the other bed.

Mr. Colton's statement was corroborated by the following affidavit :—

"I now proceed to a short detail of circumstances, to the truth of which I have voluntarily sworn, with a safe and clear conscience; I am well aware that all who know me would not require the sanction of an oath, but as I am now addressing the public I must consider myself before a tribunal of which my acquaintance constitutes a very small part. And first, I depose solemnly, that after an attendance of six nights (not successive) at Mr. Chave's house, in the village of Sampford, and with a mind perfectly unprejudiced, after the most minute investigation, and closest inspection of all the premises, I am utterly unable to account for any of the phenomena I have there seen and heard, and labour at this moment under no small perplexity, arising from a determination not slightly to admit of supernatural interference and an impossibility of hitherto tracing these effects to any human cause. I farther depose, that in my visits to Mr. Chave's house at Sampford, I never had any other motive, direct or indirect, avowed or concealed, but an earnest, and, I presume, not a culpable wish, to trace these phenomena to their true and legitimate cause. Also, that I have in every instance found the people in the house most willing and ready to contribute every thing in their power, and to co-operate with me in the detection of the cause of those unaccountable sights, and violent blows and sounds.

"Also, that I am so deeply convinced of the difficulty of proving these effects to be human, that I stand engaged to forfeit a very considerable sum to the poor of my parish, whenever this business now going on at Sampford shall be made appear to have been produced by any human art or ingenuity, collectively, or individually exerted. Also, that I have, in the presence of many gentlemen, repeatedly sworn the domestics to this effect, namely,—that they were not only utterly ignorant of the cause of those circumstances which then astonished us, but also of the causes of many other things equally unaccountable, which we ourselves did not hear nor see, but to the truth of which they also swore, no less than to their perfect ignorance of the means by which they were produced. Also, that I have affixed a seal with a crest, to every door, cavity, &c. in the house, through which any communication could be carried on;—that this seal was applied to each end of sundry pieces of paper, in such a manner, that the slightest attempt to open such doors, or to pass such cavities, must have broken these papers, in which case my crest must have prevented their being replaced without discovery; that none of these papers were deranged or broken; and also, that the phenomena that night were as unaccountable as ever. Also, that I have examined several women, quite unconnected with the family of Mr. Chave; but who, some from curiosity, and some from compassion, have slept in this house; that many of them related the facts on oath; that all of them wished to be so examined, if required; and lastly, that they all agreed without one exception, in this particular,—that their night's rest was invariably destroyed by violent blows from some invisible hand, by an unaccountable and rapid drawing and withdrawing of the curtains; by a suffocating and almost inexpressible weight, and by a repetition of sounds, so loud, as at times to shake the whole room.

" To the truth of the above cited particulars, I voluntarily make oath, in the presence of B. Wood, Master in Chancery, Tiverton.

"B. WOOD, M. C."

" I shall here subscribe the names of a few, selected

from a cloud of witnesses, on whose minds a sensible experience of similar facts hath produced similar convictions; facts, which though they are willing to substantiate on oath, they are utterly unable to trace to any human agency. The names are as follows :—

    Mr. JOHN GOVETT, Surgeon, Tiverton.
    Mr. BETTY, Surgeon, Tiverton.
    Mr. PULLIN, Merchant, Tiverton.
    Mr. QUICK, Landlord of the White House, Tiverton.
    Mr. MERSON, Surgeon, Sampford.
    JOHN COWLING, Esq., Sampford.
    Mr. CHAVE, Mere, near Huntsham.

All these gentlemen are ready, if called on, to depone to their having witnessed circumstances in this house at Sampford, to them perfectly inexplicable, and for which they are utterly incapable to account.

C. COLTON."

Mr Colton published an appendix to his narrative, which was closed by the following affidavit :—

"Thursday, September 27th, 1810, John Chave, William Taylor, James Dodge, and Sally Case, voluntarily make oath this day as follows :—' That they are entirely ignorant of the cause of all those extraordinary circumstances that have and are occurring in the house of Mr. Chave, in the parish of Sampford. Also, that they have never made in or on any part of the premises, any sounds or noises, by day or night, by blows, or knockings, either with or without an instrument, in order to induce any one human being whatever to believe, or even to think, that there was anything unaccountable or supernatural in the house. Also, that they have never requested any other person so to do, and that they firmly believe no such attempts have been made by others. Also, that they have repeatedly heard in mid-day most violent and loud noises in the house, when numerous persons have been assembled, some in the upper, and some in the lower apartments, at the same time; and all of them anxious and eager to discover the cause. Also, that the marks on the ceiling have been made by the persons trying, but in vain, to imitate the same sounds. Also, that to the best of their knowledge and belief, there are no subterraneous passages in or about the house.'—Sworn before me, the 28th of September, 1810.

J. GOVETT, Mayor of Tiverton."

Talley, the landlord of the house, whose interest it certainly was to rid his property of such visitations at the moment that he brought it into the market for sale, now pretended to have discovered the whole affair; but this was on his own surmise, and not on the confession of either party. The house was certainly in a shattered condition, and somewhat out of repair; to this he ascribed the shaking, &c. A cooper, a mopstick, and a bludgeon, were likewise found concealed in the house one night when Talley had arranged to sleep there; but forsooth! might not the cooper and his implements have been placed there by Talley? With the broomstick and bludgeon the cooper was said to have produced the noises! One Taylor, a young wag, was magnified into a necromancer on this occasion, and was said to have communicated his cabalistic attainments to Sally the servant; thus attempting to prove they were both in the plot. This pretended exposure drew down the vengeance of the populace on Chave at Tiverton, insomuch that he narrowly escaped with life. Chave was even compelled to fire a pistol on his assailants, and one man fell dead on the spot.

Soon after this Mr. Colton writes thus : * " An affair is still going on in this neighbourhood, and known to the public by the title of the Sampford Ghost, which might puzzle the materialism of Hume, or the immaterialism of Berkeley. Here we have a visible and incomprehensible agent, producing visible and sensible effects. The newspapers were not quite so accurate as they might have been in their statements on this occasion. First, the real truth is that the slightest shadow of an explanation has not yet been given, and that there exist no good grounds even for suspecting any one. The public were next given to understand that the disturbance had ceased ; whereas it is well known to all in this neighbourhood, that they continue, with unabating violence, to this hour. Soon after this, we were told, by way of explanation, that the whole affair was a trick of the tenant, who wished to purchase the house cheap—the stale solution of all haunted houses. But such an idea never entered his thoughts, even if the present proprietors were able to sell the house ; but it happens to be entailed. And at the very time when this was said, all the neighbourhood knew that Mr. Chave was unremitting in his exertions to procure another habitation in Sampford on any terms. And to confirm this, these disturbances have at length obliged the whole family to make up their minds to quit the premises, at a very great loss and inconvenience, as Mr. Chave had expended a considerable sum in improvements, and could have continued on a reduced rent.

" When one of the labourers on the canal was shot, the newspapers informed us that this took place at the house of the Mr. Chave above mentioned. The fact

---

* Notes to " Hypocrisy," a satire, 8vo, 1812. Mr. Colton is the author of " Lacon, or many things in few words " (crown 8vo., published by William Tegg), universally allowed to be one of the most piquant works in modern literature.

is, that this circumstance happened in another part of the village, at the house of another Mr. Chave, neither related nor connected with the Mr. Chave in question.

"If these nocturnal and diurnal visitations are the effects of a plot, the agents are marvellously secret and indefatigable. It has been going on more than three years, and if it be the result of human machination there must be more than sixty persons concerned in it. Now I cannot but think it rather strange, that a secret by which no one can possibly get any thing, should be so well kept; particularly when I inform the public, what the newspapers would not or could not acquaint them with, namely, that a reward of two hundred and fifty pounds has been offered for any one who can give such information as may lead to a discovery; nearly two years have elapsed, and no claimant has appeared. I myself, who have been abused as the dupe at one time, and the promoter of this affair at another, was the first to come forward with one hundred pounds, and the late mayor of Tiverton has now an instrument in his hands empowering him to call on me for the payment of that sum to any one who can explain the cause of the phenomena.

"Many circumstances, if possible still more extraordinary than those I have related, have also occurred, but as they do not offer the least clue that may enable us to discover the cause that produced them, I shall do the public no service by relating them. A gentleman who commanded a company in the Hereford Militia, was stationed at Sampford: his curiosity was much excited, and he sat up in Mr. Chave's house, at different times, thirty nights. I dined with him at Ottery Barracks; his brother officers were anxious to know his opinion of that affair. He immediately replied, 'Mr. Colton, who sits opposite, has engaged to give one hundred pounds to any person who can discover it. If he will hand me half a guinea across the table, I engage before you all to pay the money instead of him, whenever he is called upon.' I did not take his offer. A clear proof that neither of us think a discovery the most probable thing in the world."—*From H. Welby.*

XCV.

A Dream Fulfilled.

During the present year (1874) the following has appeared in the *Hartford Times*, the Editor vouching for the truth of it :—" Mr. John Eiswirth, a resident of this city, is a German by birth. He came to this country in 1849, bringing his wife with him. They had been here about a year when they received a letter stating that a brother of Mrs. Eiswirth was *en route* to America; but from that time to this they have never seen their relative. About three weeks ago Mr. Eiswirth had a dream. He thought he was seated in a car at the depot in Asylum Street. He didn't want to go anywhere, but in spite of this feeling he was rolled out of the depot, and whirled away at lightning speed. It seemed to the dreamer that he was being carried, much against his will, thousands of miles from home. At last the train slackened its speed and came to a halt, and John found himself moving along with the passengers who were making their exit from the cars. When once outside he discovered that he was in a strange city, and among strangers. He asked a man where he was. He was told, 'St. Louis.' 'But,' says John, 'I live in Hartford. I want nothing in St. Louis.' The stranger smiled and passed on, leaving our Hartford friend as perplexed as ever. While standing in his tracks wondering what to do, he saw at a distance a figure which sent a thrill of joy through his frame. It was his long-lost brother-in-law. It had been more than a quarter of a century since John had set eyes on him, and time had worked a great change in his appearance, but for all that our friend recognized him, and ran towards him hallooing at the top of his voice, as if afraid he might disappear. The meeting was a cordial one, and the pair celebrated the event at a stylish saloon, where foaming mugs of 'lager' played a prominent part. The next John knew he found himself awake at his home in Park Street. But his dream had made a strong impression, and, do what he would, he could not forget it, and when he got up the next morning the remembrance of that long ride and the happy meeting clung to him still. That very day some clerk in the Hartford Post-office might have seen a letter addressed to Mr. ——, of St. Louis, with the instruction on the end of the envelope—' If not called for within ten days, return to John Eiswirth, Hartford, Conn.' Mr. Eiswirth says that he sent the letter addressed to his brother-in-law without the remotest expectation of hearing from him. He sent it to relieve his mind. But after the missive was sent he might never have thought of it again if something startling had not occurred a day or two since. John was at home with his family when the postman came to the door and delivered a letter. It was postmarked 'St. Louis.' It was torn open with tremulous fingers, and to their great joy it was found to be from their long-lost relative in answer to the letter which John had forwarded in obedience to his dream. It appeared by the letter that the St. Louis German had been as much in the fog as to his sister's and Eiswirth's whereabouts as they had been in regard to him. The St. Louis man writes that he shall soon come to this city on a visit, and his Hartford friends are delighted at the prospect of a happy *réunion*. When he does come, John proposes that what he dreamed about the 'lager' shall become a reality."

XCVI.

A New Miracle.

We extract the following from the *Hour* newspaper, London, where it appeared under the authority of a Prussian correspondent:—

For some time lately, a young girl named Louise Lateau has created quite a sensation in Belgium and the Rhenish provinces of Prussia. She is said to be "stigmatized," and pretends in her moments of ecstasy to see God in His glory. Under the term "stigmatization" the Catholic Church understands the miraculous peculiarity of persons bearing on their body the five principal wounds of Our Saviour, and bleeding from them on certain days. Bois d'Haine, the village in which Louise Lateau lives, is now the place of pilgrimage for many pious persons coming from Holland, Germany, and Belgium, to witness with their own eyes the performance of the miracle. Majunke, being some time since in Treves on a visit to his constituents, made also a call upon Louise Lateau, and remained several days in Bois d'Haine, where he also met with Bishop Mermillod, and Lefevre, a medical professor at the University of Louvain. After his visit, Majunke gave a lecture on what he beheld, from the reports of which in Ultramontane papers the following items are extracted:—"Louise is a very simple girl; she has seen very little of the world, and spent the greater part of her life in a solitary country cottage. She daily receives the Holy Sacrament, which is her only nourishment. For two years she has neither eaten or drunk anything else. When she does not receive the Communion she is seized with deadly faintness, so that even on Good Friday she is allowed to partake of the Lord's Supper. Every morning at six o'clock she visits the church, at some distance from her abode, except on Friday, when the Holy Sacrament is brought to her. Last Friday it was administered by the Very Reverend the Bishop of Tournai. I myself assisted. In the little room, floored with bricks, we found everything prepared as for a person dangerously ill. Louise was kneeling at the table, and bleeding profusely. The bleeding by Louise Lateau begins at midnight on Thursday, and terminates at midnight on Friday. First the forehead bleeds, as when the crown of thorns pierced the head; the blood streams from under the hair down the cheeks; and then the hands, side, and feet bleed from above and below." On the day Majunke was at Bois d'Haine, Louise Lateau took the Holy Sacrament almost ravenously. "In the afternoon, about two o'clock, she fell in ecstacy. The Bishop of Tournai went to her previously, to see if, perhaps, in conversation she would forget the time. But, no. Punctually at two o'clock she became silent, and her eyes fixed. The *cure* of the village declared that Louise often during her excitement saw apparitions. First, she saw God in His glory, and later on, the sufferings of Christ, especially in the last stages. Shortly before three o'clock, Louise fell to the ground, and at three she extended her hands. Strange to say, during these convulsions—when the spirit is transported to other regions—it still lives for the things surrounding the body. A consecrated article, for instance, being placed in the immediate neighbourhood of Louise, a gentle smile was seen to play on her features. Also during the prayers she smiled at certain moments—fourteen of us were present, and the priests were praying; when the words *Gloria Patri, Misericordia*, or *Misericors*, were uttered, she smiled in a most remarkable manner, no matter if the prayer was delivered in the French, German, or Hebrew, for in her ecstacy she understood all languages, and consecrated or unconsecrated articles were immediately distinguished by her. Professor Lefevre convinced us, by plunging a pen-knife, into her extended hand, that Louise was insensible to all the laws of the natural world; for the hand was not withdrawn, nor flinched; neither did any blood proceed from the place penetrated. When during prayers the names of Jesus and Mary were mentioned, the upper part of the body of Louise arose from the ground; but this movement was no voluntary one, as generally the case; she seemed to be borne up invisibly. On the Bishop uttering the words, 'Oh, my Jesus, I kneel to Thee,' she turned round so quickly, and fell down so suddenly before the Bishop, that I and the Bishop were quite concerned, fearing she was going to spring out of the window. On the episcopal cross approaching her, she seized it with her hands. At the termination of the prayers, she again fell down —or rather was invisibly placed down, for by falling she would have wounded herself on the pavement. 'Indeed' (states Majunke) 'our language has not the proper word for expressing the act of this prostration. On the next morning, at six o'clock, although she had lost so much blood on the previous day, Louise was nevertheless in the church. I called again upon her. On entering I found her occupied with her sisters in needlework. She offered me a chair, and was somewhat reserved. Her face was rather pale, but seemed transfigured. I said I was a priest from Germany, where the Church had now so much to suffer; and begged her to pray for me and the Catholics in Germany, and that I would remember her when offering up mass. She replied, 'Je vous remercie, monsieur,' and nothing further. She has been so much visited by theological and medical commissions, by men of learning, princes, and distinguished personages, that she is quite insensible to the external world; she receives no presents whatever, and is living in very poor circumstances. Among other trials, she was shut up for a month without receiving the whole time the least nourishment." These are the words of Majunke literally translated, and to add to the force of his statement, he finished by declaring, " All this I have witnessed with my own eyes: so I found Louise Lateau."

Printed and Stereotyped by A. King & Co., Aberdeen.

ב"ה

LIST OF

PUBLICATIONS.

⁎ *Booksellers can be supplied with this Catalogue, with their Name and Address, to the extent of* 150 *Copies.*

LONDON:
12, PANCRAS LANE, CHEAPSIDE.

Two Vols., Crown 8vo.

THINGS NEW & OLD:
OR,
A STOREHOUSE OF SIMILES, SENTENCES, ALLEGORIES, APOPHTHEGMS, ADAGES, APOLOGUES, Etc.
WITH THEIR SEVERAL APPLICATIONS.

Collected and Observed from the Writings and Sayings of the Learned in all Ages to this Present.

By JOHN SPENCER,
A LOVER OF LEARNING AND LEARNED MEN,
WITH
A PREFACE BY THE REV. THOMAS FULLER, D.D.

Price 12s. 6d.

Crown 8vo.

THE
LIFE OF PETER THE GREAT,
CZAR OF RUSSIA.

By J. BARROW, F.R.S.,
Author of "The Mutiny of the Bounty."
ILLUSTRATED.

Price 6s.

Demy 8vo.

ASTRONOMY SIMPLIFIED

FOR GENERAL READING,

WITH

NUMEROUS NEW EXPLANATIONS AND DISCOVERIES
IN SPECTRUM ANALYSIS, ETC., ETC.

BY J. A. S. ROLLWYN.

With Twenty Full-page Coloured Illustrations and suitable Diagrams. Price 10s. 6d.

Two Vols., Crown 8vo.

LORD CHESTERFIELD'S LETTERS TO HIS SON.

NEW EDITION.

Edited, with Translations of all the Latin, French, and Italian Quotations, with Notes, and a Biographical Notice of the Author, by CHARLES STOKES CAREY.

Price 10s. 6d.

Crown 8vo.

THE
MUTINY AND PIRATICAL SEIZURE OF H.M.S. THE BOUNTY.

By J. BARROW, F.R.S.

ILLUSTRATED BY LIEUT.-COLONEL BATTY.

Price 6s.

Imperial 16mo.

THE CHASE:
A POEM.

By WILLIAM SOMERVILLE.

ILLUSTRATED BY JOHN SCOTT.

Price 5s.

Crown 8vo.

QUARLES' (FRANCIS)
EMBLEMS,
DIVINE AND MORAL.

ILLUSTRATED.

Price 4s. 6d.

Royal 18mo.

LEGENDS OF KILLARNEY.

By THOMAS CROFTON CROKER,

Author of "The Legends of the South of Ireland."

NEW EDITION.

By T. WRIGHT, M.A., F.R.A.S.

ILLUSTRATED.

Price 2s. 6d.

Two Vols., Demy 8vo.

PRIDEAUX'S (H.)
HISTORICAL CONNECTIONS
OF THE
OLD AND NEW TESTAMENT.

Price 10s. 6d.

Two Vols., Demy 8vo.

SHUCKFORD'S (SAMUEL)
SACRED AND PROFANE HISTORY
OF THE
WORLD CONNECTED.

Price 10s. 6d.

Two Vols., Demy 8vo.

RUSSELL'S (M.)
CONNECTION OF SACRED
AND
PROFANE HISTORY.

COMPLETING THE SERIES, PRIDEAUX, SHUCKFORD, AND RUSSELL'S CONNECTION.

Price 10s. 6d.

Royal 18mo.

COMMON-PLACE BOOK OF EPIGRAMS.

WITH A COPIOUS INDEX.

By CHARLES STOKES CAREY.

Price 2s. 6d.

Royal 18mo.

EPITAPHS,

QUAINT, CURIOUS, AND ELEGANT.

WITH REMARKS ON OBSEQUIES.

Collated by HENRY JAMES LOARING.

Price 2s. 6d.

8vo.

SELECT THOUGHTS

on the

MINISTRY & THE CHURCH.

GATHERED FROM THE LITERARY TREASURES OF ALL TIMES, AND ARRANGED FOR IMMEDIATE CONSULTATION AND USE.

By the Rev. EDWIN DAVIES.

Beautifully printed on Toned Paper.

** *No Clergyman should be without this Work for reference or Study.*

Price   .

Demy 8vo.

MILTON'S (JOHN)
POETICAL WORKS,

EDITED BY SIR E. BRYDGES, BART.

Illustrated by J. M. W. TURNER, R.A. *New Edition carefully corrected.*
Price 15s.; morroco, 24s.

8vo.

THE KORAN.

TRANSLATED INTO ENGLISH IMMEDIATELY FROM THE ORIGINAL ARABIC, WITH EXPLANATORY NOTES.

BY GEORGE SALE.

A NEW EDITION, WITH VARIOUS READINGS AND NOTES (SAVERY'S VERSION), WITH PLAN AND VIEW OF BEIH ALLAH.

Price 8s. 6d.

Royal 18mo.

THE CRUET STAND;

OR,

SAUCE PIQUANTE TO SUIT ALL PALATES.

EDITED BY WILLIAM TEGG.

Price 2s.

Royal 18mo.

GAY'S FABLES.

ILLUSTRATED.

A NEW EDITION, ENLARGED, WITH LIFE OF THE AUTHOR BY DR. JOHNSON.

Price 2s.

Imperial 16mo.

PARLEY'S (PETER)

TALES ABOUT ANIMALS, BIRDS, FISHES, INSECTS, ETC.

NEW EDITION, EDITED BY WILLIAM TEGG

500 *ILLUSTRATIONS.*

Price 6s.

Square.

PARLEY'S (PETER)

UNIVERSAL HISTORY

ON THE

BASIS OF GEOGRAPHY,

CORRECTED TO THE PRESENT TIME.

Price 5s., School Edition; imperial 16mo., price 6s.

Crown 8vo.

GURNEY'S (Rev. W.)
DICTIONARY OF THE HOLY BIBLE,

Containing an Historical and Geographical Account of the Persons and Places, and an Explanation of the various Terms, Doctrines, Laws, Precepts, Ordinances, Institutions, and Figures in the Sacred Oracles.

Newly Revised and Edited by the Rev. J. G. WRENCH, M.A., Camb.

With Coloured Map of Palestine, and 16 full-page Illustrations.

Price 5s.

Foolscap 8vo.

ROBERT BURNS'S LIFE.

By JOHN GIBSON LOCKHART, D.C.L.,

Author of "The Life of Napoleon," and Editor of "The Spanish Ballads," &c.

A NEW EDITION, WITH NOTES AND MEMOIR OF THE AUTHOR.

Price 2s. 6d.

Three Vols., Crown 8vo.

THE CHURCH HISTORY OF BRITAIN.

FROM THE BIRTH OF JESUS CHRIST TO THE YEAR 1648.

Endeavoured by THOMAS FULLER, D.D.,

Sometime Prebendary of Old Sarum, and Author of " History of the Worthies of England," "Abel Redivivus," &c., &c.

Price 21*s.*

Also the following Works of FULLER:—

	s.	d.
ABEL REDIVIVUS. Two Vols., crown 8vo.	9	0
CAUSE AND CURE OF A WOUNDED CONSCIENCE. Crown 8vo.	4	6
COMMENTS ON RUTH. Crown 8vo.	4	6
JOSEPH'S PARTI-COLOURED COAT. Crown 8vo.	4	6
PISGAH-SIGHT OF PALESTINE. Crown 8vo.	15	0
HISTORY OF CAMBRIDGE. Demy 8vo.	7	6
HOLY AND PROFANE STATE. Demy 8vo.	7	6

Crown 8vo.

HISTORY OF NAPOLEON BUONAPARTE.

REPRINTED FROM THE

"FAMILY LIBRARY."

ILLUSTRATED BY G. CRUIKSHANK, &c.

Price 6s.

Demy 8vo.

STRUTT'S SPORTS AND PASTIMES

OF THE

PEOPLE OF ENGLAND.

WITH 140 ILLUSTRATIONS.

EDITED BY WILLIAM HONE,

Author of "The Every-day Book,' "Year Book," &c.

Price 4s. 6d.

Crown 8vo.

SIGNS BEFORE DEATH.

A RECORD OF STRANGE APPARITIONS, REMARKABLE DREAMS.

A NEW EDITION, ENLARGED AND CAREFULLY CORRECTED.

Price .

Foolscap 8vo.

BLUNT'S (Rev. J. L.)

HISTORY

OF THE

REFORMATION.

ILLUSTRATED.

Price 3s. 6d.

Two Vols., Crown 8vo.

THE RAMBLER.

By Dr. SAMUEL JOHNSON.

WITH A

COMPLETE INDEX AND TABLE OF CONTENTS,
CAREFULLY FROM THE BEST EDITIONS.

Price 10s.

4to.

PASSAGES FROM ENGLISH POETS.

ILLUSTRATED BY THE JUNIOR ETCHING CLUB.

47 in Number.

⁂ A SPLENDID GIFT BOOK.

Price 15s.

Crown 8vo.

QUEEN BERTHA

(*OUR FIRST CHRISTIAN QUEEN*)

AND HER TIMES.

By E. H. HUDSON.

ILLUSTRATED.

Price 5s.

Crown 8vo.

RUINS OF MANY LANDS.

By NICHOLS MICHELL.

A NEW EDITION, CORRECTED.

Illustrated with Eight fine Engravings.

Price 3s. 6d.

4to., Fancy Boards.

CRUIKSHANK (GEORGE)

(EIGHTY-TWO ILLUSTRATIONS BY), ON STEEL, WOOD, AND STONE;

WITH DESCRIPTIVE LETTERPRESS.

*** Uniform with LEECH's Sketches.

Price 10s. 6d.

4to Fancy Boards.

LEECH'S (JOHN) SKETCHES:

CONTAINING

FIFTY-THREE ETCHINGS ON STEEL, WITH DESCRIPTIVE LETTERPRESS.

*** A Drawing-Room Edition.

Price 8s. 6d.

Crown 8vo.

CHRISTIAN THEOLOGY:

A SELECTION OF THE MOST IMPORTANT PASSAGES IN THE WRITINGS OF THE

REV. JOHN WESLEY, A.M.

Arranged so as to form a complete body of Divinity; with a Biographical Sketch by the

REV. THORNLEY SMITH.

Price 3s. 6d.

Imperial 16mo.

THE HISTORY OF A SHIP FROM HER CRADLE TO HER GRAVE,

WITH A SHORT ACCOUNT OF STEAM SHIPS FROM THEIR FIRST INTRODUCTION.

NEW EDITION, CAREFULLY EDITED, WITH NUMEROUS ILLUSTRATIONS.

Price 5s.

Crown 8vo.

MANLY GAMES FOR BOYS:

A PRACTICAL GUIDE TO THE INDOOR AND OUTDOOR AMUSEMENTS OF ALL SEASONS.

By CAPTAIN CRAWLEY.

ILLUSTRATED BY

JOHN PROCTOR AND OTHERS.

Price 6s.

Crown 8vo.

HISTORY OF THE PLAGUE.
By DE FOE.

A NEW EDITION, WITH HISTORICAL NOTES BY
EDWARD WEDLAKE BRAYLEY, F.S.A.;
WITH
G. CRUIKSHANK'S ILLUSTRATION ON STEEL;
TO WHICH IS ADDED

SOME ACCOUNT OF THE GREAT FIRE IN LONDON, 1666,
By DR. HARVEY,
Physician to the Tower of London.

WITH AN APPENDIX, CONTAINING THE EARL OF CLARENDON'S ACCOUNT OF THE FIRE.

Price 6s.

18mo.

THE DESCRIPTIVE

HAND-BOOK OF ENGLISH COINS.

Giving a Concise Description of the various kinds of Coins from the Norman Conquest to the reign of Queen Victoria.

WITH 11 PLATES, CONTAINING FACSIMILES OF 64 COINS.

By LLEWELLYN JEWITT.

Price 2s.

2C

Royal 18mo.

SELECT LETTERS OF EMINENT MEN AND WOMEN.

By CHAMBERLAIN.

Price

Two Vols., Crown 8vo.

THE SERMONS OF MR. HENRY SMITH,

Sometime Minister of St. Clement Danes, London;

Including a Preparative to Marriage, God's Arrow against Atheists, Certain Godly and Zealous Prayers, &c.

Printed according to his Corrected Copies in his lifetime.

WITH A MEMOIR OF THE LEARNED AUTHOR,

By THOMAS FULLER, B.D.,

Author of "A Pisgah-Sight of Palestine," "The Worthies of England," &c.

THE WHOLE CAREFULLY EDITED BY THE

Author of "Our Heavenly Home," "Life at Bethany," &c.

Price 7s.

Two Vols. in One, Crown 8vo.

THE LIFE & TIMES OF JOHN WESLEY:

Embracing the History of Methodism, from its Rise to his Death; and including Biographical Notices and Anecdotes of his Contemporaries & Coadjutors.

By ABEL STEVENS, LL.D.

New Edition, carefully revised and corrected, with Notes, Copious Index, and an Appendix containing an Account of all the Writings of JOHN and CHARLES WESLEY, &c.

Price 6s. 6d.

Vol. II., Crown 8vo.,

CONTAINING THE

HISTORY OF METHODISM FROM THE DEATH OF WESLEY TO THE CENTENARY YEAR.

By ABEL STEVENS.

New Edition, with Notes and Copious Index.

Price 5s.

Crown 8vo.

WOMEN OF METHODISM:

OR, MEMOIRS OF ITS THREE FOUNDRESSES, SUSANNAH WESLEY, THE COUNTESS OF HUNTINGDON, AND BARBARA HECK.

By ABEL STEVENS.

Price 3s. 6d.

Small Post 8vo.

THE CHRISTIAN'S PATTERN:

Or, a Treatise of the Imitation of Jesus Christ.

By THOMAS À KEMPIS.

Translated from the Latin by Dean Stanhope.

New and Revised Edition.

Price 2s. 6d.

Crown 8vo.

HISTORY OF THE ANGLO-SAXONS.

By Sir FRANCIS PALGRAVE, F.R.S., F.S.A.

PROFUSELY ILLUSTRATED.

Price 6s.

Imp. 16mo.

EVERY MORNING.

A TRIPLET OF THOUGHTS FOR EVERY DAY IN THE YEAR.

INTERLEAVED.

Price 3s. 6d.

Crown 8vo.

ADDISON'S ESSAYS

From the SPECTATOR.

NEW EDITION, WITH NOTES ILLUSTRATIVE OF THE TEXT.

Price 3s. 6d.

Crown 8vo.

LETTERS ON NATURAL MAGIC,

Addressed to Sir WALTER SCOTT, Bart.

By Sir DAVID BREWSTER, K.H.,

LL.D., F.R.S., V.P.R.S.E., ETC., ETC.

New Edition, with Introductory Chapters on the Being and Faculties of Man, and the more Recent Wonders of the Material World.

By J. A. SMITH,

Author of a Treatise on the "Structure of Matter," &c.

Price 6s.

Crown 8vo.

LIFE OF SIR ISAAC NEWTON.

By Sir DAVID BREWSTER,

LL.D., F.R.S., V.P.R.S.E., ETC.

NEW EDITION.

By W. T. LYNN, B.A., F.R.S.,
Of the Royal Observatory, Greenwich.

Price 6s.

Crown 8vo.

DEMONOLOGY AND WITCHCRAFT.

By Sir WALTER SCOTT, Bart.

WITH FIVE ILLUSTRATIONS ON STEEL.

A NEW EDITION.

Price 6s.

Imperial 8vo.

THE HORSE:

HIS BEAUTIES AND DEFECTS.

With a Few Hints to Inexperienced Purchasers.

By "A KNOWING HAND."

Illustrated with Nineteen Coloured Plates.

Price 5s.

Crown 8vo.

MELANCHOLY ANATOMISED,

SHOWING ITS CAUSES, CONSEQUENCES, AND CURE;

With Anecdotic Illustrations drawn from Ancient and Modern Sources.

Abridged from the larger work, entitled

"BURTON'S ANATOMY OF MELANCHOLY."

Price 3s. 6d.

*** The complete 8vo. Edition, enriched with **Translations** of the Classical Extracts, price 8s. 6d.

Medium 8vo.

THE SPECTATOR,

WITH

BIOGRAPHICAL NOTICES OF THE CONTRIBUTORS.

Price 6s.

Square 16mo., fully Illustrated.

THE BOY'S HOLIDAY BOOK.

By the Rev. T. E. FULLER.

Containing Simple Instructions How to Play all Kinds of Games, whether in the Fields, the Woods, the Rivers, the Playground, or at the Fireside; with a Copious Guide for Breeding and Rearing Home Pets—their Treatment in Sickness and in Health, &c., &c.

Price 4s. 6d.

Crown 8vo.

FAIRY LEGENDS AND TRADITIONS OF THE SOUTH OF IRELAND.

By THOMAS CROFTON CROKER,
Author of "The Legends of Killarney," &c.

EDITED BY

THOMAS WRIGHT, Esq., M.A., F.S.A.

A New Edition, Fully Illustrated.

Price 6s.

Two Vols., 8vo., Library Edition.

CARLETON'S (W.) TRAITS AND STORIES OF THE IRISH PEASANTRY.

WITH THE FINAL CORRECTIONS OF THE AUTHOR.

Thirty-seven Illustrations on Steel, and numerous Woodcuts.

Price 15s.

Also, just out, in One Vol., Large Post 8vo., the People's Edition, with Illustrations by Maclise, R.A., 6s.

Four Vols., Medium 8vo.

HONE'S (WILLIAM) EVERY-DAY BOOK, TABLE BOOK, & YEAR BOOK;

Or, Everlasting Calendar of Amusements, Times, and Seasons, Solemnities, Merry-makings, Antiquities and Novelties.

Forming a Complete History of the Year, and a Perpetual Key to the Almanacs.

730 *Engravings and Portrait.*

Price £2 10s.

TEGG'S CABINET SERIES.

Illustrated, Imp., 32mo., 2s. ; gilt edges, 2s. 6d.

Beauties (The) of Washington Irving.
Butler's (S.) Hudibras.
Gulliver's Travels. Coloured Illustrations.
Life and Voyages of Columbus, by Washington Irving.
Popes' Poetical Works, with Notes.
Ritson's Songs and Ballads of Scotland, with Glossary.
Robin Hood's Songs and Ballads. Edited by John Hicklin; with Notes by J. M. Gutch, F.S.A.
Seven Champions of Christendom (Complete Edition).
Southey's (Robert) Life of Nelson.
Sterne's (L.) Sentimental Journey.
Syntax's (Dr.) Tour in Search of the Picturesque.
Tale of a Tub, and Battle of the Books, by Jonathan Swift.
Voyages and Discoveries of the Companions of Columbus. By Washington Irving.
Bampfylde Moore Carew, King of the Beggars, with Vocabulary of the terms they use.

Small Crown 8vo.

SCIENTIFIC TERMS

(THE DICTIONARY OF).

Explanatory of all the Terms used in the Arts, Sciences, &c., &c.

By W. M. BUCHANAN.

A NEW EDITION.

Price 6s.

LONDON:
WILLIAM TEGG & CO., PANCRAS LANE, CHEAPSIDE.

www.ingramcontent.com/pod-product-compliance
Lightning Source LLC
Chambersburg PA
CBHW030732230426
43667CB00007B/682